SERIES EDITORS:
Stewart R. Clegg &
Ralph Stablein

C000072185

Edited by
Peter Case, Simon Lilley and Tom Owen (eds)

ADVANCES IN ORGANIZATION STUDIES

The Speed of Organization

Liber
Copenhagen Business School Press
Universitetsforlaget

The Speed of Organization

ISBN 978-91-47-07766-3 (Sweden)
ISBN 91-47-07766-3 (Sweden)
ISBN 978-82-15-01071-7 (Norway)
ISBN 82-15-01071-7 (Norway)
ISBN 87-630-0188-8 (Rest of the world)
© 2006 Peter Case, Simon Lilley, Tom Owen and Liber AB

Publisher's editor: Ola Håkansson
Cover design: Fredrik Elvader and Designlaboratoriet
Typeset: LundaText AB

1:1

Printed in Slovenia by
Korotan Ljubljana, Slovenien 2006

Distribution:
Sweden
Liber AB, Baltzarsgatan 4
S-205 10 Malmö, Sweden
tel +46 40-25 86 00, fax +46 40-97 05 50
http://www.liber.se
Kundtjänst tel +46 8-690 93 30, fax +46 8-690 93 01

Denmark
DBK Logistics, Mimersvej 4
DK-4600 Koege, Denmark
phone: +45 3269 7788, fax: +45 3269 7789
www.cbspress.dk

Norway
Universitetsforlaget AS
Postboks 508
0105 Oslo
phone: +47 14 75 00, fax: +47 24 14 75 01
post@universitetsforlaget.no www.universitetsforlaget.no

North America
Copenhagen Business School Press
Books International Inc.
P.O. Box 605
Herndon, VA 20172-0605, USA
phone: +1 703 661 1500, toll-free: +1 800 758 3756
fax: +1 703 661 1501

Rest of the World
Marston Book Services, P.O. Box 269
Abingdon, Oxfordshire, OX14 4YN, UK
phone: +44 (0) 1235 465500, fax: +44 (0) 1235 465555
E-mail Direct Customers: direct.order@marston.co.uk
E-mail Booksellers: trade.order@marston.co.uk

Advances in Organization Studies

Series Editors:
Stewart Clegg
Professor, University of Technology, Sydney

Ralph E. Stablein
Professor, University of Otago, New Zealand

Advances in Organization Studies is a channel for cutting edge theoretical and empirical works of high quality, that contributes to the field of organizational studies. The series welcomes thought-provoking ideas, new perspectives and neglected topics from researchers within a wide range of disciplines and geographical locations.

www.organizationstudies.org

Table of Contents

SECTION I
THE SPEED OF ORGANIZATIONAL IDENTITY

SECTION II
THE SPEED OF ORGANIZATIONAL TECHNOLOGY

SECTION III
THE SPEED OF ORGANIZATIONAL IMAGERY

Chapter 1

You Shall Know Our Velocity

Peter Case, Simon Lilley and Tom Owens

The threat of our contemporary speed of organisation, explicit in the title of this opening chapter, is writ large for us all. But real as the threat certainly is, it is also a little laughable, a little *un*real as well. It is somehow too Biblical, and thus too inchoate with that of which it speaks, to be taken really seriously. Except of course by those who seek the serious in the portentous pronouncements of the characters of such contemporary classics as *Yu-Gi-Oh*[1] and indeed all manner of less animated, but equally absurd, so-called 'action' movies.

In the novel *White Noise* some rather different characters are confronted with an 'airborne toxic event' (as it is 'officially' described) and the ways in which Don DeLillo renders their reactions to it rather delightfully epitomise both the horrors and the absurdities of not only the contemporary speed of organisation but also of the causal reversals and impossibilities to which its hyperrealities give rise:

> Babette's head appeared at the top of the stairway. She said a neighbour had told her the spill from the tank car was thirty-five thousand gallons. People were being told to stay out of the area. A feathery plume hung over the site. She also said the girls were complaining of sweaty palms.
>
> 'There's been a correction', Heinrich told her. 'Tell them they ought to be throwing up.' (DeLillo, 1986: 112).

In the tumult of the hypermediated, hurdy gurdy world that the novel describes, the protagonists live not as simple subjects of old, inhabiting an environment that affords them certain possibilities whilst precluding others. Rather this world is one in which the throttling tautness of the speed of the narration of the times becomes increasingly productive of world and times themselves through feedback loops so accelerated that they begin to feed forward. When media messages reach Heinrich to inform him that the symptoms deemed consequent upon the 'airborne toxic event' now include vomiting, the lack of this activity on the part of the girls is read not as a

---

[1] Ask your own or your neighbour's kids!

deficiency of this information, nor of its source. It is not even read as mere prediction, as a disinterested account of a future yet to come to be. Rather the reality in which vomiting is not yet present, and the girls who participate in that reality and not the one described, authorised, and indeed prescribed by media messages, are all to be seen themselves as deficiencies. The girls and their reality are outmoded, out of date and out of time, in the face of the new account, in relation to which they are so clearly lacking. They are realities incongruent with and inimical to the really, *really*, *real*, real that is the hyperreal. Simply too slow to take place in the hypermodern world.

It is, it seems, *Hasta la Vista, Baby* to the present, and increasingly so, in an ever accelerating pursuit of terminal velocity. A contemporary condition of sufficient significance to warrant organising, for and against, a 'postmodern' condition – captured by Harvey (1989) in terms of a radical increase in the compression of time and space. In such circumstances time apparently increasingly becomes a competitive issue, and the speed and responsiveness of an organization becomes that which delivers comparative advantage. (See, for example, Kreitzman, 1999: 121–2 and the critical commentary of Armitage and Roberts, 2002). And we are cursed and blessed to live in times so interesting that they are 'speeded up so as to make, as the saying has it "twenty-four hours a very long time"' (Harvey, 1989: 285).

Increasing speed – of production, of information flow, of capital moving through deregulated financial and trading systems – couples with the more familiar increasing speed of transportation rendering, perhaps more explicitly than ever before, economies as systems of time and space as well as of value (Lash and Urry, 1993: 10–11). But with so much going on, and going on – and thus apparently changing – so quickly, how can it all, indeed any of it, be attended to? As Paul Virilio, perhaps the foremost theorist of speed, puts it: 'The twin phenomena of immediacy and of instantaneity are presently one of the most pressing problems confronting [us]' (1995; see also Virilio, 2000). Virilio sees this not so much as the result of the forces of capitalism, favoured as explanation by Harvey, but rather as the result of the imperatives of war, played out through a military industrial complex. The racing of information through its ever new circuits and the problems associated with such racing, Virilio terms *dromology*.

Although somewhat pessimistic, nostalgic and conservative (Kellner, 1999, particularly 103), Virilio is far from alone in seeing danger in our thrall to speed, not least in terms of our ability to grasp and grapple with the realities so created. For Harvey, for example, the 'time-space compression' attendant upon our acceleration 'always exacts a toll on our capacity to grapple with the realities unfolding around us' (1989: 306), thus leaving us in a world accelerating out of control. Or at least a world in which control is increasingly carried out (solely) in the symbolic realm – material being simply too lumpy and sticky to move fast enough. A world increasingly

8

realized through economies of signs, cultural developments within which identities can be formed and commitment seduced into being (see Lash and Urry, 1993; Baudrillard, 1990).

It seems that the speed of organization can be studied, then, from many points of view. In this book we have selected themes which resonate with Marxian thought. Like him or hate him, Marx has dictated the basis of intellectual debate on economics, business organization and sociological issues in general for the past hundred and fifty years. Our first theme concerns the manner in which capitalism becomes perceived as common sense, rather than as a social class which must be overthrown, through the identity of (largely but not exclusively) business organizations as permanent institutions serving the public good, thus our first section 'The Speed of Organizational Identity'. Our second theme deals with technology, by which labour and information are transformed into commodities and power, respectively. Indeed, the organization itself is the 'machine' of capitalism, suggesting a technology of organization structure and behaviour superimposed on the transformation technologies. In 'The Speed of Organizational Technology', our contributors examine technologies of representation, structure and information processing. The final theme is reification, the unconscious process of regenerating abstract ideas as concrete objects, which turns brand names into things-in-themselves and stifles questioning with the sedimentation of layers of agreement and acceptance. Branding, of course, applies to ideas as much as to products, through which we think we know the concept through deep familiarity with its name.[2] Our contributors examine this process in our final section 'The Speed of Organizational Imagery'.

Organizational identity is the public perception of an abstract entity, which is regarded as distinct from the collection of single individuals which created it. Gramsci says:

> 'If each of the single components thinks of the (organization) as an entity extraneous to himself, it is evident that this organism no longer exists in reality, but becomes a phantasm of the intellect.' (Forgacs, 1988: 243)

Elsewhere in the prison notebooks, Gramsci says that reality cannot be seen as something existing on its own, of itself, but only in a historical relationship with us, who modify it. We accept our need to distance our organizations from ourselves in a kind of philosophical space. We understand our need to have these organizations project themselves on to our consciousness so that we can provide boundaries for them there. Does this provide an opportunity for our exploitation? So that we remain unwitting of our exploita-

---

[2] Kearney (1986: 151) tells the story of Berthold Brecht throwing up his hands in dismay when 'Walter Benjamin informed him in 1938 that he had been writing and reflecting on the Marxist revolution for over twenty years without ever having read *The Capital!*'.

tion, must the exploitation process, the hijacking of organizational identity, be carried out very fast indeed?

According to our first contributor, Ben Agger, the exploiter is capitalism, succeeding through its very pervasiveness. It reaches into every aspect of our lives, so that we perpetuate it unwittingly. To observe its advance we need distance. Agger prefers temporal distance to distance in space. Spatial distance is easy enough to conceptualise and operationalise. But distance in time? Historicity has been a useful construct, back to the time of Marx. However, Agger believes, perceives, that capitalism has put on speed since that time, particularly post world war two and even more so since the advent of the Internet. To create the necessary temporal distance so that we can 'see the big picture' we need to slow down time itself. This means slowing down the pace at which we live our lives. As an old-time radical, Agger finds this easy enough to accomplish. Having directly experienced the dropping-out and turning-on social phenomenon of the 1960s, he has produced himself as an actor of his own philosophy. Authentic, existential, Marxist Agger suggests slow-modernity as counter-hegemony to that of capitalism.

This is a brave step. We know, from Althusser (2001) that capitalism gained its hegemony through becoming the dominant ideology of society. It achieved this through the integration of individuals into the system through membership of trades unions and political parties (Althusser, 2001), by manipulating public opinion through exploitation of religion and education (Gramsci, 1971) and by harnessing morality itself (Weber, 2001). How could 'slow-modernity' replace capitalism as the dominant ideology?

Slow-modernity is a concept of modernist manufacturing and information technologies being utilised to decelerate the pace of existence. We need to slow things down because the stability of our own identities is under threat from fast capitalism. We learned in the 1960s that self matters, that everyday life, food, sex, exercise and culture are political. Presentation of certain behaviours become political statements, political acts. Today these items are better seen as battlefields. On one side we have fast capitalism attempting to gain new markets and depersonalising us in the process. On the other side, we have the revolutionary or dropping out impulse fighting against, or effectively ignoring, the colonising forces of capitalism. This fight is not easy for us. Today everybody is involved in performance – essentially so that the existing order can be reproduced. Our focus on the big picture is blurred through forced concentration on tiny aspects or dimensions of being. By slowing down the world we can understand it and re-order it.

The first place to start is with children. Slowing down children's lives in combination with enriching them creates a 'delicate but not impossible balance'. Children can learn that capitalism 'need not endure forever'. Second, we can help ourselves by concentrating on ways of fighting capitalism through behaviours which mimic performativity. We can attempt to change ourselves and in that process, collectively, change society. Ironically the Internet can be a powerful tool in the advancement of a hegemony counter to that of capitalism. Ironically, for Agger, because the Internet is undecidable. Is it an instrument which destroys discourse? Or one which produces greater democracy? Might this speedy tool help us to slow things down?

Can we help ourselves through the 'slow food' movement? Perhaps not, if this simply leads us to a 'supposed golden age of pre-modern life'. As metaphor 'Slow-life' is appealing. The problem is that it risks an anti-technology posture crystallising in switching off the TV and computer, sending the kids out to play and having family meals prepared from scratch. 'The problem is not technology but its uses', as Marx had it. Slow-food and slow-life are goals to be situated in modernity. The slow-food movement means nothing if it does not result in the demise of agribusiness and supermarket chains. If it is simply lifestyle, it changes nothing. We need to reconceive progress as productive harmony with nature, not as conquest. Slow modernity, a stage of civilisation in which the best of the modern and pre-modern coexist will 'restore and redeem nature as a standard by which other activities and arrangements are judged'.

Ever the optimist, Agger concludes with a 10-point self-help 'agenda' to guide us through the 21st century. His work is erudite, eclectic and sheer fun to read. And his final image of Marx, brandishing a bowl of pasta as protest, lingers long in the memory.

In the first chapter of Capital, Marx (1999) writes of commodity as fetish. A fetish is an object of some kind or a principle, reverenced for possessing a magical property. Marx used the term to highlight the separation of the worker from his work. Commodities appear in the market as if by magic; capitalism encourages us to focus on the goods, not on that which brought them into being. We learn to develop an unnatural devotion to things and their acquisition. If we use that perfume we will become attractive, if we drive that car we will become powerful.

Adrian Carr uses the language of psychoanalysis to explain the fetish concept and the manner in which certain individuals develop fetish attachment. His focus is on the generally observable pre-occupation with speed, which for some is raised to the level of fetish. That there is a modern pre-occupation with speed is evidenced by the terms we employ for everyday items. Our telephones have speed-dial facilities, we eat in fast-food restaurants. Carr is fascinated by the process whereby general pre-occupations emerge, providing a reading of the present based on Freud's theories of the psyche.

From initial studies of adults displaying inordinate, 'extravagant', devotion to physical objects, Freud could identify erotic, perhaps sexual, impressions formed in childhood. Leaving the full implications of this aside, as pertaining to the few, Carr traces Freud's development of theory through his second model of the psyche, as pertaining to the many. The technical language of the model has since entered mainstream speech. Although Carr believes we are mostly familiar with terms like id, ego and super-ego, he reminds us of the tensions set up by interaction between these elements and between the ego and reality. Conflict between the ego and the superego, where we are prevented by conscience from doing something we might otherwise have done, can be eliminated through group processes, whereby we replace superego imperatives with the need to achieve group ideals. In that same process, the ego has identified with others in the group according to the extent of gratification received.

Carr's argument, to this point, creates a platform on which he builds a discourse on pre-occupation with speed and its social consequences, based on a reading of critical theory. Citing Marcuse, he argues that the superego can be shaped to fit in with social restraints set by others. The individual's behaviour in affirming and reaffirming these restraints becomes instinctive. Following Atkinson, we see that the individual not only wants to conform to societal norms but must, to avoid feelings of guilt. Societies may produce a 'reality principle', according to Marcuse, arising from their material conditions. In capitalist societies, the reality principle is based on competitive economic performance, output determining social strata. Carr draws our attention to Gramsci's earlier conclusion that the power of a dominant group cannot be maintained indefinitely by force alone, needing also the consent of the subordinate group. This consent is enlisted through persuasion that interests are served through acceptance of the prevailing order.

This brings to mind Lukács' (1971) observation that consciousness is reified as commodities are fetishized. The idea is that products become our lives, rather than exist in them. We assert ourselves through the brand names of the food we eat, the clothes we wear, our 'life-styles'. But as this happens our consciousness freezes, we lose our criticality. We are non-people, consumers merely, persuaded that this state leads to our happiness.

Carr turns to Debord for suggestions as to the triggers and mechanisms used to persuade us. Entertainment, it seems, creates our reality for us through its images. These show us how we should live, how we want to live. They inform us, perhaps, of the group's ideals, to which we surrender our sense of self. The current reality principle emphasises speed as a characteristic of performance efficiency. Speed, itself, can become elevated in our consciousness to the level of fetish. We all become preoccupied with it, as an object of our devotion. Carr fears that this preoccupation may lead to the condition of stimulus entrapment, a psychological disability, which permits no inner life to the individual. The concept itself is a fitting metaphor for the condition of a society that has lost its internal reflective, or moral, mechanisms.

Being fast is being sexy, being powerful. Fast organizations and instant messages serve the public good, surely? The speedier organization is identi-

12

fied as more admirable, speedier products are more valuable, speed itself is pure magic.

Critical theory and psychoanalysis are two routes to understanding our economies of signs and the identities they support. They share objectification of the problem as an approach to a solution. They place distance between the observer and the phenomenon observed. They try to be on the outside, looking in. The ethnographer, on the other hand, writes from the inside out, sending out observations of the inside world. The ethnographer is part of, and apart from, the culture observed. Tuomo Peltonen observes the culture of mobile professionals and managers as a highly mobile academic. His study contains descriptions of mobility in an absolute sense, in that he provides insight into the joys and problems associated with travel itself. Peltonen goes further, determining the existence of that other who informs – indeed forms – the culture observed relativistically. Since his culture is essentially dynamic, the other is, perforce, static; his people are nomads, the other is rooted; the nomads are constantly moving, the other permanently stuck. Once we accept mobility, speed and distance as positive factors, those with access become superior to those without.

In passing, Peltonen notes that capitalism confers these values on its more senior practitioners, increasing in magnitude with higher positioning in capitalism's hierarchy. Owners and senior managers are the most mobile, the most unburdened; made most powerful in consequence. Capitalism moves faster in our times, it circulates faster, with faster meaning more successful in the rhetoric of speed. Perhaps this means that capitalism is becoming more successful. First, because we become less pervious to its encroachment on our private lives; second, because workers increasingly emulate capitalist practice. A new elite is formed of those with access to 'speed', shaped through 'speedy' performance, objectified through the necessary comparison with those who are slow, those denied access. Peltonen tightens his focus on the frequent-flyer, of which he himself is one. He explains his research methodology as being in the spirit of actor network theory rather than as 'pure' inductive ethnography. The appropriateness of this choice becomes obvious as he helps us to see the culture of this new elite in terms of its dependence on supporting technology and infrastructure. Furthermore, it may be a culture in relative terms only.

As we read, we are drawn into Peltonen's world. This is as much a testament to his wit as to his methodology, for Peltonen is more than alive to the absurdities of our current velocities. We are reminded of the 'hurry-up, slow-down' aspects of modern air travel, of our dependence on the support systems being made obvious only when they fail. The method of exposition includes boxed paragraphs of Peltonen's lived experience. These present themselves as windows on the world of the new elite. As they (we) gaze from the window of the airliner they can feel their power, their literal superiority.

13

And as we peer through Peltonen's boxes, we too gain power voyeuristically. Certain conclusions are reached in the course of our travel. We learn that the meanings of speed and mobility are formed through the participants' discourse. We learn that speed's dependence on technology produces two effects, of which humans becoming more machine-like is the first and the granting by us to machines of faculties of wisdom and potency, the second. Finally, Peltonen confronts his own standpoint. Since he is an observer of the new, speedy elite, he is made 'heavier' and 'slower' by his research, than those who are totally immersed in the liquid world of lightness, speed and mobility. They are not troubled by the 'inner dynamics of subjectivity' as Peltonen is. This leads logically to questions of the separation of research from research objects, of science from practice. Scientists may experience envy of those 'faster' than they can be. Developers of theory may feel 'somehow incomplete and impure' relative to the actors of speed.

It seems reasonable to claim that this first section establishes capitalism as the dominant ideology of our times. Capitalism works faster than in Marx's time, the ethos of performance has become the reality principle, business executives literally move faster than before, as work and reward simultaneously. We recognize success, of organizations, of their executives, of their products, according to their ability to construct an identity of speed.

In the second part of our edited collection *The Speed of Organizational Technology* takes centre stage. Marx approved of technology. Indeed, he seems to have been pleased with the speed with which capitalism employed new technology in the production process, because this would tend to bring its demise closer. During the formative years of industrial capitalism (generally regarded as the fifty years from 1870 to 1920), technology meant production operations technology, typically mass production and continuous flow production. Engineering of machines to process materials has latterly given way to the engineering of machines to process information. And the speed fetish is at work in information technology as obviously as in the production of organization identity.

We open here with Scott Lawley whose fundamental concern is reality itself – which is no bad place to start! Is there such a thing as objective reality and if there is, can we know it? His intellectual forebears are metaphysicians, for all that he locates his argument in the discourse of post-structuralism. And Lawley is a realist, his starting point and his touchstone is the existence of reality independent of our perceptions. The problem for him, then, is the correspondence between our perceptions of the real world and its objective existence. Reality is difficult to perceive because of its ephemeral nature. Constantly changing, omni-present, it refuses to be pinned down. It is as if reality were moving so fast that we may only perceive a blur. Lawley cites Lee's metaphor of infinite speed for the movement of reality – a speed beyond the concept of measurement, making perception impossible.

For Lawley, these two positions are reconciled through mediating structures. Reality exists. It cannot be perceived directly. Our perceptions are formed, therefore, by representations of reality, enabled through technological structures. Representations are substitutes for reality in the sense of role; representations are performances of aspects, or facets, of reality, in the sense of event, or object. For the latter sense to be operative, reality must be 'slowed down', 'frozen in time'. A photograph freezes reality at the camera's shutter speed. The photograph is a performance of reality and reality's 'representative'. The more 'realistic' the photograph, the more we are willing to accept it as real. Magritte's image of a pipe becomes a pipe, according to its degree of realism, as it were. Lawley argues that the 'photographer', in choosing one snapshot from the infinite number possible, controls our perception of reality. By extension, those who construct representations of reality exercise power over those who receive them. This is an insidious power. On the receiving end, we imagine we are looking at reality when, in fact, we are looking at chosen instances of reality. Furthermore, our perceptions inform our actions and these constitute elements of reality. So in this way, controllers of representations of reality tend to control reality itself.

Lawley's text is complex and challenging. He assumes, perhaps demands, a readership of a high intellectual order, well-read in philosophy, linguistics and semiotics, in addition to his vehicular discourses of post-structuralism. Inevitably, in his short treatment here, these texts not only resonate in a post-modern manner but positively interrupt each other. His usage of hyperreality is contingent on specific discourses, although simply epithetic of reality, in the aggregate. Yet, that a train timetable is hyper-real, in the sense that it is 'more real' to us than the entire system, or its infrastructure, cannot be in doubt. The printed timetable is a representation, therefore, of the hyper-reality of the transport schedule. This step lets us see how control is exercised over reality. The hyper-real facet is selected from reality, then promulgated through a broadcast representation. The selection activity slows reality down but then accelerates the hyper-reality. The Internet is the most recent acceleration device, which Lawley considers as much for its internal workings as for its role in this power performance. Aspects of the Internet infrastructure enable the slowing-down of representation broadcast (from its own speed of light) and the creation of private zones for representation reception. The boundaries of these zones become the new boundaries of organizations.

Lawley's chapter forces us to consider the most basic questions of philosophy. What is the world in which we live? How do we know that world, how do we interpret it, how do we communicate it? All approaches to these fundamental problems can be placed in two categories: idealism and realism, labelled by Heidegger (1997) as studies of being by a worldless subject and of a subjectless world, respectively. We seem not to be able to do both at once, because of our presence as subjects in the world. The interested reader will find Eco (2000) instructive on the development and current state of this argument. Nobody seriously suggests a lack of objective reality anymore. The issue is the meaning of 'being there'. What does it mean to study the world as it is, by us, as we are? History is in our consciousness, there is only a constant fleeting present. Photographs are representations of things no longer true. The speed factor we must contend with is intimidating. Virilio (1997) says that speed leads to collision, greater speed leading to bigger collisions. The digital reality of information technology produces a different concept of time and space. The internet world has no concept of night and day; no concept of a topos. The study of 'being there' implies an ethnographic methodology, axiomatically.

Good ethnographers are good story-tellers. Living within their host cultures, they tell the history of that culture as it unfolds. Through their stories we learn of their feelings and impressions of people and events as well as of those people and events themselves. Whereas Peltonen might represent the accidental ethnographer, Sam Warren is deliberative. Nonetheless, they share an interest in people who move faster than others; whose faster movement characterises them as successful, progressive, achieving individuals. Both researchers identify alienation symptoms. In Warren's observation, their employer's goals and methods oblige employees to be in constant motion, thereby preventing any sense of rootedness, of belonging, to develop.

Warren concentrates on 'Dept. X', an organisational unit of a large firm in the information technology industry. 'Dept. X' designs web-sites for the firm's customers. The firm is convinced that customers have 'an expectation of immediacy' regarding the satisfaction of their needs. The company response is to work faster, using 'hot-desking' as a speed device. Warren understands the short-run economic benefits of this usage but worries about long-run diseconomies caused by employee resistance and disaffection. Hot-desking, as she explains the term, means employees sharing desk space with each other. Because of the varying demands on employees' time and the opportunities provided by online work operations, employers found investment in desks and desk-space wasteful. The provision of this space becomes economical when organised on a shared basis. A further benefit may lie in reorganising such (reduced) space so that, for example, employees working as a team may be grouped together physically as well as strategically. The root source of benefits to the employer, Warren concludes, is speed. Speed of online communication and project-sharing means employees can work from home. Speed of responsiveness to clients means employees can work on clients' premises. Speed of project completion means speedy regrouping for the next project.

Here we see three distinct technologies in play. The first, and most obvious, is a work-space optimalization technology used to reduce investment in fixed overheads, Marx's 'constant' capital; the second is a production process technology used to provide a more valuable product to the customer, which means more utility for the same price, in a narrow economics sense; the third is a productivity enhancement technology used to derive additional value from the labour cost, Marx's 'variable' capital. Marx's labour theory of value states that labour is the only ingredient of cost that can yield a surplus. The worker is exploited according to the expropriation of surplus. Warren's study sheds light on the ways in which the Internet facilitates the exploitation of the worker, through its pervasiveness and its speed.

There are though, clear benefits to the employees – flexibility of working, excitement, novelty. What is not so clear is what the disadvantages are and this is what engages Warren the most. Among these are the loss of the concept of home as haven, the loss of symbolism of personal office space – in terms of size, location, furnishings, and the loss of a sense of individuality and control associated with the loss of a personal place at work. It is this latter issue which prompted Warren to use photographs as a research tool. Her sample of sixteen employees photographed their current work-space and used the photographs (displayed on a computer monitor) to discuss their concerns. The photograph is, at once, explicit of its content and a stimulus for memories and associations. Furthermore, it enables a sharing of data with the reader of the research. As a research tool, therefore, it generates rich data. Like Lawley she thus sees photographs as both performances of reality and propulsion towards further performance. And in her desire for her subjects to 'own' the process of research in which they are engaged, she buttresses Lawley's claim that the photographer, in selection of shot, controls the perception of reality so produced.

We learn, through this study, of the respondents' needs to aestheticise and personalise their work-spaces and thereby, establish a sense of community, seen as vital for productivity. Indeed, there is evidence suggestive of an informal push-back against the hot-desking requirement enforced by these needs. Warren is clear that her conclusions are not capable of extrapolation, for all that they resonate with those from other studies. It is tempting, though, to believe that the workers in 'Dept. X' may be attempting to slow down the carousel of capitalism.

Lawley argues that information technology (IT) has the potency to misrepresent reality, Warren provides a sketch of the worker in a modern IT environment and now Tamar Zilber deals with the IT industry directly, at the time of the 'dot.com Bubble', in Israel, a country whose economy is hugely dependant on the Hi-Tech sector. She discovers through her research that speed is the informing term of Hi-Tech discourse and that Hi-Tech rhetoric came to pervade all published discourse. As she deconstructs speed in Hi-Tech, therefore, she offers insight into 'the broader cultural world', as well as into Hi-Tech itself. In Zilber's context, Hi-Tech is a general term for the information industry, including both hardware and software sectors as well as information disseminators and managers. Hi-Tech firms are characterised as operating under extreme time pressures, within an environment characterised as risky, dynamic, uncertain and highly competitive. In this context, speed becomes a 'technical, or functional requirement'.

Zilber identifies four dimensions of the Hi-Tech discourse through her research. These are technology; change of scale; competition; and crisis evaluation. She postulates that speed acquires symbolic power in its reference within these dimensions. Under technology, we find employment advertisements using speed rhetoric as smoothly as product advertisements. Faster product speed can be a unique selling proposition. In job ads, speed is coupled with wealth, with progress, with wisdom. Zilber reflects on the circumstance of product improvements being too much, too soon for consumers, yet not impeding the speed of speed rhetoric's social acceptance. Under change of scale, Zilber focuses on economic time scales, organisational trajectory and presentations to funders. Although the Hi-Tech industry is, at least, thirty years in existence in Israel, the widely shared perception is that it is a mere two to five years old. One element of this perception is that Hi-Tech success occurred within that time-frame; another element is the 'exit' strategy of transformation into a public company or of being acquired by another firm. Either form of exit ends the history of the start-up enterprise.

When these firms presented their plans to funders (typically venture capitalists), they did so in '15 minutes or less', in 'one sentence, one bullet-point'. Change of scale produces increasingly smaller technological 'gadgets', increasingly higher start-up valuations, increasingly younger owners and managers, increasingly inexperienced. Zilber wonders if the sense of the future becomes lost in the process of celebrating youthfulness and disregarding experience.

Under competition, Zilber finds the rhetoric of comparison. To be fast means being faster. So that one competitor can be faster, another must be relatively slower. Finally, under crisis evaluation, the final irony: an industry characterised by speed collapsed 'at the speed of light'. The same rhetoric of speed that had been used to glorify the Hi-Tech industry was now used to mourn it. And yet another irony is to be found in the aftermath of the dot. com bubble. It seems the subsequent recession will prove to have been the shortest ever. The rhetoric of speed may prove to be the Hi-Tech industry's lasting legacy.

This means that speed itself becomes valuable and morally correct. The imagined value of speed during the dot.com bubble may have been based on a new productivity technology, leveraging substantially more labour value through full or shared ownership of intellectual property. In the new economy of the Internet, slow equals bad, fast equals good. Speed has become a virtue.

The third and final part of our text deals explicitly with *The Speed of Organizational Imagery* and we begin the end with Jo Brewis and Gavin Jack's special offer: an account of the development of fast and convenience foods and their role in modern society. They counterpoint this development with a commentary on the slow-food movement, a phenomenon we have already encountered with Agger. Their exposition centres on a study of television advertising of 'fast' foods and a deconstruction of these messages.

Messages of speed and convenience are valuable to those pressed for time. Brewis and Jack explore western notions of time and locate these in a discourse of dialectical materialism. New oppositions are found, as for Peltonen, between being time-bound and space-bound, between being time-poor and time-rich. In the latter case, they trace development of conspicuous commodity consumption through leisure consumption and back as characteristic of varying stages of capitalism.

Fascinating though the account is by itself, just like the toy that comes with a Happy Meal, it is the style that engages our attention most. The narrative hurtles along, with a mixture of bullet-points, journalistic section-headings, references drawn from popular media as well as from respected academic sources. They find faux-nostalgia, a longing for a past that never existed, and time-poverty, being impressively busy, as Hallmarks of our culture. Capitalism asserts, confirms, echoes these mental states through marketing.

Their argument starts with a depiction of the spectacular growth of the McDonald's corporation worldwide. The best-known product in the world is perhaps, McDonald's Big Mac, a fast-food item. Two factors are suggested for this development. The first is that society seems to have changed its eating habits, turning eating at home into a weekend or special occasion event. The second is that fast-food consumption may transcend cultural preferences or indicate cultural assimilation and/or convergence.

To what extent are these factors caused by marketing or simply, reflected by marketing? Brewis and Jack tackle this argument full-frontally, juxtaposing Marx (and others) with those, like Toivonen and Mort, who emphasize the autonomy of the consumer. Consumers can 'resist and subvert' marketing messages, in a way, surely, to be hoped for. But perhaps these are merely 'Culinary Luddites'.

Next, they turn their attention to the relationship between consumption of fast-food and living a busy life. The concern is clear. The busier we are at work, the less time we have for 'ourselves'. Brewis and Jack trace the discussion through the study of cultural attitudes to time, and cultural differences between the developed and developing parts of the world. Successful people in the developed world are Peltonen's frequent fliers, Kivinen's speedy cyclists (of whom more in a moment), Zilber's IPO promoters, all 'time poor'. Those who want to be successful, or be regarded as such, can emulate the time-poverty syndrome, at least. Grabbing a Big Mac, for example, can suggest our success since we don't have enough time for anything more complicated. As general support for their arguments, they outline a series of television commercials for fast and convenience foods through the adoption of a couch potato methodology. The commentary is always witty, sometimes hilariously so. Finally, if consumption of fast-food can be interpreted as rebellious the slow-food movement is a further stage in revolution. They remind us of the distinction between speed and acceleration. Speed is transformative, radical; acceleration is adaptive, conservative. We may only be conscious of the effects of acceleration, since speed has already become an accepted element of life. Speed is a fetish, our consciousness of it is reified.

Nina Kivinen declares her interest to be an understanding of visual representations of concepts, things and people. Her attention in this chapter is focussed on the representation of corporate identity through images of the corporation (corporate imagery). She stresses her lack of care with outcomes of these projected or broadcast images. In other words, she is concerned with a translation of the image's meaning and not with the variety of effects on human behaviour such images (or their meanings) might have.

An image on an Internet home page is doubly provocative to her, since the image and its medium of expression are both objects of study in themselves. Her work resonates with the Internet argument – effective circulator of signs (information), new technology predicated on existing conventions, agent of fast capitalism – but is not preoccupied by it. Rather she reflects on the ease with which images are used and circulated on the Internet. Inevitably this increases the number of images surrounding us, rendering those images as things in themselves, rather than repositors of meanings. Consequently, we may be losing our ability to 'read' images, leading, perhaps, to 'stimulus entrapment' as described by Adrian Carr. Kivinen's own ability to read images is centred on her understanding of semiotics. There are two aspects to this, being the identification of objects in an image and the ideas and values expressed through objects (and their composition).

Her reason for choosing the precise image treated here is that it was the only image on Enron's home page in the autumn of 2001, an image of a young man on a bicycle. The image has been created with a 'blurred' effect, so that certain features of the cyclist are indistinct, as is the background. According to Kivinen's ekphrasis, it is suggestive of a city-scape, the cyclist appearing to move against a fixed background. There is a grid superimposed on the image with certain 'squares' of different colour to the overall scheme. She interprets the composition and construction of the image as intending reality and 'high tech'. She responds to the image by adding values and probabilities to the image from her own cultural inheritance, as this technique requires. She interprets the cyclist as representative of the company. This, in turn, presents more possibilities for interpretion, in the sense of Barthian connotation. The bicycle is an old invention but confers an advantage of relative speed (possibly its only advantage) over other road users. The company, it seems to say, uses old technologies in new ways to create competitive advantage. Chief of these is relative speed. Naturally, for one to be faster, another needs to be slower, pace Peltonen.

The bicycle speaks of the past, as a mode of transport, or of leisure; it is not an icon of speed. The bicycle may then be used as a trope of nostalgia, ala Brewis and Jack. The company may be hoping to suggest old-style, willingness to use traditional methods, conservatism.

Enron was an energy trader. The cyclist provides a faster way of delivering certain packages than other methods. Enron could, the image suggests, deliver energy from one with excess to one in need, faster than its competitors. Kivinen points out that the cyclist's relative speed depends, in part, on 'cutting corners' and in part on disregarding certain traffic regulations, which slow others down. To assess the inherent risk in this approach, we need not look elsewhere than, in hindsight, at Enron. Kivinen contributes to the current study by organisational theorists of aesthetic phenomena, using semiological tools and her rich imagination.

We close with Steffen Böhm, for whom the essence of capitalism is its expansion, achieved through circulation. Without circulation, the surplus value created in the production process sits in inventory. Böhm roots his argument on circulating capital firmly in Marx. He points out that Marx knew indeed that distribution and marketing are essential factors for capitalism's success. Böhm searches for a metaphor for capital, which needs to circulate constantly and which needs to return constantly to the fixed point of production. His love for Benjamin leads him to the image of a child on a carousel.

Engagingly, Böhm treats us to a discourse on Benjamin's political awakening. We learn of his early academic life and his frustrations. We are helped to form a picture of Benjamin writing, on the one hand, to secure university tenure and on the other, to develop his own understanding of the world in which he finds himself. This more subjective writing required a new, different method. Images of modern city life would present the materiality of the world, its concreteness, in a way that 'coherent argument' could not. As Benjamin became more interested in the relationships between people and things he read more deeply into materialist philosophy, notably that of Lukács. Benjamin resonated to Lukács' account of reification, finding human relations in modern cities increasingly thing-like. From this, it is a short step to commodification of human relations and the elevation of ordinary things to spectacles and presentations.

Böhm now revisits Marx. His reading shows that Marx sees capital as a process rather than an entity. The process transforms labour commodity into material commodity into money into increased transformation of labour and so on. Capitalism thrives on the productivity of the capital process. The more efficient the process, the greater is the increase in capital. Nor is efficiency limited to labour productivity, since technology creates benefits of scale as well as speed. Given competition between firms as a reality, advantages created by one are soon reduced by equivalent development by rivals. As a consequence, there is an enhanced need for new technology and methods, which will spur relative productivity gains. The carousel keeps turning but moves faster with each turn.

Again from Marx, we see that capital can prosper through market expansion, indeed markets must expand if no further improvements are obtainable within existing demand. Capital *needs* to be in a constant process of circulation. Capital *needs* to increase as it circulates. Ironically, this signals the inherent weaknesses of capitalism. If demand is lacking, Böhm offers as example, capital freezes in time. Consequently, the speed of circulation, the speed of the carousel, is produced by expanding markets, an expansion of the system itself. As this takes place, capitalism becomes the entire social system. The boundaries between private life and capitalist endeavour become blurred.

We go back to Benjamin. Or, perhaps like the carousel, we go forward to arrive at the point we left. The carousel shows us a changing world with every second but brings us back always through the same point. 'The carousel of capital give the impression of speed and change, but for Benjamin this is only a phantasmagoric illusion.' The image of the child on the carousel can, nonetheless, be an image of hope. Children, for Benjamin, can make the most creative connections. They may find a way, through riding it, of transcending the carousel.

So capitalism really is conservative. The logic of capitalism is to demonstrate apparent rather than real speed, or perhaps acceleration rather than speed, since the carousel ride doesn't actually take us on a trip to anywhere. The real, transformative speed is already reified. Capitalism provides an exciting life, not a worrying one.

If we question this, we need method. Böhm's moral is in his method. He introduces his chapter with a short section on translation. We cannot translate adequately from one language to another. Rather, we can attempt to understand text by going through an author's experience and expressing that in the target language. Böhm demonstrates this in relation to Benjamin by bringing his readers on a carousel ride. Böhm's text progresses and returns to its starting point. His discourse on capital is, itself, in constant circulation, expanding with each turn and culminating in a valiant attempt at transcendence. His fixed-point of Benjamin starts with a quotation from One-Way Street; turns through front covers of his work; turns again through Benjamin style quotations (from Marx, Blumenfeld, Toynbee); again a Benjamin quotation; a pictorial image of a carousel; finally an image of a child on the carousel, the image of hope. This is entertainment for the intellect and a fitting non-end for a collection reflecting on the speed and acceleration of organisation. All aboard!

References

Althusser, L. (2001) *Lenin and Philosophy and Other Essays*, New York: Monthly Review Press.

Armitage, J. and Roberts, J. (2002) 'Chronotopia', pp. 43–54 in J. Armitage and J. Roberts (eds) *Living with Cyberspace: Technology and Society in the 21st Century*, New York and London: Continuum.

Baudrillard, J. (1990) *Seduction*, Basingstoke: Palgrave Macmillan.

DeLillo, D. (1986) *White Noise*, London: Picador.

Eco, U. (2000) *Kant and the Platypus*, tr. A. McEwen, London: Vintage.

Forgacs, D. (ed) (1988) *A Gramsci Reader*, London: Lawrence and Wishart.

Gramsci, A. (1971) *Selections from the Prison Notebooks*. London: Lawrence and Wishart.

Harvey, D. (1989) *The Condition of Postmodernity*, Oxford: Blackwell.

Heidegger, M. (1997) *Kant and the Problem of Metaphysics*, tr. R. Taft, Bloomington: Indiana University Press.

Kearney, R. (1986) *Modern Movements in European Philosophy*, Manchester: Manchester University Press.

Kellner, D. (1999) 'Virilio, war and technology: some critical reflections', *Theory, Culture and Society*, 16(5–6): 103–26.

Kreitzman, L. (1999) *The 24 Hour Society*, London: Profile Books.

Lash, S. and Urry, J. (1993) *Economies of Signs and Space*, London: Sage.

Luckács, G. (1971) *History and Class Consciousness: Studies in Marxist Dialectics*, tr. R. Livingstone. Cambridge Mass.: MIT Press.

Marx, K. (1999) www.marxists.org/archive/marx/works/1867-c1/, consulted November 15th 2005.

Virilio, P. (1995) 'Speed and information: Cyberspace alarm!' *Le Monde Diplomatique*, August, tr. P. Riemens and included in D. Trend (ed.) (2001) D. (ed.) (2001) *Reading Digital Culture*, Oxford: Blackwell: 23–7.

Virilio, P. (1997) *Open Sky*, tr. J. Rose, London: Verso.

Virilio, P. (2000) *The Information Bomb*, tr. C. Turner, London: Verso.

Weber, M. (2001) *The Protestant Ethic and the Spirit of Capitalism*, London: Routledge Classics.

SECTION I

The Speed of Organizational Identity

Chapter 2

Fast Capitalism and Slowmodernity

Ben Agger

I (Agger 1989a) have argued that capitalism has quickened since WWII, especially with the advent of the Internet. People work harder and more; their private space has been eroded; kids are doing adult-like amounts of homework and activities; people eat badly, on the run, and then embark on crash diets and exercise programs. The world is ever-present and omnipresent, saturating us with stimuli, discourses, directives. It is difficult to gain distance from the everyday in order to appraise it. Our very identities as stable selves are at risk. We need to slow it all down.

Tuning In, Turning On, Dropping Out

Slowing down is easier said than done. The self is so embattled, bombarded from all sides at all hours via all media, that reclaiming it, as if we ever had it in the first place, is a tall order. Heroic measures are usually futile. And yet the 1960s taught us, first in the anti-war and civil rights movements and then the women's movement, that the self matters. The self is political, as are everyday life, the body, food, sex, exercise, and culture – even if not all politics involves the personal, sexual, dietary, and cultural. Critical theory and postmodernism powerfully teach us that discourse, language, writing, media, cultures, bodies and bedrooms are the new contested terrain of post-WWII, post-Fordist, fast and now faster capitalism. The forces of capital and control, those who benefit from disempowering selves, have colonized what used to be off limits to the social and political. They have done so, as I have been arguing, largely to find new markets and at the same time divert people from the revolutionary deed or, as Timothy Leary and hippies preferred during the sixties, from dropping out (and perhaps dropping acid). Marcuse (1955) said it well when he talked of the late-capitalist performance principle, according to which all life, experience, diet, sex, and leisure are mobilized in order to reproduce the existing order, denying a Dionysian desire that would recognize the prospect of liberation inscribed in advanced technologies capable of finally delivering us from scarcity. Performativity is

27

the logic of faster capitalism, subjecting all of life, and even children's existence, to scheduling, producing, connecting, messaging, immersing oneself in the quotidian and therefore losing sight of the bigger picture.

This bigger picture, like a complicated jigsaw puzzle or mosaic, can only be grasped from the vantage of distance. Adorno (1978) and his Frankfurt colleagues preached distance as the vantage of critical reason from which we can appraise our damaged lives, figuring out what bonds us and then what we can do to burst free. Marcuse argued that distance, and thus critical consciousness, was being reduced because in late capitalism people are so immersed in everyday life that they can't stand outside of it in order to appraise it. This is one of my main contentions about a fast and faster capitalism: People's lives are so accelerated that they cannot slow down sufficiently to take stock let alone begin to change things. It is all people can do to keep up with the frenzy of cyberspace – e-mail, cell phone calls, instant messaging, directives from the boss, children's frantic schedules, a substantial and growing work load that respects neither temporal nor physical boundaries.

Adorno chose the spatial metaphor of distance and closeness to characterize the predicament of the social critic who must work hard to separate himself from the everyday in order to gain a critical vantage on it. I choose the metaphor of time, passing rapidly or slowly, in order to suggest that social critics must slow down their worlds in order to grasp and then reorder them. We must turn off television and the cell phone; we must not obsess about our e-mail; we must insulate our children against an incipient, premature adulthood; we must slow down and think things through, carefully evaluating modernity for its strengths and weaknesses and not simply accepting existence as a plenitude of social being.

Although people in modern cultures are better educated than in Marx's time, Marx could gain the vantage of social criticism more easily than we can because the issues were more basic then – getting enough to eat, finding shelter, providing for one's family, escaping political tyranny. Today the issues seem more nuanced as we live amid abundance, if not for everyone. Let us not forget that one out of every four Americans lives near, or below, the poverty line, which is currently considered to be an annual income of $17,900 for a family of four. Try to buy groceries, pay rent, perhaps maintain a car, acquire health insurance, and even save modestly for future education on that pitiful sum! And without education one's children will be destined to relive one's own penury, locked into a cycle of poverty that seems natural, inescapable, for its tenacious hold on minds and bodies.

Barbara Ehrenreich documents the working poor who subsist at the margins of our economy and society, desperately clinging to the edge of subsistence while doing exhausting, degrading part-time jobs without benefits. But the lives about which Ehrenreich writes do not include her own, which affords her not only distance – and with it education, time, hope – but also the luxury of shedding her life and taking on another, "going underground" to experience first-hand what it's like to live as the working poor do. Ehrenreich does this as a literary methodology, a way of getting inside other selves much more desperate than her own. But no matter how bleak her lot while working at Wal-Mart or for a maid service, she always knew that she was "going home", out of penury and back to security, from the vantage of which she could engage in important social criticism. Ehrenreich masterfully combines distance and immersion in order to tell the stories of selves denied the privileges of time, food, housing, health care – stability.

For the poor and desperate, distance, and with it hope as well as systematic anger – expressed as theory – is unattainable and probably even unimaginable. For the comfortably college educated and middle class, distance, contemplation, and critical thought are rejected as a violation of utility and performativity. They are "good for nothing", a waste of time. As the vast majority of my students ask me and my colleagues, "Is it going to be on the test?" "Am I responsible for the lectures or the readings?" "Do I have to have footnotes?" "Exactly what pages do I have to read?" Some of my colleagues, in utter frustration, give objective tests, supposing that real understanding can be sacrificed for a modicum of content, given that most of our students are unmotivated, turned off by the intellectual life. They merely imitate their parents and the culture at large, which substitute performance for thought and utility for intrinsic value. The theoretical life won't pay the mortgage, car note, tuition, or credit-card bill.

My argument risks being a romantic one for distance, contemplation, and quietude – life lived at a snail's pace in order to take stock and then take action. Our culture needs romanticism in order to arrive at the electric moment when thought becomes action, first on the personal level and then collectively, even globally. It also needs humanism, as I will explore later, at the risk of offending postmodernists who have given up on selves. We need to contemplate utopia and implicitly our distance from it, even as we acknowledge that fantasies often turn into nightmares if accompanied by hubris, arrogance. It takes dexterity, subtlety, and nuance to engage in social criticism and visionary theory without being prescriptive; our problems are common, but our solutions may vary with context, culture, race, gender, generation. Most visions end up being hallucinations, distorting and deceiving. And yet not to fantasize condemns one to the quotidian, to what I am calling immersion and instantaneity, which block distance, critique, and action. My students are so utilitarian because the culture at large elevates performance and production over evaluation and reflection. Again, this is the meaning of Marcuse's concept of one-dimensional thought.

Worldliness has become a plague, blunting critical insight by bending it back toward earth and not into outer space, with utopian reach. We are too worldly not only in the sense that we have too many experiences and know too much trivia but also in that our experiences rush by so quickly that we cannot pause to consider what is happening to us, and why. Worldliness involves immersion and instantaneity, being swallowed up by things that, in themselves, are coveted, and living in the moment instead of considering many moments, both past and future. The present becomes eternal, devoid of history, which includes the possibility of a different, better future. The character trait best suited to this everyday world of instant, all-encompassing experience is versatility, the ability to adapt to whatever comes one's way, rapidly. We learn quickly, even as children, that we must be flexible, roll with the punches, compromise, accept what we cannot change. Of course, this acquiescence has always been taught by religion, which, as Marx knew, blunts critical consciousness and discourages utopia as well as revolution.

We begin to learn these lessons in school and in our early play groups (see Bowles and Gintis 1976). Many report cards have grades for "citizenship", which combines conformity and obedience. As kids we are also taught instrumental rationality, how to study for tests and turn in homework in order to earn good grades that will ease our way into comfortable adulthood. By the time we get to high school, many American kids already know what they want, which are essentially lives like their parents' – suburbia, white-collar jobs, vacations, cars, electronic technologies for entertainment and communication. Our needs have already been determined, indeed overdetermined, by peers, parents, and the media. It is already far too late to become critical theorists, let alone political activists. Childhood and adolescence have rushed by, barely allowing kids pause to locate themselves in a world not of their making and to question the value of values, let alone ask the question of questions. It is for this reason that we must turn to childhood and schooling in order to slow down the virtual self.

Raising Different Kids

My kids are already different from their peers. They aren't yet allowed to stay home alone. They don't know much about cars or colleges. They don't have boyfriends or girlfriends. They don't have their own phone line, or televisions in their rooms. They have traveled beyond North America, and they eat weird foreign food, but they aren't worldly in the sense of knowing what is on late-night television or the plots of the latest R-rated movies. We talk about sex, and define scatological terms for them in order to sate their curiosity, but they aren't yet sexualized. They play instruments, and sports, too, but not on "select" teams that require monthly fees, a contract, emotional intensity and rigorous practice and travel schedules. They go to bed early by their classmates' standards, and they never stay up overnight in order to toilet-paper houses. Sometimes, they say they feel deprived by neighborhood and schoolroom, but we know better.

My wife and I are purposely slowing down our kids' lives where we can. Although they often have mountains of homework, we keep their schedules fairly clear so that they can decompress from the accelerated pace of school and of life. We want them to play, to rest, to explore, to think, to be kids. We know other parents who recognize that kids grow up too fast, and we encourage our kids to play with their kids and not with worldly, jaded kids. We put a premium on studiousness, but not on grades or test scores. As academics, we recognize that test taking is an art and that much homework, especially the taxonomic kind requiring mere memorization, adds little, if any, value (see Kralovec and Buell 2000). We want our kids to read, and to want to read. We want them to be creative, writing stories and plays, which they enact. They go to theater camp in the summer, and art classes during the year.

This combines a slowing down of life with enrichment, a delicate, but not impossible, balance. There is a difference between being worldly, in a superficial sense of knowing the "latest" cultural trends, and being firmly situated in the world and then being curious about it. We want our kids to ask questions, to interrogate authority and rules, to think critically and not accept what is given to them. We want them to be expressive and not passive or downtrodden. In the American south, including Texas, kids are often taught to call their elders "sir" or "ma'am". When I first heard this, I immediately read Southern "manners" for the social-psychological underpinnings of authoritarianism, involving deference and idolatry. We are Yankees (a Southern pejorative for states on the wrong side during the Civil War), and we want our kids to be Yankees! We also want them to be respectful. The challenge is to inculcate respectfulness while teaching children not to be submissive.

The challenge of raising kids, then, is to insulate them from the world while teaching them about the world. They need Adorno's precious quality of mind called distance, differentiating knowledge and the knower from the everyday in order to question its rightness and permanence. The key philosophical term here is *historicity*, a way of viewing the present, and facts, as grounded in the past, which bore them, and opening to a possible but not necessary future. Thus, one can analyze today's capitalist economy as stemming from feudalism and the beginnings of the Industrial Revolution, and stretching into the immediate and perhaps even distant future. But the economy, like everything else in the world that bears the human imprint, is defined by "historicity". That is, just because we have known capitalism for over a century, and know it today, does not mean that it must endure forever, as non-Marxist social theorists such as Durkheim, Weber and Parsons allege. History's final chapter has yet to be written.

We teach our kids to view the world through the lenses of historicity, recognizing "why" things are the way they are, rooted in the past, but at the same time recognizing that the social world is fluid and can be transformed. This transformation must pass through selves, people like you and me who inhere in everyday life and aren't oblivious to it and yet who grasp the big picture, necessarily known through paradigms and not simply through the accumulation of piecemeal evidence. After all, evidence is a text, a mode of rhetoric, argument for one state of affairs or another. Positivism is a text urging people to give in and give up, to accept the given instead of recognizing their own potential for "giving" it, and giving it differently.

This argument for (or perhaps, better, from) agency risks being another politics of subjectivity, issuing in self-improvement and individual attainment, all the way from better jobs to better bodies and better mates. Although the personal matters, as feminism has taught us, so does the political, which, in these postmodern times, positions the personal as its accomplice. False needs are imposed on the self, and then internalized so that they appear to be one's own choices. But politics is not exhausted by the personal, even as it mobilizes everyday life, sexuality, bodies, desire, even the unconscious. It is all too easy for our children to hear our arguments from agency – "you can be anything you want to be" – as personal and not also political arguments, which in some cases they certainly are. Todd Gitlin (2003) recently published a book, sold tellingly in the self-help section at Barnes & Noble, offering advice to young radicals and activists. Gitlin wants the next generations to commit the revolutionary deed, but with gentle guidance and admonitions from ancient 1960s radicals such as him and me! When I first saw the book, I realized that Gitlin and I were, in parallel ways, addressing the post-baby boom generations who, we hope, can learn to connect personal and political agency.

Self-Care, Alternative Lifestyles, Counterhegemony

The weight of what anthropologists call culture bears down heavily on all of us, unless we live on a desert island. The movie *Castaway*, in which forsaken airline passenger Chuck Noland (played by Tom Hanks) is stranded on just such a desert island, showed how culture and the self were called into question in its depiction of Noland's struggles to stay alive and remain hopeful about his rescue. Noland had to create a modicum of civilization for himself, not just finding food and building shelter but also creating myths of meaning that revolved around his past life and his hope of regaining it by being found. He had little to sustain hope, apart from a picture of his wife that survived the airplane crash and a ball that he fashioned into a totem that he animated by giving it a name. He created his own culture, in solitary confinement on that distant island, and thus he saved himself, giving himself the psychic resources with which to embark on a desperate but ultimately successful voyage home.

Even on this deserted island, Noland wasn't inured to the effects of culture. He brought with him both the material culture of his few remaining possessions and the ensemble of his ideal culture, including his values, impulses, priorities, and pragmatism – his theory, by another name. Culture – theory – saved him by giving him both hope and a game plan for escaping the island's lonely hold. Even the most isolated and forlorn among us, in prison or the mental prisons of our own making, can exercise Sartrean agency and change ourselves and even begin to change the world around us (see Sartre 1976). As Hegel and then existentialism demonstrated, consciousness can never be entirely imprinted by the edicts and structures, which often appear intractable, of the outer world (see Poster 1975). Marx seized on this insight and argued not for a solitary consciousness but for collective consciousness, of the proletariat, with which to uproot old orders and create new institutions.

Marx assumed that workers would communicate effectively with each other, beginning on the factory floor and in the everyday sites of their daily existences, about the evils of capitalism and how to overcome them in a new society. They would write and read pamphlets and theoretical treatises, opening themselves to political education that would overturn the falsehoods of bourgeois ideology. This ideology argues that the world cannot be changed, toward a communist utopia, and thus workers – everyone – must content themselves with their meager lot. People could hope for modest self-betterment, through savings and the acquisition of skills, but not for radical changes in social structures.

At stake in a faster capitalism is the status of consciousness, and then communication. Marx did not foresee the extent to which people's minds and needs could fall prey to advertising and pro-capitalist political theories. He assumed a mode of consciousness that could distinguish between true and false claims, and thus overthrow all ideologies. He assumed reason and rationality, where today they are very much at stake. He assumed the ability to engage in clear discourse and to achieve consensus. Fast capitalism, and its accelerated Internetworked version, has laid waste to reason and reasoning, requiring selves to work hard in order to escape the gravitational pull of the everyday in order to imagine, and work towards, different worlds.

The Internet is a literary vehicle, composed of, and calling forth, millions of literary and interpretive acts. One cannot find definitive answers if by that we mean we can find Web pages we can simply trust without questioning their authority and digging beneath their claims for what is left unsaid. Internet postings are no less literary, indeed fictional, than other literary versions. One finds contradictory, incomplete, question-begging, carping, purposely deceiving and made-for-profit pages. This can be confusing for amateur surfers interested in finding out the truth of things, whether the cheapest airfare to Orlando or the best way to treat tennis elbow. The inherent ambiguity and indeterminacy of the Internet – of course, of all knowledge – is *undecidability*, by which Derrida means that sentences don't end other sentences but instead beget new ones, in questioning and clarification. Even science, as I and others have written often (Agger 1989b, 2000; Aronowitz 1988), is susceptible to a Derridean deconstruction, revealing science's text to be every bit as undecidable, as a poem, novel or music video.

This doesn't defeat self-education, and thus alternative lifestyles, via the Internet, in effect slowing down capitalism. It doesn't mean that we must be cynical about writings, and thus all theoretical systems, as nihilist deconstructors sometimes are. Rather, the occasion of the Internet's inherent democracy and polyvocality should be seized on as an occasion for new texts and thus new worlds – new ways to live, work, raise families, become educated, get fit, and eat better. Today, the weight and speed of capitalism compel private solutions to our problems, for which we consult self-help pages and enter chat rooms devoted to single issues. But it is conceivable that Internet-based reading and writing can do more than change individual lives, instead shifting power and building community in ways that defy the commodifying, conformist tendencies of capitalism.

As long as we understand that the self's experiences are fundamentally social, stemming from overbearing social structures of work, family, education, leisure, and diet, we can deal with the self's problems as social problems. Eating more fish and less meat, working out regularly, finding jobs that don't require dishonesty and alienation, and decelerating the pace of children's lives and schooling can become not only personal adjustments – alternative lifestyles – but genuine modes of counterhegemony, by which I mean fighting capitalism and figuring out alternatives to it that have meaning and momentum (Gramsci 1971). This risks being heard as a timeworn utopianism, a long journey beginning with a single step. I remain convinced, by feminists, existential Marxists and the Frankfurt School, that social change must change people – and requires people to be changed for it to occur, in the fateful simultaneity of self- and social change. What is so difficult today is imagining that self change can occur so massively, globally and rapidly that incremental changes cumulate into major structural transformations. And yet the Internet makes this easier to imagine than even 15 years ago, when I wrote *Fast Capitalism*, and certainly than 150 years ago, when Marx published *Capital* (1967, originally published in 1867). The Internet helps us imagine, and then exploit, the protean connection between selves and social structure as we enter others' worlds, and affect them, with quick keystrokes using DSL connections.

The Dialectic of Discourse: Decline or Democracy

As Garfinkel's (1967) ethnomethodology helps us understand, discourse constitutes social structure – the ways in which we talk about, and then resolve, social quandaries, such as how to make ourselves understood in a rapidly moving, complex, imperfect, noisy world. We find ways to "do" social structure – of families, work, schools – from the ground up, using our ingenuity, inferential abilities, empathy and especially our literary skills, decoding what others and the media say, and then communicating with others. Garfinkel helps us understand that underlying social structure are discourse, consensus and sense making, not abstract social laws identified earlier by Parsons (1951) as the moving force of a sociological invisible hand. Parsons' law-like "pattern variables" of adjustment, integration, boundary maintenance and goal setting are fictions, just terms for what people ordinarily do as they read the paper in differentiating truth from fiction, help their kids with homework, finesse a micromanaging boss, or conduct themselves at neighborhood meetings. People "do" these things using their powers of discourse, inferring, interpolating, imagining, signifying – deconstructing, by another name.

The Internet is a sprawling, global, nearly instantaneous vehicle of discourse, and thus of social structure. It is replacing newspapers, magazines, television, movie theaters, stand-alone CD players and tapes and even books. It is replacing pulp, which comes from trees. When I chaired a faculty job search in my department, we no longer write letters of acknowledgment to applicants or to their references. We used e-mail to do the search, saving on postage, stationery, and telephone bills. Using e-mail helps speed up the process of a faculty job search, which, in this case, is probably a good thing because we are helping candidates sort out their job-market options more efficiently. But replacing pulp in other respects is very problematic, preventing people from writing and receiving letters, which they peruse and savor, attending public theaters and concerts, and reading and writing books that matter. The Internet, a frictionless vehicle of discourse and thus of social structure and self-change, has the potential for enhancing democracy and overthrowing capitalism, which thwarts democracy, but, in its conformist, commodified version, accelerates what I have called the decline of discourse. Democratized discourse resists and reverses discourse's decline, yet again demonstrating that the Internet is dialectical, possessing the contradictory potential for liberation and domination.

It is tempting to call for a return to pulp as a panacea – an era of slow publishing, transportation, mail, journalism, entertainment, education. Here, pulp is a metaphor for considered reflection, which takes time and requires distance from its object. But pulp can be a conservative metaphor where we return to a mandarin or high culture in which very few have the opportunity to write books, let alone wield political and economic power. It is a contemporary metaphor for the elite organization of academic social science in which the opportunity to publish articles in refereed journals is restricted to a lucky few who sport the correct letterhead, have friends in high places and use the quantitative methodologies prevailing in midwestern empiricism. Pulp, as counterpoint to the Internet, is also dialectical, requiring the distance and time necessary for critique or reinforcing elite codes of disciplinary and cultural power closed off to nearly everyone.

Imagine Adorno answering his email or putting up a personal Web page! This is a credible image, given his interest in technologies of culture and art. I suspect that he would have been skeptical, as I am here, of digitality, in Negroponte's sense, as a panacea for personal and social problems, just as he would have rejected the technological utopianism of Daniel Bell's postindustrialism (which is a veiled attack on Marxism, from which Bell [1960] broke). And the Frankfurt School, writing for the most part before Garfinkel's ethnomethodology and French postmodern theory, did not place emphasis on discourse as a basis of social structure. They were more traditional Marxists who retained Marx's original 19th-century concept of ideology, even as they addressed an accelerating capitalism of state intervention and the culture industries. But I can envision Adorno not only sending emails to Horkheimer, separated by their travels, but also theorizing the Internet – pixels and/or pulp, decline and/or democracy – as a stage of faster capitalism in which we can no longer assume the separation of text and world (subject and object). Our inability to assume this separation would have led Adorno to address what I am calling the decline of discourse, but it might have led him, and it certainly would have led Marcuse (always more upbeat and engaged), to seize on the permeable boundary between culture and society, critique and social structure, as an occasion for what Gramsci (1971) first called counterhegemony – critique and action bridging the self and structures within which selves are constituted.

This work has already begun as latter-day critical theorists such as Luke, Kellner, Poster and I have addressed a virtual, postmodern, faster capitalism, and its contradictory potentials for further decline or greater democracy. Inspired by the Frankfurt School but conditioned by television, music and movies, we recognize that the decline of discourse occasioned by the Internet and media culture might reverse itself toward greater democracy, even undoing capitalism as we know it, if people learn to use information, communication and entertainment technologies in order to live different lives and become different selves. It cannot be ignored that as I am writing these words, millions of people in the U.S. and abroad are not lying on their couches watching television while drinking beer but busily composing – themselves – on the Internet, even if few of them have read *Capital, Fast Capitalism, Screens of Power* (Luke 1989), *What's the Matter with the Internet?* (Poster

2001), or *Media Culture* (Kellner 1995). They are learning how to live better and they are creating community. It is easy to see the political potential of this discursive activity, which is, above all, literary work – reading, interpreting, writing, revising.

As capitalism speeds along, people use the Internet and other information technologies to connect to and organize their work, home, school, kids, friends, and leisure activities. As I have been arguing, this sucks people into hurried, unstudied lives immersed in the everyday. What I am trying to do here is not abandon everyday life but connect it to utopia. The casualty of capitalism's acceleration since the late 1980s has been reason, a word inimical to instrumental rationality and even to postmodernists, who fear dogmatic reason. But the Freudian Marxism of the Frankfurt School, especially Marcuse, the embodied existential Marxism of Sartre (1956) and Merleau-Ponty (1964a, 1964b) and left-wing feminist theory demonstrate convincingly that one can develop reasons and rationalities that do not trample the self or defoliate nature. This embodied, humane reason was grounded in the body subject by early Marx, who begins critical theory, from which I draw here.

By partaking of the Internet's opportunities for busy textuality (both as readings and writings), people enticed to live the fast life can also slow it down by developing the capacity for discourse and thus citizenship, both understanding and mastering their everyday worlds. The Internet is a trap, but also a vehicle of practical reason and critique. Garfinkel, contrary to Parsons, helps us understand social structure as the contingent everyday practices of people situated in their lifeworlds. People don't necessarily possess perfect information, advanced degrees, endless leisure, and ample resources. They cannot always make themselves understood, or understand. Yet, as Garfinkel demonstrated, people create meaning out of chaos, becoming adept at a communicative competence that helps them make sense of indeterminacy, imperfect information, and misunderstandings, as well as poverty, racism and sexism. Garfinkel's self is similar to Sartre's efficacious agent of *Being and Nothingness* (1956), both of which derive from early Marx's self of praxis – he who imprints himself on the world through work and achieves communion with others and with nature.

The literary self isn't always already political but can become political as we write and read our way out of bad habits, unreflected rapid routines. I am not saying that chatting online is a paradigm, or embryo, of liberation but rather that chatting is an example of an embryonic textuality or literariness that models self-determination and communicative competence. This potential to do discourse, to write, read, chat critically, can become political when oriented to building community and rearranging power. Garfinkel showed that everyday selves create social structure which, by implication, they can transform using different political frameworks. His – and phenomenology's – point is that the constitution of social structure always begins from the ground of everyday life and is not simply foisted on people from above, by the custodians of alleged social laws (of differentiation, stratification, modernization and so on) promulgated by 19th and early 20th century positivist sociology. To ignore people's capacity for what Sartre called agency – authorship – is an act of bad faith, abandoning the constitution of social structure to others, who are experienced as dominant.

Slowmodernity

The critique of fast, and even faster, capitalism, much like the critique of fast food (Petrini 2003; Schlosser 2001), risks returning to a supposed golden age of premodern rural life. The "slow food" movement is a case in point, although Petrini implies a critique of capitalist mass production in his argument for local cuisine savored over a glass of indigenous wine. Who can disagree with his critique of McDonald's, especially where he brandishes bowls of pasta in metaphorical opposition? Schlosser's critique of the economic, workplace and health perils of fat-laden, meat-driven fast food is an important part of my perspective on capitalism's acceleration. However, in embracing slow food and slow life we risk regressing behind modernity, which, as Habermas argues, needs to be defended, even if, as he also notes, modernity's project has yet to be fulfilled. At issue here are metaphors of modernity and the implications they bear for a critique of a faster capitalism heavily reliant on the Internet and other social technologies of acceleration and globalization.

The speedup of social technologies and everyday lives breaks down important barriers between public and private required for people to engage in self-reflection and communication. People lose the vantage from which critique is possible. This has always been the argument of the Frankfurt School. In my book *Fast Capitalism*, I revised Marcuse's critique of the eclipse of reason by noticing that capitalism has sped up, under sway of further Taylorism and Fordism, threatening the very status of *the book* as a vehicle of critique and persuasion. Today, things have gotten more perilous for critical reason because the Internet and other information and social technologies such as the cell phone and courier services make it even harder to gain the distance and time necessary for reflection and reason. The Internet and media cultures not only cause the book to decline further, but also enable the penetration and colonization of everyday life, of consciousness itself. The wired world tempts us to abandon not only books in the traditional sense of texts that stand apart and require us to work at their meanings, but all quiet time – here, the metaphor of slow life – during which we are not "connected".

The average American child spends five and a half hours a day using information and entertainment technologies, all the way from television (by now almost a traditional medium) to computers and video games. This attenuates childhood and negates other developmental activities such as playing outside with other kids, reading, studying, and practicing music. The sheer health risks are abundant as children who surf also gorge themselves on fatty fast foods and convenience foods. It seems obvious that the solution is to turn off the television and computer, to send kids out to play, and to return to family dinners with meals prepared from scratch.

The metaphor of slow life is appealing, but it risks an anti-technology posture that regresses behind modernity to a postmodern pastoralism. Petrini sometimes implies that the good society would be a wine-tasting circle or dining club. Although I share his critique not only of fast food but also of fast life, requiring standardization, mass production and globalization, the pastoral, almost premodern alternative is fundamentally bourgeois; it would change very little, except for Yuppies able to travel and savor regional wines and goat cheese (or, while they are at home, to shop and eat with a cosmopolitan sensibility). The problem, as Marx always recognized, is not technology, but its uses. It is not the machine or factory system, or now the Internet, but the social contexts in which these technologies are deployed. At issue, then, as it was for Marx, is power, and notably the power accruing to wealth.

Postmodern critiques of the modern tend to focus on industry, factories, technology, science, and the loss of meaning (see Davis 1990; Harvey 1989; Soja 1989). These are compelling issues, but they can be better addressed within a modernist critique of modernity – Marxism. This is because Marx had no illusions about the superiority of the capitalist-modern over its premodern predecessors. Who doesn't prefer electricity over candlelight, hospitals over hospices, public schools over homeschooling? Of course, the upper-middle class take these amenities for granted, which is why they can embrace "slow food" defined as regional cuisine and wine whose prices are necessarily prohibitive. Marx was a modernist, but he argued that capitalism doesn't exhaust modernity; indeed, it is the penultimate stage of prehistory, after which real history, modernity, can blossom, harnessing technology to human needs and pacifying our relationship to nature.

Slow food and slow life are important goals, but they must be situated within, and not before or beyond, modernity. I term *slowmodernity* a stage of civilization in which modernist manufacturing and information technologies are utilized to decelerate the pace of existence, thus redrawing the boundaries between private and public, self and society, that an accelerated postmodern/Internet capitalism has nearly dissolved. Petrini is correct to oppose agribusiness, pesticides, Taylorized fast-food restaurants, and supermarket chains in the name of slow life, but we must insert slowness into modernity in such a way that we don't eliminate certain fast technologies, including media culture and the Internet, that enable a literary democracy of the kind I have been describing. The slow must coexist with the fast – the modern – as we formulate a new vision of the end of history, which is neither the fast-modernity of capitalism nor a postmodernity that abandons the project of modernity altogether. I side with Habermas (and Marx) on the value of modernity; I side with Derrida and Adorno on the hidden arrogance and dominance of a version of modernity springing from the Enlightenment; I side with Petrini on the superiority of penne pasta lightly tossed with olive oil and parmesan or doused with marinara over the Big Mac. Together, these theoretical, existential and culinary tendencies define what I am calling the slowmodern, a society as yet unfolding in which fast technologies, providing for basic needs and making electronic democracy possible, coexist with slower technologies of pulp books and old-fashioned letters, family dinners, long walks, and unencumbered childhoods.

The dilemma of the "slowing down" metaphor is that it risks Luddism, regressing to a premodern past. A technological utopianism based on speed fails to extricate capitalism, which pits speed against thought and text, from modernity, which has yet to be fulfilled. A modernity that remains capitalist, even using the Internet, thwarts Marx's projection of a society in which technology could be used to master nature in fulfilling human needs, allowing people time for praxis – self-creative work on a pacified nature. *Modernity as an image of the end of history needs to be transformed into slowmodernity, a final stage in which frictionless community building and literary work via the Internet and other informational and entertainment technologies coexist with the simple pleasures of slow life, slow food, slow bodies, slow families, and slow work.*

The issue, thus, isn't only pace or speed. In slowmodernity, the fast and slow coexist: People enjoy the slow life amidst rapid cybercommunications and instant technologies that free them from scarcity (see Dyer-Witheford 1999). The issue, rather, is the ways in which fast technologies break down boundaries and barriers that used to insulate the self, and reason, against a forbidding outside world. Of course, as critical theory, deconstruction, feminism and psychoanalysis all demonstrate, there is neither an unsullied "inside" nor impinging "outside" that are not somehow implicated in the other. The self, and its critical reason, was never a world apart, nor can it ever be, given its saturation with the social. And, as Marx demonstrated, we can create an "outside" – economy and culture – that doesn't thwart reason but instead embodies it.

Slowmodernity involves restoring certain boundaries, including those between public and private, self and society, text and world, and reason and its object. It also involves breaking down other boundaries, such as those between friends, neighbors, colleagues, and cultures. In a supposedly global era, ethnocentrism is arguably the greatest barrier to completing the project of modernity. The premodern threatens to undo culture and civilization, even as they bear the scars of inhumanity.

Retreat behind a boundary restores the self, who can dine, love, and exercise, *slowly*, without time compression and acceleration. But one can also venture forth into the world, with minimal resistance, embracing globality, universality, and totality especially via the electronic prostheses that de-privatize the self. In fast capitalism, the self has the worst of both worlds: He is dominated in public, by fast work, fast food, fast cars, even fast diets – fasting. This is the intensely social, saturated self (Gergen 2000) that cannot resist its constitution by, and as, the social object. And yet the self is denied a healthy and communitarian – no, communist! – privacy, that includes the moment of publicity – friends, family, even colleagues. The person feels very much alone when the public/private boundary is assailed by media culture and the Internet, cut off from meaningful relationships, including, as Petrini reminds us, the experience of convivial dining.

In slowmodernity, people could live as quickly or slowly as they like, traveling far to sample regional cuisines and cultures or staying home to compose letters, read newspapers and books, author the culture – and themselves. Authorship is citizenship in slowmodernity, which combines the project of modernity – industrial production, democracy, cities, medicine and science – with certain valuable premodern elements such as community, intimacy, ceremony, low-fat diets of organic, unprocessed foods, exercise and physical exertion, papyrus and then pulp. The premodern is not to be condemned simply because mythology and dogma prevailed. There were important premodern counterforces that humanized agrarian Europe, affording what Weber called "enchantment" (1978). The subsequent disenchantment of the world by science, technology, industry and globality eliminated these premodern vestiges that could have saved the project of modernity, notably capitalism, from itself, indeed from its pace and its destruction of boundaries, including the boundary between the self and world.

Although postmodern theory affords invaluable insight into the power and opportunities of discourse, revealing apparently non-discursive accounts such as science to be decisive, deliberate authorial choices (that could have been made differently), the metaphor of the postmodern – "after" modernity – abandons slow life in favor of an informatic instantaneity. Fast life is assumed as either late-modern or genuinely postmodern, and utopia is depicted, by non-leftist postmodernists, as "life on the screen", not as life with others. But slowing things down can be formulated as a postmodern agenda if by postmodernity we understand the fulfillment of modernity's promise once modernity is no longer allowed to assail all boundaries.

This is another way of saying that fast and slow life – lives – can coexist, distinguishing between what is worthy about a modernity inextricably bound up with capitalism – medicine, health care, democracy, science, transportation, material and information technologies – and the premodern, which includes low-fat diets rich in processed foods, conviviality, community. Indeed, this communitarian, agrarian premodern, less anchored in reality than in a Luddite, pastoral mythology of yesteryear before the machine age, *transforms* the modern by shattering its capitalist framework. As he well understands, Petrini's argument for slow food and slow life amounts to nothing if it does not destroy agribusiness, slaughterhouses, supermarket chains, food and lifestyle advertising, and the exploitation of minimum-wage labor. It is harmless, even conformist, to suppose that one can change the world by boiling one's penne pasta, sprinkling aged cheese over it and washing it down with a regional wine. That changes nothing if it remains lifestyle, enjoyed by a few while the rest are locked into alienated labor, fast lives, fatty food, obesity and meaninglessness.

The argument for a slowmodernity, thus, breaks from capitalism without abandoning the project of modernity. It borrows a premodern image of slow life that it then blends with fast-paced information, communication and material technologies freeing people from what early Marx called alienation. Images of slow life from premodernity help us disentangle modernity and capitalism, issuing in a slowmodernity that can be viewed as a desirable utopian endpoint. The slow purges the fast of its boundary-shattering tendencies, instead allowing people to rebuild boundaries and blend slow with fast in ways that facilitate human needs – precisely Petrini's image of slow life, as I understand it. It is remarkable that his imagery of a slow life and slow food, which refreshes critical theory at a time of its impasse, comes not from communication theory (Habermas 1984, 1987b) or aesthetic theory (Adorno 1984) but from *food theory*. I found Petrini's book in the cooking section of an Austin bookstore!

Food theory becomes critical social theory where we allow diet and shopping to illuminate key issues of the public/private relationship, global markets, and the body. I am inserting the argument for slow food and slow life into the discussion of modernity and postmodernity. I conceptualize the completion of the project of modernity using images from both the premodern and capitalist-modern (slow and fast, respectively), issuing in a notion of slowmodernity that doubles back on capitalist alienation and boundary shattering in order to return to a perhaps mythic notion of slow food, slow life, and slow community. In this light, we find the premodern inadequate because it is penurious and irrational; we find the modern inadequate because it is bound up with capitalism's conquest of nature and otherness; we find the postmodern inadequate because it disqualifies utopia. We retain from the premodern the notion of slow life, from modernity a promise of technological abundance and electronic democracy and community and from the postmodern a questioning about the Enlightenment's dubious equation of reason and science.

All of this is to suggest, with Petrini, the Frankfurt School and various leftist postmodernists and feminists, that progress needs to be reconceived not as conquest *of* but productive harmony *with* nature. Adorno viewed the desired end of history as the redemption of nature, which reflected his Nietzschean critique of the Enlightenment's Promethean will to power. Nature has its seasons and rhythms, to which all things return. Alienation from nature, especially in urban life and via interstate highways and expressways, takes its toll on the slow life, which needs to measure itself against nature's cycles of eternal recurrence. In slowmodernity, we will restore and redeem nature as a standard by which other activities and arrangements are judged. This is why food theory opens the way to a broader understanding of society and culture: Food is nature, and it reveals to us our own nature as sentient beings. The early Marx, Marcuse in his Freudian Marxism, feminist theorists of the body subject and now Petrini help us theorize the body in nature, especially via food, diet, and exercise.

This is not puritanism, preaching abstinence, as Petrini indicates. One can revel in the reproduction of one's body through eating, especially, I would add, if one works the body hard, both in vocation and recreation. The spent body, toned and purged of the poisons of fast life, relishes cuisine and the conviviality of dining. Since most of us don't work with our hands and bodies, we require exercise – preferably sport – in order to be fit. But it is not only good health I am urging here; it is the experience of oneness with nature that comes from experiencing our bodies as both body subjects and objects, at once humanity and nature. Sartre and Merleau-Ponty well understood that existence is embodied, helping their existentialism move considerably beyond Descartes' thinking subject. I add here that the subject is also an eating and exercising subject, and a loving subject, that experiences full humanity when working on itself and replenishing itself with the fruits of slow life, cooked and eaten slowly, in sync with nature.

From Food Theory to Critical Theory, Body Politics to the Body Politic

In his argument for slow food and slow life, Petrini gives the impression that we can change the world by choosing a different restaurant, an *osteria* or small, independent establishment specializing in local cuisines and devoted to gourmets and gourmands. Or one might imagine that by turning off the television, unplugging the alarm clock, abandoning the cell phone and going to the gym we can overturn established political power. These are but beginnings. The limitation of food theory and a body politics is that they tend to lack a firm foundation in critical social theory that links bodies to the body politic, even though they illuminate crucial ways in which we are dominated by food production, diets, lethargy, compulsive working – fast life generally. The opening of food theory to critical theory, of Petrini to the Frankfurt School, is the concept of boundaries, vital to good life but at risk when the body has been colonized and accelerated by injurious external forces.

I have argued that a fast capitalism dismantles boundaries shielding the self, its critical reason and even its body, from the impinging world. Information, entertainment and communication technologies tether the person to the world and make it nearly impossible to stand apart and gain distance necessary in order to think and then act. Although sometimes physical and involving space, boundaries are largely temporal, either insulating us or exposing us to a 24/7 world that streams through us and binds us to it. Food theory joins feminist theories of the body and existential perspectives on embodiment in illuminating the ways in which everyday bodies are damaged by a world that bursts through boundaries: We eat unhealthful prepared food; we use expensive and self-objectifying cosmetics; we cannot escape the Internet and cell phone; stress and fatigue are chronic.

It is not enough, however, to illuminate the damaged self in a world without adequate boundaries. One must not only shield the self but also remake the world *through* the self, who, in slowmodernity, makes better choices, models good choices for others, and begins to build community and thus transform social institutions of culture, work, home, school, food, exercise, and bodies. Adorno, in exploring the extent to which the self has been damaged and reason eclipsed, draws attention to the public sphere's domination of private experience and existence. Accordingly, he wants to shield the self against what the Frankfurt School called domination. This is laudable and necessary. But, to shift metaphors, it is not enough for the person to choose pasta and exercise over fast food and lethargy. One must extend transformed existence into social change, a rebuilt public sphere that no longer stands against the person as controlling and external forces. Once boundaries are protected sufficiently to harbor and nurture the self, the self must then move outward and live – slowly and quickly at once – amongst others who become partners in what I am calling slowmodernity.

We thus go beyond the Frankfurt School's theme of domination to an existential, Marcusean and feminist theme of transformation, not only undoing the public sphere's hold over privacy but also allowing the private to become public in its own right. Utopia begins at home. Indeed, what counts as "home" is no longer the same as for earlier generations, and centuries, in which the barrier between private and public was clear, and relatively impermeable. Home is now work, and work curiously home-like in its intimate collegiality. Both venues are open to the world, often too open, allowing the tentacles of discipline to choke off individuality and reason.

44

Struggling toward slowmodernity requires us to re-boundary and de-boundary our worlds at once, acknowledging that public and private, outside and inside, are now thoroughly implicated in each other. This insight is the bridge between food theory and critical theory, which swallows food theory whole, both preserving and extending its alimentary insights into the importance of body politics for the body politic. What should life be like in this, a new century? Let me offer an agenda, if not the only possible one:

1. *Periodically shut down the electronic prostheses dictating our worlds and lives to us.* If we must use them – think of the Internet – we should be selective and pragmatic, not allowing the possibility of connection to become an occasion for checking compulsively to see if we are connected. Shut off the cell phone; ignore email; disable the answering machine and caller ID. Watch an hour of television, or less. If television must be watched, watch it with your kids so that you enjoy their worlds and help explain yours to them.

2. *Don't let home become a job, or be overwhelmed by the job.* Set priorities that minimize work – time spent away from family, friends, personal projects. Nearly nothing we do in the way of paid work will have lasting impact. Articles and books published by academics over fifty take time away from avocations, family, children, the community. It is okay to work, and even necessary, but workaholism drowns the spirit. Don't leave your kids in after-school care, or by themselves, unless you absolutely have to. Don't obsess about leaving work early, lest you miss an "important" meeting. All meetings are useless, by definition. And sucking up to the boss is inauthentic and ephemeral; bosses change, and you have to start all over again. Marx shrewdly recognized that zero work was to be the goal of his utopia. He also said that in a good society people would pick and choose among jobs that express themselves; they would become artisans again, and craftspeople. This includes writing, my chosen field.

3. *Eat healthful foods, both carbohydrates and proteins, preferably purchased from organic sources. Defy the supermarket chains and advertising for fast food and prepared food. Become athletes as a way of toning the body, restoring joie de vivre, overcoming depression and lassitude.* Athletes know what to eat; their bodies tell them: We need broccoli, rice, beans, some chicken. Athleticism overcomes alienation, as George Sheehan wrote in his inspiring *Running and Being* (1978), a meditation on the 1970s running boom (also see Rodgers 1980 on marathoning). You don't have to run, or even to like broccoli. But achieving a oneness with the body, what early Marx called the organic body, allows one to become intimate with nature, and thus to de-stress. One sleeps better, dreams better, loves and lives better, feels stronger and more vital when one eats healthfully and exercises. The goal in this is not the body beautiful, if that means anorexia. The beautiful body is the body with which you feel at one. It is tireless, energetic, self-

confident. And it dictates its own diet, which combines carbs (for energy) and protein (for the restoration of muscles). Fast fad diets are fake. They are tailored to people who don't exercise. Athletes know that you cannot eat only or mainly meat, as the Atkins diet counsels. Without carbohydrates as fuel, fatigue defeats the will to exercise. We must break out of the feast/fast dynamic in order to experience our bodies as vehicles of our humanity and our opening to nature.

4. *Don't overschedule – oneself or one's kids.* People have insufficient time for relaxation and avocation, let alone contemplation. As wealth increases (although not for everyone), time compresses and becomes scarcer. This should be no surprise, given the logic of capitalism: time is money precisely because it is through labor time that labor power transfers value to commodities, and hence makes way for profit. Only the poor have time on their hands, too much time, given their unemployment or underemployment. But those who are above the poverty line need to reassess their exhaustive and exhausting commitment to paid work, shaving away hours that could be spent in more fulfilling ways than composing memoranda, typing e-mails, or networking. Few jobs afford flexible time, but this is exactly what people need in order to make good choices about vocation and career, trading time for money at the margin. School teachers enjoy the summer off, but few can afford to drive Lexuses. They are the richer for all that because they can travel, read, write, work out.

One needs time in order to be human. One also needs much of this time to be unstructured, not necessarily time for which one has planned. Well-managed selves "build" time into their hectic lives, for example reserving two hours on Thursday afternoons (barring office emergencies) "for themselves". Although those two hours are better than nothing, one needs *unplanned* time in order to enjoy the serendipity of real recreation and avocation – the time during which people discover themselves, often in surprising ways. I appear idle much of the time, reveling in the unplanned time of the academic leisure class. During this time, I think, play, work, and enjoy sociability with family and friends. It is a hallmark of our late-capitalist productivism and early-capitalist puritanism that we view such idle hours as purely "personal" time and not also time that is productive in the sense that it produces selves if not commodities.

5. *Defy productivism – use time to produce not commodities for market but selves for civil society and for family.* Viewed this way, the self is a creation and a self-creation, precisely the sensibility early Marx (1964) discussed in his veneration of "praxis", self-creative and productive activity. The production and self-production of the self displaces and then altogether replaces commodity production as a societal goal. This assumes not necessarily high technology (complete automation and the total elimination of human toil) but *high-enough technology*, a central feature of slowmodernity

as I intend it. This borrows from E. F. Schumacher's (1973) notion of appropriate technologies that spring from local cultures and levels of development. Sometimes, with Petrini, these can be "slow" technologies, whereas there can also be "fast" technologies, tending toward the elimination of human work altogether. The point is that we replace commodity production with self and community building as economic and societal goals, fundamentally displacing the value systems of western societies.

6. *Actively work to transform our education systems, which should deal with "a mind at a time" (Levine 2002) instead of promoting a mass-production model of education for which there is a single fixed curriculum and accompanying standardized tests.* Mass-market education and standardized testing reflect a one-size-fits-all attitude toward education, and they betray a Fordist approach to schooling and curriculum. This is counterproductive even within a postmodern, post-Fordist capitalism, let alone a post-capitalist society. Fordist education produces standardized students as commodities, using the assembly line as both metaphor and reality. In a post-Fordism edging towards slowmodernity, we must uncouple education and production, no longer educating young people "for" the workplace but helping them develop selfhood – identity, by another name. I tell my students that college, in addition to being about future vocation, is a time during which they can learn to be free and learn who they "are", also acknowledging that they can change who they are. They can learn to be free of assembly-line expectations, of confining social norms, of the quotidian. They can learn to take intellectual risks, to think outside the box, to question and to criticize.

Levine's notion of a mind at a time is a critique of a standardized curriculum that ignores children with certain learning disabilities, such as Attention Deficit Disorder (ADD). Indeed, ADD, as a symptom of childhood distraction in the busy classroom, is an outcome of an accelerated world in which it is difficult for almost everyone to "focus", given the many, and rapid, stimuli bombarding us. The ADD child is the accelerated child; indeed, ADD can be viewed as the mind's and body's protest against the speed up, a way of disengaging from the harmful, hurtful world of a fast-paced, fill-in-the-box approach to education. Levine insists that kids diagnosed with ADD are often the more creative ones, able to think outside the box but not to do well on timed standardized tests. High test scores and grades might actually signal intellectual dullness and rigidity.

7. *Return to a view of the lifecycle and childhood development that prolongs the pre-adult phases and shields kids from the intrusion and acceleration of adulthood.* Removing productivism from education is not enough to liberate children. We must take additional steps to reverse the abbreviation of childhood in slowmodernity. Kids not only have too much unimaginative homework, designed both to prepare them for a Fordist workforce and to occupy their time but also too many other "activities" that are designed by

parents and educators to position them advantageously for college admission. And kids are too worldly, knowing too much about adult topics such as sexuality, crime, violence, shopping, brands, and professional sports. In some measure, the attenuation of childhood reflects the privatization of children, who no longer fill their after-school hours with aimless neighborhood play but have their hours structured for them by parents, teachers, coaches, and activity mentors. We need to remove *structure* from childhood, which, by definition, defies structuring and needs to be shielded from structure so that kids can learn, acquire and construct their identities using an approach that Kant called "purposively purposeless".

This involves both time compression and work expectations. Children need guidance and structure, to be sure, but they also need serendipity, which is one of the hallmarks of slow life in slowmodernity. They need unstructured play, and they need opportunities for creativity in school. My son learns more from voracious reading and from writing his own "books" than he does from most worksheets with empty blanks that are supposed to be filled in with a single correct answer. My daughter derives more benefit from writing and staging a play with friends than from her literature class in which she must try to remember (in case of a quiz) what happened to a marginal character in chapter 2 after she has read ahead in the book. The underlying issue here is structure, and kids' need to be free of it regularly. Time and work/homework combine to thwart serendipity, which is the joyful and often mercurial process of finding and creating a self.

8. ***Deprogram your kids from being overly concerned with their futures, and with success*** – and this from a faculty member who values academic accomplishment! The attenuation of childhood involves shortening the life cycle of kids so that they must view virtually all K-12 activities, inside and outside the classroom, as "counting" toward college admission and thus successful adulthood. Very few things really count, as long as the child learns fairly normally, not falling behind. Indeed, what matters are not the traditional markers of academic success, from grades and test scores to extracurricular activities, but the opportunities kids need to discover what they like and are good at, and then to pursue these activities and avenues. Not everyone has a knack or taste for geometry, or grammar, or public speaking, or shooting baskets. Emphasizing "everything" courts the child's disinterest in things she feels are being thrust on her by parents and academic authorities. This is not an elitist argument against mediocrity but simply an observation that kids need to be able to discover their calling, which is tantamount to discovering what they are potentially good at, acknowledging, of course, that becoming good at something, whether the viola or computer science, requires a lot of hard but fulfilling work. Today, a lot of kids work hard, to the point of mental exhaustion, but they are intellectually lazy because their hard work doesn't answer to their muse.

I am not arguing against all childhood work, only against compulsive homework and resume building. I am in favor of hard work where it allows the child to become good at something, excelling, and where the child enjoys the work, the practice, for its own sake, a crucial lesson for adulthood. I am against career building where it substitutes for, and obstructs, building a life and a self – the real challenge for all of us. An instrumental rationality, whereby every activity is designed to meet a goal, defeats the purpose of childhood, which is to discover different rationalities, sensibilities, ways of living and relating.

9. *View and enact our everyday lives as always already political, not as irrelevant to, or beneath, politics.* I have struggled, as we all must today, with the multiple levels of self. In order to bring about social change, we must change ourselves; but we cannot change ourselves without promoting changes in others and in our institutions. At stake for this personal/public politics is time – how we spend our brief passage on earth, not hurriedly but with heart. Faster capitalism involves a certain production of time, which must be opposed. The overriding argument of this chapter is that we must re-boundary the self, slow down our lives and conceptualize and enact social changes that will take us to a higher level of modernity – slowmodernity. This level is not a Luddite retreat (slow), nor a digitized, cybernetic utopia (fast). It involves going back and moving forward, mastering time so that it serves us and not the other way around. In *Being and Time* ([1927] 1962), in which Heidegger launched existentialism just four years after Lukacs founded Western Marxism in *History and Class Consciousness* ([1923] 1971), Heidegger argued that the greatest existential problem is for people to accept their mortality. Once this was accomplished, people could live meaningful, authentic lives, making everyday choices that define them. Time does not defeat the human project, on this account, but enriches it, much as Marcuse transformed the so-called death instinct into an impulse to overcome alienation.

As the Frankfurt School understood, alienation involves forgetting – losing contact with the damaged lives that made this world possible. These lives, haunted by Gordon's (1997) ghosts, are being expended today, around the world and at home, and they were expended for most of human history, as travel to Mayan ruins, Cambodian killing fields and the Holocaust's crematoria demonstrate. We are taught to forget so that we remain on task. Time is compressed into an eternal present so that we forget what brought us here. It is also compressed so that we extrapolate the present as we know it – malls, highways, schools, bodies – into an infinite future, forgetting the possibility of utopia, of radical rupture with the past and present. Time is at stake in the way we imagine ourselves as caught up in the contemporary, which is a postmodern form of consciousness. Immersion in the everyday isn't necessarily a truer form of experience, a phenomenological bracketing of the inessential, especially where everyday life is simulated by advertisers and ideologists in order to elicit it – the everyday – from consumer/workers overwhelmed by working, spending, eating, and schooling.

Time is cluttered precisely so that we won't spend time pursuing the past and imagining a different future. As Weber understood, capitalism emerged from the Protestant Reformation, which placed value on busyness as well as business. In this chapter, I have addressed the production of time – its framings by dominant institutions, and the selves who sustain them – using categories such as Fordism, post-Fordism, fast capitalism, and faster capitalism. In effect, this is to deploy Marx's central categories in ways appropriate to a late capitalism in which economic exploitation and alienation become intensive as well as extensive. It is not enough for people to work and spend within 19th century parameters of officially boundaried institutions, such as employment, family, leisure, religion. They can't produce and consume enough to sustain capitalism. Global capitalism finds new markets and new producers, but that is only a partial solution. People in first-world capitalist countries must also be accelerated through the colonization of their life-worlds, to use Habermas' turn of phrase.

We must break the clocks, resisting and refusing the quickening of our lives. This is political protest and reconstruction where it emerges from a theoretical understanding of faster capitalism. We must not allow ourselves to be overscheduled, hurried, hassled; we must take our sweet time, daw-dling in order to slow down the flow. This was well understood by Walter Benjamin (1969) as he theorized the *flaneur*, who strolled through Paris in order to drink deeply of cosmopolitan urban life as a mode of enjoy-ment, of existential being. We must treat every day as a holiday, reading the newspaper slowly, lingering over coffee, thinking through our plans, and being flexible enough to change them as circumstances and opportunities dictate. The flaneur is the antonym of the postmodern self who can multi-task, juggle time and projects, prioritize, set agendas and work the room. The postmodern business/busyness self dresses carefully, posturing the body as commodity, whereas the flaneur recognizes that identity lies deeper than mere appearances. Above all, wear an inexpensive, expendable watch that you can fling aside when it becomes too confining.

10. *Refuse a disengaged social science, reject positivism and a post-po-litical postmodernism, and insert theory into practice. We must embrace a leftist humanism – again.* The self who initiates social change from within everyday life, recognizing that History is made body by body, family by family, workplace by workplace, must think theoretically, conceptually, about society and selves. Theory is understood here as generalizing activ-ity, rising above the particular without sacrificing particulars – selves – to a transhistorical Reason or other abstractions that elevate liberty above lives. But theory is not a contemplative posture, or value free, as Marx and

Engels understood in the last of their Theses on Feuerbach (1947). By the early 21st century, both positivism (midwestern-empiricist journal science) and postmodernism (Lyotard 1984; Rorty 1997) condemn politics either as bias or as authoritarian, grand theory having become grandiose. In our post-political age, what Jacoby (1975) called the politics of subjectivity re-emerges as a studied posture, for example in postmodernism and post-feminism, both of which reject the eleventh thesis. This responds to the identity of political and personal, at the expense of the person, with a rejection of politics. Instead, as I have been arguing, the political and personal must be re-boundaried without failing to understand their interpenetration; Adorno called that non-identity. The personal is political, but not entirely, just as politics extends beyond family, home and body.

Post-political quietism is tempting in faster capitalism, especially where official political institutions are hollow; think of the Supreme Court, the presidency, the Politburo. But politics can be reframed in slowmodernity as the simultaneous identity and non-identity of public and private. This neither sacrifices bodies to a millenarian conception of progress, as we have done for over two thousand years, nor fails to recognize that our jobs, families, children, schools, diets and bodies have fallen under the spell of what the Frankfurt School, following Weber, called administration. That politics has colonized the lifeworld – cultures, jobs, families, schools, bodies – doesn't mean we must withdraw from politics. Instead, we must reconfigure the polity and public sphere in a way that makes the self (see Bay 1958) the measure of all things, neither violating the self's ultimate interiority nor avoiding the self's responsibility to enter regularly the public sphere as a transforming and contributing agent.

Total administration or domination has de-boundaried the self in relation to the public sphere, which is experienced as threatening or irrelevant. As such, the self must be re-boundaried lest it simply dissolve, deconstruct, into nothingness. But the self's re-boundarying should be matched by a de-boundarying of private and public, person and politics, so that we recognize, and act upon, the inherence of politics in everyday life, again making man and woman the measure of all things. Petrini is absolutely correct that how and what we eat are political acts, and have impact on the public sphere; the osteria always trumps the fast-food franchise as a locus and paradigm of humanity or what I am calling slowmodernity. If this is humanism, so much the worse for anti- or post-humanist philosophies of history, whether Althusserian (history without a subject) or postmodern (self merely as subject position). This humanism is the humanism of early Marx, who would have joined Petrini in fighting fast-food capitalism by brandishing bowls of penne pasta in protest and reconstruction.

Postmodern cynicism and irony are not adequate postures. Nor is liberalism, which dissolves the crushing weight of social structures into good intentions and rational choice. Don't be ashamed to be political, humanist, activist, Marxist, feminist. Embrace the eleventh thesis and oppose positivism. Retain, but also reclaim, modernity, recognizing that its project can only be fulfilled in a utopian stage I call the slowmodern. Fast and slow, modern and pre-modern, blur to the point of identity. Technologies will serve human needs, people will pursue projects that define and enrich them, their children will be allowed to find their ways, and people will be at one with their bodies.

References

Adorno, Theodor W. (1978) *Minima Moralia*. London: Verso. 1984. *Aesthetic Theory*. London: Routledge and Kegan Paul.

Agger, Ben (1989a) *Fast Capitalism: A Critical Theory of Significance*. Urbana, IL: University of Illinois Press.

Agger, Ben (1989b) *Reading Science: A Literary, Political and Sociological Analysis*. Dix Hills, NY: General Hall.

Agger, Ben (2000) *Public Sociology: From Social Facts to Literary Acts*. Boulder: Rowman & Littlefield.

Aronowitz, Stanley (1988) *Science as Power: Discourse and Ideology in Modern Society*. Minneapolis: University of Minnesota Press.

Bay, Christian (1958) *The Structure of Freedom*. Palo Alto: Stanford University Press.

Bell, Daniel (1960) *The End of Ideology*. Glencoe, IL: Free Press.

Benjaimin, Walter (1969) *Illuminations*. New York: Schocken.

Bowles, Samuel and Herbert Gintis (1976) *Schooling in Capitalist America*. New York: Basic.

Davis, Mike (1990) *City of Quartz: Excavating the Future in Los Angeles*. London: Verso.

Dyer-Witheford, Nick (1999) *Cyber-Marx: Cycles and Circuits of Struggle in High Technology Capitalism*. Urbana, IL: University of Illinois Press.

Ehrenreich, Barbara (2001) *Nickel and Dimed: On (Not) Getting By in America*. New York: Metropolitan Books.

Garfinkel, Harold (1967) *Studies in Ethnomethodology*. Englewood Cliffs, NJ: Prentice-Hall.

Gergen, Kenneth (2000) *The Saturated Self: Dilemmas of Identity in Contemporary Life*. New York: Basic.

Gitlin, Todd (2003) *Letters to a Young Activist*. New York: Basic.

Gordon, Avery (1997) *Ghostly Matters: Haunting and the Sociological Imagination*. Minneapolis: University of Minnesota Press.

Gramsci, Antonio (1971) *Selections from the Prison Notebooks*. London: Lawrence and Wishart.

Habermas, Jürgen (1984) *The Theory of Communicative Action*. Volume One. Boston: Beacon.

Habermas, Jürgen (1987) *The Theory of Communicative Action*. Volume Two. Boston: Beacon.

Harvey, David (1989) *The Condition of Postmodernity*. Oxford: Blackwell.

Heidegger, Martin (1927/1962) *Being and Time*. New York: Harper.

Jacoby, Russell (1975) *Social Amnesia: A Critique of Conformist Psychology from Adler to Laing*. Boston: Beacon Press.

Kellner, Douglas (1995) *Media Culture: Cultural Studies, Identity and Politics Between the Modern and the Postmodern*. New York: Routledge.

Kralovec, Etta and John Buell (2000) *The End of Homework: How Homework Disrupts Families, Overburdens Children and Limits Learning*. Boston: Beacon.

Levine, Mal (2002) *A Mind at a Time*. New York: Simon and Schuster.

Lukacs, Georg (1923/1971) *History and Class Consciousness*. London: Merlin.

Luke, Timothy W. (1989) *Screens of Power: Ideology, Domination and Resistance in the Informational Society*. Evanston: University of Illinois Press.

Lyotard, Jean-Francois (1984) *The Postmodern Condition: A Report on Knowledge*. Minneapolis: University of Minnesota Press.

Marcuse, Herbert (1955) *Eros and Civilization*. New York: Vintage.

Marx, Karl (1964) *Early Writings*. Edited by Tom Bottomore. New York: McGraw-Hill.

Marx, Karl (1967) *Capital: A Critique of Political Economy*. New York: International Publishers.

Marx, Karl and Friedrich Engels (1947) *The German Ideology*. New York: International Publishers.

Merleau-Ponty, Maurice (1964a) *Sense and Non-Sense*. Evanston: Northwestern University Press.

Merleau-Ponty, Maurice (1964b) *Signs*. Evanston: Northwestern University Press.

Parsons, Talcott (1951) *The Social System*. New York: Free Press.

Petrini, Carlo (2003) *Slow Food: The Case for Taste*. New York: Columbia University Press.

Poster, Mark (1975) *Existential Marxism in Postwar France: From Sartre to Althusser*. Princeton: Princeton University Press.

Poster, Mark (2001) *What's the Matter with the Internet?* Minneapolis: University of Minnesota Press.

Rodgers, Bill (1980) *Marathoning*. New York: Simon and Schuster.

Rorty, Richard (1997) *Truth, Politics and 'Post-Modernism'*. Assen: Van Gorcum.

Sartre, Jean-Paul (1956) *Being and Nothingness*. New York: Philosophical Library.

Sartre, Jean-Paul (1976) *Critique of Dialectical Reason*. London: New Left Books.

Schlosser, Eric (2001) *Fast Food Nation: The Dark Side of the All-American Meal*. Boston: Houghton Mifflin.

Schumacher, E.F. (1973) *Small is Beautiful: A Study of Economics as if People Mattered*. New York: Harper & Row.

Sheehan, George (1978) *Running and Being*. New York: Simon and Schuster.

Soja, Edward (1989) *Postmodern Geographies: The Reassertion of Space in Critical Social Theory*. London: Verso.

Weber, Max (1978) *Economy and Society: An Outline of Interpretive Sociology*. Berkeley: University of California Press.

Chapter 3

The Modernist Pre-Occupation with Speed: A Psychoanalytic and Critical Reading

Adrian N. Carr

"the world went and got itself in a big damn good hurry"

These are the words of Brooks Hatlen, a character played by the extremely talented actor James Whitmore, in the film *The Shawshank Redemption*. Brooks Hatlen is a seventy-five year-old prisoner who, after serving a long term sentence, is released from Maine's oppressive Shawshank State Prison. He soon discovers he cannot cope with the pace of the external world and hangs himself – a final act that might be interpreted as the ultimate statement of alienation.

The fact that the world has just got itself in a "damm good hurry" seems something that is undeniable. Evidence of a society in a rush is all around us – some of that "rush" and "hurry" is embedded in the very name of the evidence. For example, "fast" food, "speed" dialing, and "speed" reading. Other simple evidence of our hurry gets displayed in an almost bizarre manner. For example, studies that have been undertaken throughout Asia reveal the paint on the "door close" button in the lift wears off before any other (Linnell, 2001). In Japan, engineers have tried to 'reduce' what they refer to as the "door dwell" of lifts by installing "psychological waiting lanterns" – pressing any button instantly results in a light coming on. The mechanics of the lift do not respond any more quickly, but it is thought that the light will cause people to feel better because something has quickly reacted to their request.

The subject of this chapter is our pre-occupation with speed and the manner in which, for some, *it has become an object of blind devotion or reverence* i.e., a fetish, or at the least an ideal to be attained. Using the optics of psychoanalytic theory and critical theory, the origins and psychodynamics of this pre-occupation are outlined as is an explanation for this pre-occupation being so pervasive. In addition, it will be demonstrated that this specific pre-occupation with speed is characterized by a time-space compression in which 'cultural texts' and 'realities' are conveyed in such a manner that they displace critical reflection. Further, it will be argued that a psychological state of *stimulus entrapment* (Meares, 1992, 1997)[1] is experienced as a consequence of this pre-occupation.

Stimulus entrapment is a notion that suggests that through continual external hyper-attentiveness, a person fails to develop an "inner self voice" and, as a result, experiences feelings of "emptiness". A lack of an ability to self reflect, makes these individuals prone to external locus of control and/or to a false self that is often one dimensional. "They live as if at the mercy of the environment, in a hypertrophy of the 'real'" (Meares & Coombes, 1994, p. 66). The pre-occupation for speed demands and sustains a state of external hyper-attentiveness and maintains a need for societal personas while simultaneously militating against individuality.

The chapter concludes with a brief discussion of the implications of our pre-occupation with speed for the field of organization studies.

The nature of fetish and the ego-ideal: A psychoanalytic rendering

Budapest, January 15, 1914: Sándor Ferenczi writes to Sigmund Freud about a masochistic patient with "foot fetishism" (Brabant, Falzeder & Giampieri-Deutsch, 1993, p. 534). Ferenczi was to link this foot fetishism with sexual arousal (see Ferenczi, 1916/1994, pp. 16 & 22). In an early comment upon foot fetishism, Freud (1906/1990, p. 71) suggested more generally that "ever since Binet [1888] we have in fact tried to trace fetishism back to erotic impressions in childhood". Elsewhere, Freud (1905/1977, p. 67) expresses his view slightly differently when he says that Alfred "Binet [1888] was the first to maintain that the choice of fetish is an after-effect of some sexual impression, received as a rule in early childhood". "Sexual impression" and "erotic impression" are not precisely the same thing, but in his earliest works, Freud commented on fetish in a context that was linked to early childhood and sexuality.

From these early observations, Freud was later to revise his opinion on the adequacy of fetishism being viewed as simply in the realm of the erotic and the sexual. It needs to be clearly understood that these initial observations were made in a context in which Freud had conceived psychodynamics in terms of a *libido theory*. Freud argued that one's innate instincts create 'psychic energy' – a biological force produced in a manner akin to the way a dynamo produces electrical power. Freud viewed thoughts, feelings and

---

[1] I would like to acknowledge the extremely helpful nature of the discussions with my colleague Derek Simmons on the notion of stimulus entrapment.

55

behaviour, as powered by libido. While libido needed expression, a number of influences caused its repression, that is relegation of the ungratified impulses to the unconscious where they still sought expression. Much of this early formulation simply conceived libido as specifically related to sexual instincts and bodily pleasures. This initial conception of the psyche was evident in Freud's work in the first two decades of the last century. It was in the early part of the 1920's that Freud started to put forward a significantly revised view of the psyche which, in turn, caused him to reconsider a range of explanations he had previously advanced for various behaviours.

In an unfinished paper of some four pages entitled "Splitting of the Ego in the Process of Defence" (1940/1985), Freud moved beyond his initial notion of fetishism as an instance of sexual perversion or erotic/sexual impression. His initial idea was that fetishism was almost always a male 'perversion', narrowly related to the castration complex – that is, fetish as a non-sexual part of the body (or, another object) becomes a substitute for the mother's penis, that the son once believed in. The fetish object becomes simultaneously both a means of denying sexual difference as well as a defence against the fear of castration. In this unfinished paper, Freud (1940/1985) began to link fetish with the broader psychological processes of the ego's function and with the psychodynamics of defence – particularly those of displacement. This glimpse of Freud's intended revision of how fetish should be considered, has led some within the psychoanalytic community to include a rendering of the term as being, "metaphorically, an extravagant devotion to an object" (English & English, 1958, p. 205).

Part of the prompt for Freud to reconsider the notion of fetish was related to the revised view of the dynamics of the psyche – in what might be called his second model of the psyche. We are left to speculate upon the exact manner in which fetish would be explained in terms that related to the psychodynamic processes of the ego and, specifically, those related to defence. Notwithstanding, we can readily envisage fetish as part of a constellation of psychodynamic processes that deals with the threat and idealization of 'other'. As we have also noted, some within the psychoanalytic community would insist that a metapsychology of fetish should view fetish as simply an exaggerated response in the psychodynamics of devotion to an object. For the purposes of this chapter, the issue of fetish can remain slightly in the background. In the foreground it is the psychodynamics of devotion to an object that is the key to understanding how speed becomes at least a 'pre-occupation' – an idealized object to be attained. It is clear that Freud's second theory of the psyche contained the elements that cogently explain how speed has become an idealised object in capitalist societies – a psychologically embedded 'need' to be attained.

In his second theory of the psyche, Freud posited the now familiar realms called id, ego and super-ego. The various functions and relationships of these realms can be succinctly summarized as follows: the *id* – the various biological urges, drives or instincts that operate entirely unconsciously; the *ego* – the province that uses logic, memory and judgement in its endeavor to satisfy the demands of the id; and, the *super-ego* – the province of the mind where concern is for obeying society's 'rules of conduct', i.e. morality and social norms, the super-ego reminds the ego of these social realities. In terms of fundamental psychological processes, Freud argued that at the commencement of psychological life the infant's wishes, desires and drives are principally focused upon the development of self. The infant experiences itself as the center of a loving world in which the mother is the key figure – an experience referred to as *primary narcissism* (Freud, 1914/1984; 1923/1986; 1923/1984). The infant subsequently becomes aware that the world does not revolve around it. For example, an object such as the mother's breast is not always available and thus the infant may create a substitute satisfaction e.g., replacing the nipple with sucking a finger. The substitute satisfaction is never quite the same "narcissistic perfection of his childhood (and) ... he seeks to recover it in the form of an *ego ideal*. What he projects before him as his ideal is the substitute for the lost narcissism of his childhood in which he was his own ideal" (Freud, 1914/1984, p. 88, italics added).

The fantasized ego-ideal is established and re-established through a process of *identification* "whereby the subject assimilates an aspect, property or attribute of the other and is transformed, wholly or partially, after the model the other provides. It is by means of a series of identifications that the personality is constituted and specified" (Laplanche & Pontalis, 1967/1988, p. 205; see also Freud, 1921/1985, p. 137). In the development of the super-ego, Freud envisaged that the child would identify and internalize the values, attitudes and ideals of the parent. This positive sense of the super-ego for self-judgement represents the ego-ideal. In these same identifications, the super-ego simultaneously also develops its prohibitive aspect (or conscience). Freud reflects upon this dynamic in arguing that the super-ego's "relation to the ego is not exhausted by the precept: 'You *ought to be* like this (like your father).' It also comprises the prohibition: 'You *may not be* like this (like your father) – that is, you may not do all that he does; some things are his prerogative'" (Freud, 1923/1984, p. 374). Thus the ego is narcissistically drawn to the ego-ideal – "the target of the self-love" (Freud, 1914/1984, p. 88). However, it is also 'drawn' to yield to the prohibitive aspects of the super-ego that, from a fear of punishment, act like a censor to the ego's wishes, (see Nunberg, 1932/1955, p. 146). This punishment is a feeling of *moral anxiety*.

In this model it was the role of the ego to manage, amongst other things, the demands of the id, the narcissistic desire of achieving an ego-ideal, the prohibitive confines of the super-ego and the demands of the external world. If it failed to manage these dynamics the ego "is obliged to admit its weakness, it breaks out in anxiety – realistic anxiety regarding the external world; moral anxiety regarding the super-ego and neurotic anxiety regarding the strength and passions of the id" (Freud, 1933/1988, pp. 110–111). Indeed excessive conflict between the ego and the id would manifest in a form of hysteria or obsessional neurosis; those between the ego and reality taking the form of psychoses such as paranoia and schizophrenia; and unresolved conflicts between the ego and super-ego might give rise to manic-depressive disorders (see Badcock, 1988, pp. 112–113). These psychopathologies emerge because of a failure of the ego to cope with the intra-psychic conflict.

We do not need to explore a detailed description of all the psychodynamics that Freud suggested arose from his model of the mind. The key issue in the context of this chapter is the recognition that, in its attempt to avoid acute levels of anxiety and the danger of such psychopathologies, the ego may engage a variety of defence mechanisms that largely operate in the realm of the unconscious. These defence mechanisms are now part of the layperson's language and include: repression; regression; rationalization; denial; sublimation; identification; projection; displacement; and reaction formation. These are all familiar terms encountered in our everyday experiences.

In discussing the manner in which the ego-ideal is established and re-established through a process of identification with 'other', it was indicated that the ego is narcissistically drawn to the ego-ideal. It was Freud's view that in a group context it is through the process of identification that the individual may surrender the current "ego ideal and substitutes for it the group ideal as embodied in the leader (p. 161) ... (the group members) put one and the same object in place of their ego ideal and have consequently identified themselves with one another in their ego" (Freud, 1921/1985, pp. 161 and 147). In becoming a member of a group the individual surrenders some of their individuality. The degree to which this occurs depends upon the strength of their projective identification and the strength of their introjective identification. If these identifications are continually reinforced through various forms of gratification then the sense of a created identity can be so strong that the prohibitive aspect of the super-ego may be disregarded and, as others have commented, "its functions taken over by the group ideals" (Sandler, 1960, pp. 156–157; see also Chasseguet-Smirgel, 1976, pp. 363).

The preoccupation with speed and the ego-ideal

In understanding how the ego-ideal is established and re-established the connection with the pre-occupation with speed, at this stage, may seem more than a little unclear. To make this connection clear, and lay the further foundation for understanding the human consequences of a pre-occupation with speed, we need to draw upon the elaboration of Freud's work by the critical theorist Herbert Marcuse in particular and also some aspects of the work of Antonio Gramsci, Guy Debord and Ben Agger.

The Frankfurt School scholar Herbert Marcuse (1955) viewed the psychodynamic processes described above as holding the key to how individuals in society become, unwittingly, 'voluntary' agents in their own servitude. For Marcuse, the psychodynamics revealed how society reproduced its powers both within and over the individual. Particularly important for Marcuse were the unconscious psychodynamic processes related to the functioning of the super-ego, as both an ego-ideal and as a censor. He argued that the super-ego can be regarded as being fashioned to accept the systematic social restraints as though they are 'needs' that are to be realized. Through his explanation of the socialization process, Marcuse (1955) concludes that basic instinctual but socially patterned drives become that part of the psyche that is unconscious, "the personality" [having] been formed and key instincts repressed or divided in terms of the dominant norms and values of "institutionalized society" (Atkinson, 1971, p. 39). The logical extension of such a view is put into its appropriate context by Marcuse when he remarks:

> … in a repressive society, individual happiness and productive development are in contradiction to society: if they are defined as values to be realized within society, they become themselves repressive. (Marcuse, 1955, p. 245)

In examining the process of repression, Marcuse extends Freud's theory of the Oedipus complex (using a male child in his example) in a manner consistent with the description earlier in this chapter of the development of the ego-ideal and its relationship with normal narcissism:

> The revolt against the primal father eliminated an individual person who could be (and was) replaced by other persons; but when the domination of the father had expanded into the domination of society, no such replacement seemed possible, and the guilt becomes fatal … The father, restrained in the family and in his individual biological authority, is resurrected, far more powerful, in the administration which preserves the life of society, and in the laws which preserve the administration … there is no freedom from administration and its laws because they appear as the ultimate guarantors of liberty. (Marcuse, 1955, pp. 91–92)

The replacement of the parent by society and the laws that preserve its administration ensures obedience. The same psyche that hindered the revolt against the parent similarly discourages revolt against society. Atkinson (1971) incisively captures the essence of what Marcuse is suggesting:

The individual wants to conform with them because he has internalized the values that legitimize them. But he also has to conform with them, for to break them would involve the powerful psychological constraint of guilt.

It is only in this sense that the individual is seen as determined and his nature is being infinitely manipulable by the structure of pre-existing society. The individual does not know he is determined, openly coming to want to behave in ways demanded of him. His basic instincts are, in the process, manipulated and repressed to the extent that he may actually disown or fail to recognize them. Should he consciously wish to act at variance with himself, mechanisms inside his personality make sure that such action fails. (Atkinson, 1971, p. 39)

The psychological embeddedness of restraint and the particular nature of that restraint, Marcuse argues, must be understood in a specific historical context "and judged as to whether such systems of domination exceeded their bounds" (Giroux, 1983, p. 26). Marcuse rejected the notion that legitimate and illegitimate forms of domination were a natural and permanent feature of civilization. Marcuse was of the view that each society has material conditions that operate as a reality principle. The reality principle can take a different form in different societies. In capitalist societies the specific reality principle that applies is one based on a performance principle – under whose rule "society is stratified according to the competitive economic performance of its members" (Marcuse, 1955, p. 44). This performance principle, Marcuse believed, had outstripped its historical function. Scarcity was no longer a universal feature of society and therefore it was no longer "necessary" to submit individuals to the demands of alienating labor that were engendered through the application of this principle. It was historically outdated and was in need of replacement. In this context Marcuse noted that a degree of repression was "necessary", in that it was socially useful but in this case it was excessive – "surplus repression". Marcuse captured the relationship of these notions when he argued:

... while any form of the reality principle demands a considerable degree and scope of repressive control over the instincts, the specific historical institutions of the reality principle and the specific interests of domination introduce additional controls over and above those indispensable for civilized human association. Those additional controls arising from the specific institutions of domination are what we denote as surplus-repression ... the modifications and deflections of instinctual energy necessitated by the perpetuation of the monogamic-patriarchical family, or by a hierarchical division of labor, or by public control over individual's private existence are instances of surplus-repression pertaining to the institutions of a particular reality principle. (Marcuse, 1955, p. 37–38)

Marcuse highlights how repression is reproduced both in (through the super-ego as both an ego-ideal and as a censor) and over (through the reality principle of the ego that takes note of the institutionalized repressive agencies in society) the individual – thus, repression is in this sense, according to Marcuse, both a psychological and political phenomenon. Marcuse was of the view that the current performance principle was, in one sense, a cultural ideology that becomes so pervasive to the degree that there is no opposition – a one dimensionality, as Marcuse called it (Marcuse, 1964). Control by 'consent'. Others have also echoed this sentiment, although their pathway to such an insight may have been somewhat different – for example, Gramsci and Debord.

Antonio Gramsci (circa 1927–1937/1971), in the dynamics of his notion of hegemony, also captured this idea of control by consent in which institutionalized repression is located in similar locations to those that were to be later suggested by Marcuse. Hegemony, in the Gramscian formulation, is pictured as the equilibrium between civil society and political society, where civil society represents institutions such as the church, the family, and the schools, and political society is represented by the state (the formal political institutions and officials). In Gramsci's conception, power is both centralised in the political system and diffused across civil institutions. Consent is organised, and power exercised, not just through official political policies and practices, but also in civil society, where many aspects of social and political identity are fundamentally grounded (Carroll & Ratner, 1994). The dynamics of force and consent, power and persuasion, are intertwined. Power cannot be maintained for very long by force alone. In order to continue to exert influence, a dominant group must also gain the consent of the subordinate group by convincing subordinates that their best interests are served by accepting the prevailing order.

Given the interaction between force (power) and consent (persuasion), Gramsci argued that repressive institutions must be challenged within the context of transforming popular consciousness both as a precondition for transformation and as a central aspect of the liberation itself. As oppressed individuals and communities become aware of the (artificial) limitations placed on them by society, they may expand their perceptions of their needs and demands (for a similar argument and one methodology for penetrating hegemonic oppression, see also Freire, 1970, pp. 86–95). With this understanding, they can take the initiative to move beyond the boundaries that previously contained them (keeping them "in their place", so to speak) (see Carr & Zanetti, 2001).

The prominent situationist Guy Debord, in his work *The Society of the Spectacle* (1967), also tells us of how we encounter 'reality'. He argues that our reality is created by others through a circulation of images and delivered through the realm of entertainment. Life becomes something not to be lived, as such, but is a spectacle to be observed (consumed) from a distance. We acquiesce or are passive consumers of the spectacle that is our own alienated lives. Relationships, as part of the spectacle, are largely mediated through images. Reality is philosophized with technology saturating the world. For Debord the spectacle is an instrument of pacification and depoliticization, a "permanent opium war" (Debord, 1967, #44) in which its social subjects are stupefied as to their 'real' interests and needs. *The Society of the Spectacle* is a society that results in a profound alienation and, like Marcuse, there was need to reconstruct the world (situation) to bring back a connectedness with nature and each other, not based on commodification and use-values.

Marcuse ultimately suggested that there would be a transformation of the current performance principle as contradictions continued to emerge from the operation of the specific reality principle in the various institutions, and citizens would no longer tolerate what was in fact surplus repression – "The Great Refusal", as Marcuse dubbed it.

In the context of the current reality principle, it can be argued that concern for greater efficiency has become part of the performance principle. Speed has become, in the manner in which fetish was described earlier in this chapter, an object of blind devotion or reverence. Indeed, speed and its relationship with time is something that has become part of the commodification dynamic in capitalist societies. Debord, for example, makes this argument when discussing what he calls "consumable pseudo-cyclical time".

> Consumable pseudo-cyclical time is spectacular time, both as the time of consumption of images in the narrow sense, and as the image of consumption of time in the broad sense. The time of image-consumption, the medium of all commodities, is inseparably the field where the instruments of the spectacle exert themselves fully, and also their goal, the location and main form of all specific consumption: it is known that the time-saving constantly sought by modern society, whether in the speed of vehicles or in the use of dried soups, is concretely translated for the population of the United States in the fact that the mere contemplation of television occupies it for an average of three to six hours a day. The social image of the consumption of time, in turn, is exclusively dominated by moments of leisure and vacation, moments presented *at a distance* and desirable by definition, like every spectacular commodity. (Debord, 1967, #153)

Hand-in-hand with the quest for speed, and instant everything, has been a displacement of critical reflection. Ben Agger (1989, 1992, 1998) refers to "fast capitalism" as "our present social formation" in which "the rate at which concepts and images blur with the reality to which they bear a representational relationship" (Agger, 1992, p. 299). The distinction between textuality and reality dissolves. Agger (1998) argues:

The efficacious social texts of our time are *People* magazine, advertisements for Guess jeans, *Entertainment Tonight*, the movie *Pretty Woman*. As discourses dispersed in everyday life, they help "simulate" reality and thus in a sense become "realer" than reality "itself". That is, they have more social influence than traditional texts written to be read slowly and considered critically. Although books as such still exist, few publishers publish challenging, critical books for a general audience. (p. 141)

The modernist pre-occupation with speed, in the context of capitalism, can be seen as displacing critical reflection, but it also has other social fallout. It is to this fallout that I now wish to direct our attention.

The *psychological* fallout of a pre-occupation with speed

The elaboration of Freud's work, by Marcuse, provides the foundation for the suggestion that speed, in its various guises, has become part of the performance principle. Indeed, it is an idealized object to be realized as if it were a need. The psychological embeddedness of such needs are such that the unconscious psychodynamic processes that led to speed being an idealized object to be realized, are the same psychodynamics that carry punishment if the object is not realized. If the ego fails to attain the ego-ideal, the super-ego punished it through inducing feelings of anxiety and inadequacy. Speed is not only an ideal that each of us is to achieve, but the same ideology that served to install such an individual ideal also carried the message that we have a right to expect it of others and from our general consumable environment.

A second major arena of fallout from a pre-occupation with speed is that it may induce a psychological state known as *stimulus entrapment*. The term stimulus entrapment was coined by Russell Meares (1992, 1997), currently Professor of Psychiatry at Sydney University and Director of Psychiatry at Westmead Hospital in Sydney, Australia.

Meares (1992) argues that stimulus entrapment is a form of disability that is often quite subtle as the person experiencing such a state may present as a busy, active person who seems quite competent in situations where linear logic processes are required (cf. a non-linear associative form of mental function). The person however is experiencing "a prevailing sense of deadness" (p. 90). Those who present for treatment, who declare experiencing such deadness, Meares (1992) describes in the following manner:

> The presenting picture is dominated by categories of events, and of responses to stimuli. The patient talks endlessly of problems with the family, with work,

and of bodily sensations. Nothing comes from an interior world. In essence, the patient seems unable to imagine.

These people are truly trapped. They cannot relinquish the dependence upon stimuli, because if they were to cease nothing remains but a painful emptiness. As long as they go on seeking sensations they are protected from it. But on the other hand, since they constantly seek stimuli, there is no opportunity to develop an interior zone. Indeed, as soon as life becomes relatively peaceful, distractions are sought which break up this relative calm. In some extreme cases, in borderline patients, inexplicable crises develop when, for the first time, tranquility appears in their lives. Turmoil erupts as if it were needed. An alternative to turmoil is a preoccupation with bodily sensation.

The trap has reverberating consequences which compound the difficulty of escaping from it. Since there is no end to the impingements of the world, there is no "silence" out of which can arise something which the person feels as his own. Yet "inner" states are the basis of connectedness with others. (pp. 90–91)

Thus the condition of stimulus entrapment is one where through continual external hyper-attentiveness, a person fails to develop an "inner self voice" and, as a result, experiences feelings of "emptiness". Resonate with Marcuse and Agger's contention about our present performance principle and fast capitalism displacing critical reflection, stimulus entrapment leads to lack of an ability to self reflect, making these individuals prone to external locus of control and/or to a false self that is often *one dimensional*. "They live as if at the mercy of the environment, in a hypertrophy of the 'real'" (Meares & Coombes, 1994, p. 66). The pre-occupation for speed demands and sustains a state of external hyper-attentiveness and maintains a need for societal personas while simultaneously militating against individuality.

Of course the sentiments that we noted earlier in Debord's "consumable pseudo-cyclical time" in *The Society of the Spectacle* (1967) are also relevant here inasmuch as external hyper-attentiveness is nurtured, narcotic-like, by the spectacle. In words that bear great similarity to those of Meares, Debord makes the assessment that:

The spectacle obliterates the boundaries between self and world by crushing the self besieged by the presence-absence of the world and it obliterates the boundaries between true and false by driving all lived truth below the *real presence* of fraud ensured by the organization of appearance, One who passively accepts his alien daily fate is thus pushed toward a madness that reacts in an illusory way to this fate by resorting to magical techniques. The acceptance and consumption of commodities are at the heart of this pseudo-response to a communication without response. The need to imitate which is felt by the consumer is precisely the infantile need conditioned by all the aspects of his fundamental dispossession. In terms applied by Gabel to a com-

64

pletely different pathological level, "the abnormal need for representation here compensates for a tortuous feeling of being on the margin of existence". (Debord, 1967, #219)

Thus, the line of argument being raised here is that the pre-occupation for speed, conceived in the Marcusian sense of a psychological need or ideal to be attained; and/or in a Debordian sense of the spectacle that obliterates the self, the confluence of thought suggests the same outcome, namely that the individual experiences the psychodynamic of stimulus entrapment and is, – in the words I used earlier, "prone to external locus of control and/or to a false self that is often *one dimensional*".

In the context of the psychodynamic processes that have been described thus far, what are the implications for the field of organization studies? It is to this question that I would now wish to very briefly direct our attention and open up the issue for further comment in the field.

Organization studies and the modernist pre-occupation with speed: Commencing engaged disengagement

In the therapeutic setting it might be thought that the therapist themselves might be drawn into the stimulus-response form of interaction, that is they may feed the very condition that the patient is trying to escape, namely stimulus entrapment. Freud suggested that this form of engagement and interaction could, to a significant extent, be avoided by "evenly suspended attention". As Freud (1923/1986) expressed it, the therapist should:

> surrender himself to his own unconscious mental activity, in a state of *evenly suspended attention* to avoid so far as possible reflection and the construction of conscious expectations, not to try to fix anything that he heard particularly in his memory, and by these means to catch the drift of the patient's unconscious with his own unconscious. (p. 136)

This constructive form of engaged disengagement is empathetic, and as Meares (1987) cogently argues the empathetic therapist seeks to broaden attention from the immediacy of the words spoken, and:

> As a consequence, his more complex empathic statements are not the mere resultants of immediate stimuli. The therapist, in concentrating on trying to detect an underlying flux of feelings, images and memories, rather than fastening on the 'things' of the world – the day-to-day occurrences, the crises and problems that come from outside – helps the patient to discover what is his own. (p. 557)

In organization studies our forms of engagement with the subject material and the students of the field are such that they are already framed by metaphor, tropes and other forms of speech and language. Rather than fixing upon arguments related to speed, capitalism and the merits of efficiency (and other guises in which speed appears), we might suspend such attention and instead seek to map the symbolic (see Hopkins, 2000) and conceptual aspect of that language we are taking for granted – language that may seem to carry a reverence. This more reflexive approach might help to bring to the surface the unconscious *meaning* that is attached to language. Moreover we might better understand how we are parties to a co-construction of this meaning.

Recently, Cliff Oswick (2001) made the suggestion that perhaps we should mobilise counter-ideological metaphors – in a sense, a type of Gramscian counter-hegemony. Writing in the introduction to a special issue on the theme of "corporate predators" in a journal for which he was the issue editor, Oswick (2001) argues:

> Continuing to talk of 'corporate predators' … plays into the hands of corporate capitalism. My intention here … is merely to draw attention to the embedded implications of the 'predatorship discourse'.
>
> … in direct opposition to 'corporate-speak', we ought to mobilize counter-ideological metaphors, such as: 'corporate pillaging', 'corporate plundering', 'corporate theft', and 'corporate rape'. These descriptors clearly evoke very different metaphorical images. (p. 23)

This idea of counter-ideological metaphors is something that is very reminiscent of the way in which postmodernists invoke a clash of opposites as part of their approach to deconstructing texts. It is not that it is intended to replace one metaphor with its opposite, replacing one 'hierarchy' with another, but rather to de-center the original meaning. This is a way in which the text is used against itself, to bring to the foreground the assumptions carried by a text and reveal how the text is constructed in a manner such that its 'components' seek to reinforce one another to produce a convincing voice. Thus one metaphor being replaced by another, that clashes with the original, is helpful in showing how the metaphor is used as a *device* around which other text hangs and may seek to borrow legitimacy from the rhetorical persuasiveness that metaphor can provide.

Others such as David Boje (2001) with his eight "antenarrative" forms of analysis and Petra Schreus (2000, see also Carr, 2001) with her (re)constructive "interpretative repertoires" are other attempts, in the discourse of organization studies, to put in place tools through which the taken-for-granted of a text is explicitly revealed. Through the use of such tools of analysis, an examination of the language that seems to invoke speed may assist in lifting the veil of reverence and help us come to terms with what lies beneath.

References

Agger, B. (1989) *Fast capitalism: A critical theory of significance*. Urbana: University of Illinois.

Agger, B. (1992) *The discourse of domination: From the Frankfurt school to postmodernism*. Evanston, Illinois: Northwestern University.

Agger, B. (1998) *Critical social theories*. Boulder, Colorado: Westview.

Atkinson, D. (1971). *Orthodox consensus and radical alternative*. London: Heinemann.

Badcock, C.R. (1988) *Essential Freud*. Oxford: Blackwell.

Boje, D.M. (2001) *Narrative methods for organizational and communication research*. London: Sage.

Boje, D.M. (in press) *Theatres of capitalism*. San Francisco, CA: Hampton.

Brabant, E., Falzeder, E., & Giampieri-Deutsch, P. (Eds.) (1993) *The correspondence of Sigmund Freud and Sándor Ferenczi: Volume 1, 1908–1914*. Cambridge, Massachusetts: Belknap.

Carr, A.N. (2001) The enchantment of rationality: (Re)Constructing interpretative repertoires of rationality from the Anglo-American organization studies discourse. *Administrative Theory & Praxis, 23*(4), 652–669.

Carr, A.N., & Zanetti, L.A. (2001) Textuality and the postmodernist neglect of the politics of representation. *Journal of Critical Postmodern Organisation Science* (TAMARA), *1* (3), 14–26.

Carroll, W., & Ratner, R. (1994) Between Leninism and radical pluralism: Gramscian reflections on counter-hegemony and the new social movements. *Critical Sociology, 20* (2), 3–26.

Chasseguet-Smirgel, J. (1976) Some thoughts on the ego ideal. *Psychoanalytic Quarterly 45*, 345–373.

Debord, G. (1967) *The society of the spectacle*. Detroit: Black and Red.

English, H.B., & English, A.C. (1958) *A comprehensive dictionary of psychological and psychoanalytical terms*. New York: David McKay.

Ferenczi, S. (1994) *First contributions to psycho-analysis*. London: Karnac. (Original work published 1916).

Freire, P. (1970) *Pedagogy of the oppressed*. New York: Continuum.

Freud, S. (1977) Three essays on sexuality. In J. Strachey (Ed. and Trans.), *On sexuality* (Vol. 7, pp. 31–169). Pelican Freud Library, Harmondsworth, England: Pelican. (Original work published 1905).

Freud, S. (1984) On narcissism: An introduction. In J. Strachey (Ed. and Trans.), *On metapsychology: The theory of psychoanalysis* (Vol. 11, pp. 59–97). Pelican Freud Library, Harmondsworth, England: Pelican. (Original work published 1914).

Freud, S. (1984) The ego and the id. In J. Strachey (Ed. and Trans.), *On metapsychology: The theory of psychoanalysis* (Vol. 11, pp. 339–408). Pelican Freud Library, Harmondsworth, England: Pelican. (Original work published 1923).

Freud, S. (1985) Group psychology and the analysis of the ego. In J. Strachey (Ed.

and Trans.), *Civilization, society and religion* (Vol. 12, pp. 91–178). Pelican Freud Library, Harmondsworth, England: Pelican. (Original work published 1921).

Freud, S. (1985) Splitting of the ego in the process of defence delusions. In J. Strachey (Ed. and Trans.), *On metapsychology: The theory of psychoanalysis* (Vol. 11, pp. 461–464). Pelican Freud Library, Harmondsworth, England: Pelican. (Original incomplete work published 1940).

Freud, S. (1986) Two encyclopaedia articles. In J. Strachey (Ed. and Trans.), *Historical and expository works on psychoanalysis* (Vol. 15, pp. 130–157). Pelican Freud Library, Harmondsworth, England: Pelican. (Original work published 1923).

Freud, S. (1988) *New introductory lectures on psychoanalysis* (J. Strachey, Ed. and Trans.) Vol. 2. Pelican Freud Library, Harmondsworth, England: Pelican. (Original work published 1933).

Freud, S. (1990) Delusions and dreams in Jensen's 'Gradiva'. In J. Strachey (Ed. and Trans.), *Art and literature* (Vol. 14, pp. 237–386). Pelican Freud Library, Harmondsworth, England: Pelican. (Original work published 1906).

Giroux, H.A. (1983) *Critical theory and educational practice.* Geelong, Victoria: Deakin University.

Gramsci, A. (1971) *Selections from the prison notebooks* (Q. Hoare & G. Nowell-Smith, Trans. and Eds.). London: Lawrence & Wishart. (Original work published circa 1927–1937).

Hopkins, J. (2000) Psychoanalysis, metaphor and the concept of mind. In M. Levine (Ed.), *The analytic Freud* (pp. 11–35). London: Routledge.

Laplanche, J., & Pontalis, J. (1988) *The Language of psycho-analysis* (D. Nicholson-Smith, Trans.). London: Karnac. (Original work published 1967).

Lawner, L. (1973) Introduction. In L. Lawner (Ed.), *Antonio Gramsci: Letters from prison.* New York: Harper & Row.

Linnell, G. (2001, January 19) Life & death in the fast lane. *Good Weekend – The Sydney Morning Herald Magazine,* 16–22.

Marcuse, H. (1955) *Eros and civilization: A philosophical inquiry into Freud.* Boston: Beacon.

Marcuse, H. (1964) *One dimensional man: Studies in the ideology of advanced industrial society.* London: Routledge & Kegan Paul.

Meares, R. (1987) The secret and the self: On a new direction in psychotherapy. *Australian and New Zealand Journal of Psychiatry, 21,* 545–559.

Meares, R. (1992) *The metaphor of play.* Melbourne, Australia: Hill of Content.

Meares, R. (1997) Stimulus entrapment: On a common basis of somatization. *Psychoanalytic Inquiry, 17* (2), 223–234.

Meares, R., & Coombes, T. (1994) A drive to play: Evolution and psychotherapeutic theory. *Australian and New Zealand Journal of Psychiatry, 28,* 58–67.

Nunberg, N. (1955) *Principles of psycho-analysis.* New York: International University. (Original work published 1932).

Oswick, C. (2001) The etymology of 'corporate predatorship': A critical commentary. *TAMARA: Journal of Critical Postmodern Organization Science, 1*(2), 21–24.

Sandler, J. (1960) On the concept of superego. In *The psychoanalytic study of the child* (pp. 128–162). New York: International Universities.

Schreurs, P. (2000) *Enchanting rationality: An analysis of rationality in the Anglo-American discourse on public organization.* Delft: Eburon.

Biographical note

Dr Adrian Carr is Associate Professor and Principal Research Fellow in the interdisciplinary School of Social Sciences at the University of Western Sydney, Australia. Well published, Dr Carr is a member of a number of editorial boards, including *International Journal of Organisation Analysis; Journal of Management Development; Administrative Theory & Praxis; Global Business & Economics Review (founding editorial member); Policy, Organisation and Society; Journal of Organizational Change Management (Regional editor); Radical Psychology: A Journal of Psychology, Politics and Radicalism (Founding co-editor); Human Relations; Critical Perspectives On International Business* and, the *Journal of Critical Postmodern Organization Science (TAMARA)*. Dr Carr's areas of research interest are critical social psychology, psychoanalytic theory, critical theory, postmodernism, ethics, dissent in organizations and the management of change.

Chapter 4

Frequent Flyer: Speed and Mobility as Effects of Organizing

Tuomo Peltonen

Introduction: Speed And Mobility As Effects Of Heterogeneous Engineering

In Liquid Modernity, Bauman (2000) contemplates the centrality of movement and boundarylessness of contemporary society and organizations. His thesis is that we have moved from heavy modernity to liquid, light modernity, where the ease of movement is not only desirable, but also acts as a power resource. Thus, those who can travel without the burden of slow transport or strict immigration controls comprise the new elite, whereas those whose life is characterized by locality, immobility and slowness are often also those who have less opportunities for influence and success.

For Bauman, thus, globalization, with its famous 'time/space compression' (Harvey 1989), is a mechanism that changes the playing ground of social power so that instead of the closeness of the capitalist to the labor, the elite now rules based on its volatile presence and refusal to accept a spatial position. Liquid capitalism does not require colonization and constant surveillance of space, instead, the settled 'mass' is left to nurture its own territorial and positional identity at the same time as the speedy elite eschews any commitment to land or locality. In other words, time/space compression, especially the elimination of space in order to release time from the limits of having to 'pass' discrete slots, is the norm of the globalizing society and economy, and those who are not well equipped to eliminate 'localness' may become second class citizens in the emerging world society (Bauman 1998).

However, while Bauman's (2000, 1998) work opens new views on the cultural dynamics of globalization and the hierarchy of mobility, his theory tells little about how mobility and speed is produced and maintained in everyday action and organizational arrangements. In this respect there is a need to complement Bauman's theory by focusing the attention to the technologies and networks that construct and condition the emergence of a speedy business traveler as a distinct 'actor'. In this paper, we turn to actor network theory to look at power in action (Clegg 1989) and to introduce the role of the non-human elements in the finalization of a socio-cultural assemblage. Actor network theory is a well established social science perspective on the processes of 'social ordering' and on the role of the material artifacts in transmitting and mediating action, with stories such as Latour's (1991) key fobs case, Callon's (1998) analysis of 'tools of calculation' and Law's (1996) tales of the 'activities' of the office technologies comprising vocabularies and perspectives usable in the study of the configurations of social/technical.

Technologies and materials are regarded as crucial for the stabilization of a tentative order. Thus, while rhetorical and political action also counts in building organized networks, it is often the technical artifacts and scientific innovations that sediment the emerging order (Law 1992). The effect of the 'durable technologies' is that they institutionalize and normalize the roles and responsibilities of different actors in a system. So, for example in Latour's (1991) key fob case, the hotel owner becomes the one whose plea for returning the key is obeyed, while the customers turn into careful 'borrowers' of hotel's property. The heaviness of the key ring enables the hotel owner to enroll the customers into action he (or she) is wishing to initiate.

It is important to note that the construction of technical-social networks also shapes the agency of the more 'powerful'. Law (1994, 1996; Callon & Law 1995) demonstrates this through his deconstructive ethnography of managerial work. In the particular case of a scientific organization, while the laboratory manager appears to be an autonomous subject, in reality he is empowered and enabled by a number of arrangements. For example, he is dependent on accounting technology, which collects local information and constructs a picture of the 'whole', against which managerial targets and plans can be contrasted. He is also a product of hierarchy, electronic networks, telecommunication, secretarial assistance, etc. Law's point is that without all this, the manager is a helpless, powerless individual; it is the arrangements and technologies that constitute and equip a managerial agency, not the essential 'human' skills and competencies.

When listing the characteristics of the managerial agency, Law also notes the pervasiveness of mobility and absence: 'half the time [the manager] is not sitting at his desk. Indeed, he's not in the laboratory at all' (Callon & Law 1995, p. 483). The fact that the managers are not present is not perhaps anything new to anyone who has organizational experience, but the trend towards the managerial absence or mobility may be intensifying. For example the quantitative studies on human resource policies regarding the 'new forms of international work' (Brewster 1999) suggests that organizations prefer

71

short-term visits and long distance over the either/or decision regarding the situation where a task needs to be done by someone from abroad. While the formal reason for this is cost cutting, there may be power related aspects as well. The empirical results suggest that despite the ever-increasing volumes of business flights, frequent traveling is very difficult to put under budgetary control and that there is rarely a written policy regarding managerial mobility. This controversy suggests that business traveling is not put under administrative regulation and that informally, the rule is that the possibilities for mobility are preserved to the corporate elite and that frequent flying is seen as an element of the 'freedom' of the upper echelons[1].

One can argue, then, that being mobile is a crucial element in the making of an organizational 'tribe' that appears as inherently liquid, flowing and nomadic. However, as we have already pointed out, to reach this effect, a whole array of traveling technologies needs to be activated and implemented. Practices such as the making of a reservation, arriving at the airport, moving through the check-in, security and ticket control and the flight itself must be organized so that the 'body' of the business traveler can be transported easily through space and time. Furthermore, the networks of speedy traveling, to be 'effective', must also enroll the appropriate humans to the proposed action by persuading the Others – the non-global actors – to stay where they are and, when moving is necessary, to take the transport systems that fit better the 'needs' of the lay people not in an immanent hurry. The enrolment, however, cannot be imposed from the outside to the nominally free individuals (Foucault 1982), instead, the translation of travel identity is always a fragile and incomplete process. The supposedly slow and local Others can, for example, start moving around using alternative transport pipelines, such as the cheap flight airlines, and become speedy in the similar manner as the executive business travelers. The crucial difference is, as Bauman (1998) astutely notes, whether this kind of mobility is interpreted as 'vagabond' movement, which is born out of struggle for change, or as 'tourist' mobility, where speed and movement are thought of as natural consequences of the lightness and fluidity of the life of the people in question[2].

While these aspects of the frequent flying 'technologies' are obviously in need of empirical attention and theoretical work, 'access' to the making

---

[1] A staggering 60% of the respondents indicated in the survey I conducted that their firms do not keep records of frequent flying. However, they were willing to note that as many as 42% of the frequent flyers are senior managers, others being mainly middle managers and techno-logical experts.

[2] The speedy manager must also constantly work to keep his or her internal 'other', the dragg-ing, boundary-crossing incrementalist, in check and absent. The incrementalist, however, being that which the speedy manager is dependent on, cannot be abolished.

of the speedy business traveler can be difficult and expensive, and in some cases, even resisted because of the privileged nature of the executive lifestyle. However, alongside the busy businessmen, the tribe of the global academics can be identified as another group, which seems to have internalized the world of speed and natural mobility. Scientists are constantly on the move: traveling to a conference, to a meeting of an international network or to a PhD defence. Professors and other researchers seem to be constantly coming from or going to somewhere, and, furthermore, it often appears as if this ongoing mobility is not external to their lifestyle and professional identity, but has become an integral part of being an academic. If this is true, taking a closer look at some of our own traveling experiences might be worth the while.

However, before we go into the main story, a note about the logistics of the paper. After this section, the chapter introduces the author's personal experiences that led to the interest on frequent flying and reports on the empirical material used and the process of analysis. This is followed by a section, which looks at the processes of ordering in the particular case, frequent flying within a domestic context. The section is organized into three parts, the first being about the surrounding practices of easy mobility, with the second discussing the question of the Others in the networks of frequent flying, and the third tackling the issue of the momentary cracking of the stability of the system. The last section briefly summarizes the argument and suggests avenues for further research.

Experiencing And Studying Frequent Flying In Academic Life

A couple of years ago, I moved to work at a university in a northern part of my country ('Town'). As this was initially a temporary post, I chose to commute from my current location ('Capital'). The distance to the workplace was about 600 kilometers, which would either take some six hours by train or one hour by plane. I decided to use the plane. This was a beginning to a period of weekly commuting between home and office – a situation many academics become acquainted with at some stage of their career. While I started to enjoy the benefits of long distance commuting, such as the possibility of splitting my time between office duties and uninterrupted research work, there were also some drawbacks that made me think about the wider socio-technical setup constituting and enabling easy traveling and commuting. My reflection was unsystematic at first, but became more disciplined during the early part of my second year as a "suitcase academic". In the course of a period of five months, I tried to record interesting traveling situations and interactions by making notes on them as soon as possible.

Methodologically, the strategy I adapted is close to for example Watson's

(1994) ethnographic study of a plant where he worked as a manager and made notes about his involvement in the social processes and constitution of 'management'. Like him, I was participating in collective action I studied. Other recent studies made 'while working' include for example Van Maanen (1991) and Kondo (1990). Such participant observation approach, although often limited in terms of the available 'distance' of the subject from the objects, nevertheless offers an economical alternative to a 'proper' field ethnography as the 'compromised' design makes possible longer periods of observation and reflection than is typically possible in management studies (Alvesson & Deetz 2000). Furthermore, studying one's own work milieu is not only 'cost-efficient' due to the easy access to the field, but also because it opens an opportunity to ground scholarly work on one's everyday concerns and personally relevant ethical and political issues (Meriläinen & Katila 2002), a motivation no longer shied away from in the age of the de-centered subject of knowledge (Calas & Smirchich 1999).

Apart from note taking and participant observation, I also collected other material; for example, I took photos of the airport and my journey and gathered relevant clips from the NatAir in-flight magazine and other media. I also analyzed the booking process by recording one phone booking conversation as well as by asking – when appropriate – detailed questions about the organization of 'ticketless travel' when talking to the call center persons. In addition, I tried to reflect on my own action and motives in various contexts; at home, in the airports and on the plane, in interaction with the faculty colleagues and in conversation with the other academics.

It might be good to note that despite the broadly ethnographic nature of the material, the focus is not exclusively on the cultural creation of a community. Rather, the interest is in the making of the speedy business traveler by following the setup of a network of human and non-human elements and their connections in constituting and producing the mobile professional. Departing from traditional ethnography, the chapter does not assume a pre-given culture or organization, to which the research immerses in search of rich material on the crafting of the community. Here, much in the spirit of actor network theory (Law 1992), the strategy is to trace down the arrangements and technologies that create the possibility for the mobile commuter to exist. Like many actor network studies, the approach adapted could be described as being close to theoretically motivated case study method that organizational scholars such as Stablein (1996) have suggested as an alternative to 'pure', inductive ethnography. Thus, the aim is to use material from a particular national-local case to discuss the theoretical issues around speed, traveling and identities.[3]

---

[3] Practically, to make the following of the chapter easier for the reader, I have separated the anecdotes and ethnographic notes from the main text and present the stories from the field in the form of vignettes.

The Making Of 'Light Mobility' And 'Speedy Professional'

Arrangements and technologies surrounding speed and mobility

Many of the technological innovations made in air transport aim to remove the obstacles that are seen as constraining and slowing down the busy business travelers. One of the innovations introduced recently is 'ticketless travel', where the customer does not use a conventional paper ticket but moves through the checkpoints with the help of the electronic data stored in the airline computer systems. The passenger only needs to show his or her identification card at the gate to be allowed to board the plane. The airline clerk swipes the card and checks the reservation from the screen. In some routes, as for example in the domestic traffic, there is no seat reservation, so there is no need to carry anything other than the ID card, often a credit card or a frequent flyer membership card.

E-ticketing is often combined with the possibility to buy the tickets over the phone. The call center takes the reservation, charges the credit card and sends an electronic confirmation to a mobile phone or to an email address. In my case, I often use this opportunity to make the preparations as simple as possible. A telephone booking does not take long; a typical conversation with the sales person takes about three minutes, during which all the necessary arrangements for a return trip are made.

The booking is made very easy and it is the actual boarding that takes time and can be awkward. Therefore, NatAir has introduced an 'e-gate' system in the major business traveler routes. This is an automatic boarding machine that allows passengers with smart cards to enter much faster than is the case in the normal manned boarding. The e-gate reads the information from the chip in a frequent flyer card, matches the ID of the person with the reservation data, and opens the gate for the customer to go through the gate and to the plane. The whole boarding routine takes only three seconds, and NatAir celebrates the innovation in its in-flight publications as an advancement that significantly 'accelerates' the processes of check-in and boarding for passengers with electronic tickets.

The service is not available on all routes; instead, it is mainly used for the popular business destinations to and from Capital. In the domestic traffic, Town has most flight connections with Capital and there are some 10 daily flights on the route. The reason is obvious; Town is a high technology center, and thus forms an important node in the global network of 'new economy'. Airport is the symbol of the economic success of Town, and easy access from there to the other sites of global capitalism is a priority for the various stakeholders. Air travel between Town and other major cities is not only about 'winning time', but also embodies the social proximity between the different high-tech centers of the world and the importance of maintaining that closeness despite the geographical distance[4].

Transport by air is made relatively easy for those who are frequent flyers and use business routes. Not only is there a permanent 'green light' granted by the state and the security officials, but traveling is also designed to be as frictionless as possible. This is largely based on the idea that the world global managers and professionals inhabit is characteristically instantaneous and that the practical arrangements should focus on eliminating the obstacles that constrain or slow down movement. However, the intelligibility of the easy movement of the global elite can only be 'seen' against the Others whose lives are characterized by localness and constant struggle to cross boundaries. We turn next to the parts of the network whose role is to sustain mobility, partly by staying – and being held – immobile and under the 'laws' of space-time.

The Others of speed and 'natural mobility'

As far as space is concerned, in the focal case, my experience of the naturalness of the easy mobility is socially and culturally reinforced in the encounters with the Others. It is here that the divide between those for whom movement is essential to their character and those for whom mobility means overcoming the restrictions of their territorialist self is performed and mutually exclusive identities produced. These negotiations are, though, by no means uncontested and can lead to the challenging of the alleged superiority of the fast movers.

Some may see that my problem as a commuting colleague is the lack of commitment, defined as physical presence and the possibility to be 'seen' by the significant Others in the workplace. However, as Bauman notes (2000), this logic of Panopticon (Foucault 1979), where both the managed and the managers are supposed to stay in their positions, has faded away as globalization has taken a stronger hold on cultural and organizational life. Leaders of today rule more on the basis of 'intelligent absence'. In that setting, the powerful spend considerable amounts of their time outside of the workplace, looking for more experiences and developing themselves as the 'new managers', rather than watching over the employees.

---

[4] The frequency of flights and the idea that the route to Capital is an 'air bridge' came evident as I once checked in to a flight that had already left. I had forgotten my actual departure time and, without knowing it, was coming to check-in too late. The clerk at the check-in was first puzzled about the computer message indicating the gate is already closed. After a while, she discovered that the note was based on the fact that the plane had already left an hour ago. Despite the non-changeability of the ticket, she was willing to book me again to the next flight as if it was about taking the next bus instead of the previous one.

In the post-Panopticon order, commitment is less desirable and can even become a problem if work becomes a designed 'place', which fixes the search for new experiences and constant learning. In liquid organizations, the only real commitment is towards the continuous improvement and progressive self-transformation. In this spirit, I have not been too much concerned about the lack of belonging, a complaint some of my colleagues raise. After all, the opposite of the 'provincial' commitment is not necessarily an attachment to the circles of Capital, but can also take the form of a 'cosmopolitan' identity, in which case the 'local' or 'territorial' – in whatever way defined – comes to be seen, paradoxically, as the susceptible Other of the placeless global professional.

In this way, the struggle over the meaning of mobility can end up in a moment of re-appropriation, where the 'immoral' movement of a traveling faculty member is, instead of being understood as a sign of non-identity, connected to virile activism and to the habit of being mobile and progressive. Similarly, the idea of 'good' presence can re-appear in the ordering process as something that reminds of the heavy and slow form of life that characterizes those corners of the world that have been left out of the dynamics of globalization. In my case, it is 'easy' for me to picture the administrative staff, with their bureaucratic rules and a 'morality of a due process', as getting in the way of the quick academics, or, how students 'bother' and 'hinder' their professors with 'minor', technical worries. The inability of the students to progress without the unnecessary complications or the tedious administrative obstacles installed to block the dynamic researcher appear often in the stories my colleagues and I tell to each other as a way to perform us as 'proper' academics.

Such emphasis on speed and instantaneity is of course a performative act of self-identity that expresses the importance of keeping in check non-speed and non-instantaneity – stickiness and slowness – by excluding those aspects of being from subjectivity. Yet purifying and differentiating the self is problematic as the Other is already inscribed into the self-identity and therefore separating slowness from speed can never result in a pure 'weightless' identity. The inner demon of the immobility cannot be simply attributed to the outside, but must be worked over and kept in control. Having the 'darker' side that is known and yet denied may lead to fear that is not always conscious, but can surface in moments of crisis, or, as the Freudians would perhaps argue, in one's dreams. This may be what I also experienced in the beginning of my frequent flying career (Box 1).

At the mercy of an aero-machine

One night I dreamt about flying. Obviously, it was a work trip to the north. We lifted off as normal, but then suddenly I realized we were in a small plane and that the plane started making extreme turns, like in an air show. I became scared.

Later, I had another dream. This time, we were landing. I think I have had this kind of dream a long time ago, but this time it was more concrete. We were approaching the airport but there were other planes right ahead of us. The pilot flies lower and waits for the instructions. No instructions for a new approach come, and we face a hill. The plane glides along the hill, but cannot rise enough and we make an emergency landing on the top of the hill. Luckily, the landing is smooth and we are all okay.

Box 1.

Another important element that sustains speed and mobility is technology, especially the new electronic means of identification and quick air transport. These materials and arrangements are often viewed as relatively inert objects, but there is more to them than just their instrumentality. Speed is made possible by the new technologies which themselves are relatively stable and durable (Law 1992). The main purpose of the electronic networks and the automated boarding systems is to act as effective throughput elements or pipelines that transport information and human bodies as smoothly as possible. The wide bodied airplanes and pressurized high speed trains try to create an illusion of the controlled 'inside' of traveling that can be separated from the 'outside', where the 'means' of transportation defy gravity, friction and the other well known 'forces of nature'.

However, the role of air travel technology may not be as determined and one-sided as intended. As actor-network theory has argued again and again (e.g. Latour 1991; Callon & Law 1995), machines and material objects also influence the user by arousing a distinct pattern of action and suppressing alternative kinds of thinking and behavior. There is often some sort of social force coded into the design and working of the machines and it is this logic that gets decoded into the human body as the individual 'uses' technology. Thus, the human becomes more machine-like at the same time as technologies seem to be wise and capable of action (Brown 1999).

One concrete manifestation of the agency of the machine is the rule according to which the 'traveling bodies' need to arrive at the airport – to the starting point of the transport 'process' – at a certain point in time. Quick transport is promised only if the passenger checks in or arrives at the gate within the announced time. Thus, the boundary between the airport/aircraft world and the 'life on ground' is organized by a timetable concerning when the traveler needs to enter into and be present for the system. The logic of the speedy movement overruns the human sensitivity for pace and rhythm. The technologies want to separate the 'slow' aspects of the 'humanly' organized being from the 'fast' realities created in the materials and arrangements of the global business traveling. However, as I experienced, this is not always uncomplicated due to problems such as queues (Box 2).

Whose problem is a slow queue when there's hurry?

I am arriving at Capital airport to take my flight to Town. As I have some luggage to check in, I need to be at the counter 25 minutes before the departure (with just hand luggage the time is 15 minutes and there is no need to do a prior check-in, provided one is flying with an 'e-ticket'). The flight leaves at 11.20 and as I arrive to the check-in hall it's 10.54, meaning I am just in time to hand in the luggage. However, it is the skiing season, and there is a plane bound to a resort in Lapland. There is normally no queue to the domestic check-in, but now there are quite a few waiting for their turn, many with both luggage and skiing equipment. It takes more than 5 minutes to reach the counter and by that time, I am late for the 25-minute buffer. I go to the counter, where a man processes my luggage without mentioning anything about the lateness of my check-in. However, as I look at my luggage receipt, it states that the baggage has been turned in late. I am a bit worried this may mean NatAir takes no responsibility in case my bag misses the plane. At the gate I ask the clerk about the meaning of the luggage slip. She says it means the luggage may miss the plane due to the lateness. I explain that I was in time, but the queue took so long and that's why I was a bit late. I also ask whether this means I have to pick it up in case it comes with the next flight. The clerk says it's still at my cost. I repeat, with slight aggression, that queue is not my problem; I was on time and NatAir should take care that their check-in service is properly manned and efficient. Just as we begin to develop an argument, another clerk intervenes. He asks where I am bound to, and as I tell my destination is Town, he says convincingly that my luggage is on the plane and that there will be no problems. I walk to the plane and wonder why is it that there is no mention in the formal information whether the queues are the customers or NatAir's worry.

Box 2.

The fact that the systems of frequent flying not only enable but also condition and govern the subject requires some second-order stabilization and purification work on behalf of the passenger. For example, there is often an inclination to tell stories where the machine is just an instrument for the realization of a mobile agency, not an integral component in the network of speedy traveling. As I reflect on my own everyday language use, it is easy to note how I tend to separate the 'freedom to move' from the material bits that sustain my mobility in many different ways. While the movement and dynamism essentially belongs to the category of 'I', technology is seen as the passive 'thing' that 'serves' me in my project of being light and liquid. Perhaps the turbulent world situation during the last couple of years has made some to reflect on the existence of the Others and to see that as some of the taken for granted practices are 'tightened' security wise, the changes reach also the everyday life of the business travelers.

Cracks in the networks sustaining easy traveling

The struggle over interpretation of speed reminds of the fragility of the setup around business traveling. Different sorts of cracks and tilts provide concrete examples of the incompleteness of ordering that is always implicated to any projects of building socio-technical 'networks'. When talking about air travel, terrorism and terrorists are a key figure in the discourse after the events of September 11th 2001. One of the most disturbing issues in the attacks was that the 'wrong' persons were allowed to board an aircraft meant for 'normal' people. To prevent this, airports have tightened security measures with new guidelines for both service personnel as well as for the technical rigor of screening. So, for example in my case, there was practically no x-ray control prior to 9/11. Since then it has become a permanent procedure, which takes time and disturbs the 'process' of check-in and boarding.

Because of the inconvenience occurring to the frequent flyers, the air transport industry is trying to eliminate altogether the access of unwanted nationalities and ethnic, social and racial groups to the important routes with a state-of-the-art identification system. Unlike passports, which suffer from potential forgery, recognition of identity based on biological characteristics is thought to be reliable as it is based on the facts of the body. The plans to introduce the so-called biometric identification, for example the checking of identity on the basis of the facial figure, are now on the way. It is the intent of the air authorities and the airlines to apply the new recognition technologies first among the crewmembers and, after that, among the frequent flying business passengers.

Despite these radical methods, the safety of air transport, especially in the US, has been damaged for many years to come. This is because terrorism is no longer 'over there', in the struggles of the Third World, but has become an enduring feature of the sense of the Western self. Today, anyone can be a terrorist in disguise, and therefore, air travel must constantly remind itself of the danger, as well as of the need to distinguish the 'normally' mobile businessmen from the masses of suspicious immigrants and people with a 'wrong' passport, outlook or color.

The dangerous Other is thought to have blended into the relatively esteemed crowd of air travelers, making the whole idea of separating those who are safe from those who are not. But there are also other mutative elements that threaten to change the travelable air into a piece of concrete, solid space that slows and resists movement. One example of such resistance I encountered in my trips is fog; since the Town airport is by the sea, there is a chance of thick fog that may make approach to the airport too risky. Sometimes the pilots wait for the fog – which is more typical in the mornings – to clear before they take off from Capital. Such delay is of course highly frustrating, and an object of daily workplace discussions in the Town region. Even more embarrassing is the situation where, due to a delay, two consecutive planes from Capital land almost immediately one after another. And not only fog, but also the 'technical problems' and the later arrival from the previous route can cause the aircraft to come a bit late to the gate, with the consequence that what is thought of as the invisible 'enabler' of easy transport and light mobility turns out to be, in reality, heavy and imperfect.

The service technologies related to the overall 'process' of flying can also crack and, that way, show their importance as conditions of possibility in the speedy life of a global professional. The fragile points in this respect are especially the electronic networks and call centers that enable the 'ticketless travel'. In the booking process, several crucial instances in the movement of information can fail because of minor technical problems or human errors. A less dramatic inconvenience I have encountered is the impossibility to receive an electronic confirmation to the computer. At least once NatAir was not able to send me a confirmation to my email address and also the routes to the mobile phone text messaging system were down. This means problems, as this document may be asked at the security check, and it is through this that the passenger can prove his legitimacy to fly.

A more hideous incapacity took place when I was trying to buy a ticket only a couple of hours before the intended flight and the phone lines assigned for booking were not answering. The 24/7 service, an important feature in the making of the 'timeless' world for airline customers, did not seem to work as promised and only after some rather complicated maneuvers could I manage to buy a ticket and get onboard (Box 3). What is normally a routine thing took now over an hour, a reminder of the 'manual' labor and 'backstage' operations taking place in service processes implemented through call centers.

Phone reservation that does not answer

I am in Town and I want to use a NatAir Frequent Flyer offer to Capital and back. It's 3 pm and the flight I am looking for leaves at 6.30 pm, so I am already in a hurry. The problem is that I need to book the flight from the Frequent Flyer call centre (because the offer involves a deduction of some points from my F.F. account). I call the centre but the lines are busy. I try again and wait for about 30 minutes. Nobody answers. Then I try the normal phone booking number. It is busy as well. Next I try the ticket office at Town Airport, but there is no answer (the phone keeps ringing without any sign of attendance). It's 4.20 pm and I start getting worried. After all, I must take a 5 pm bus from the University to catch the flight. I try both the Frequent Flyer number and the phone sales (simultaneously, keeping my 'wired' office phone on one ear and the hands-free mobile phone on the other). After 10 minutes, the phone sales answers. I explain my situation, but the lady in the other end just notes that I must book this flight from the Frequent Flyer centre. I repeat the situation and get more serious ('who will take the responsibility if I fail to get onboard this flight?'). As I ask how is it possible that someone is kept hanging on the phone lines for half an hour, she tells that several of the staff are 'in training'. Again I try to make it clear that I will not end this conversation without a guarantee of a ticket. We then talk about my Frequent Flyer account and she is suddenly silent for a minute. I think she looks at my flight records and sees that I fly a lot in this route. Now she starts asking again about the details of my planned flights and checks something. Yes, she will do it for me! Finally, everything should be in order and the lady even promises to send the reservation number as a text message.

I get to the airport and go straight to the ticket sales. I ask for the ticket, but there seems to be nothing under my name. I also notice that there is no text message from the phone sales lady. After some hassle, the reservation pops up to the computer. It turns out that the flight is booked for the following day. To my luck, the ticket salesperson is a pragmatic being, who corrects the date by hand to the actual ticket and promptly processes my purchase.

Box 3.

While the technologies and even nature can slip from their 'support' role and become obstacles to speed, the resistance of the human others is also evident. Those who do not (or cannot not) move, for example the administrative staff, the localized faculty, the family, can voice their discontent about not having the possibility to escape from the burden of here and now. On the other hand, they can also try and imitate the speedy professional by enhancing and upgrading their 'mobility status' by going to the kinds of places that the frequent flyer visits. To an extent, this is being made easier with the introduction of the cheap travel businesses and with the increasing opportunities for virtual tourism with the help of the Internet and the electronic networks. For example, doctoral students are nowadays encouraged to attend international seminars and to visit the foreign universities, and it is through this exposure to the global 'networking life' that they are supposed to learn the ropes of the academic world.

A more immanent confusion to the cleanliness of the frequent flyer networks emerges from the presence of the physically immobile – children, handicapped, elderly, etc. – in the air routes that are normally packed with sporty businessmen and businesswoman. The 'disabled' represent that part of the mobility arrangements that are destined to stay as fixed and non-moving, and their co-existence in performance of high mobility in the air transport situations can cause inappropriate slowness and appear probably as a blockade to the speedy business traveler. The concrete immobility of a handicapped person within the context where easy movement is the norm is not only about to cause awkwardness but even bursts of aggressive tantrum as the 'divine' freedom to locate and relocate freely is hampered by someone who 'reserves' space (Box 4).

The disabled Others in a world of high mobility
In Capital, I enter the plane ahead of the others and get a nice 3rd row place. There are two seats empty in front of me in a three-seat row. The man in the first of the three seats is disabled; he is a wheel chair user and cannot move his legs. As the plane starts to get full, incoming passengers ask whether the two seats next to him are free. The man patiently explains that he cannot move and therefore it is not possible to pass him and take the free seats (he was sitting by the aisle). Then a tanned, youngish foreigner comes, probably on his way to an IT company. He asks if the seats would be free, and the man answers in English that he cannot move. The tanned businessman to that: 'You are joking, right?' The disabled kindly says that he is not joking; he is really unable to move. The businessman is confused. He persists on taking one of the empty seats and suggests that he climbs over the disabled. The disabled explains that he is completely paralyzed from the waist down and that he really cannot move. After a couple of attempts, the tanned businessman says, with a lot of irony (if not bitterness and hatred): 'Okay, I will have to take a seat somewhere else.' Just seconds later another entering businessman tries to claim an empty seat in a row across the aisle. As the young boy inhabiting the seat in front of the empty one does not react to the request and the older man gets impatient, a flight stewardess comes to the man and says: 'Sorry Sir, but this boy cannot hear anything you say.'

Box 4.

Last, but not least, perhaps the most intimate challenge to the idea of a traveling academic being fully and unequivocally 'global' comes from the inner dynamics of subjectivity, especially from the impossibility to cleanse all vestiges of heaviness and slowness from one's sense of self. So, although I feel proximity to the liquid world that surrounds the speedy traveler, I also acknowledge the gap between 'we' the researchers and 'them' the ultra-fast management consultants and business leaders. Thus, I still experience the state of flow as something that requires more work and personal betterment as I compare myself to those who seem to have reached zero gravity in their professional lives.

This unnoticed but no doubt actual habit of 'problematization' (Callon 1986) along the lines of slowness and stickiness suggests that despite the rather heroic story narrated in the chapter about the unique world of easy movement inhabited (also) by us the academic workers, the scholars may not have an unconditional access to the 'neo-nomadic' elite, but could be seen as remaining in many ways still a group whose work is characterized by a commitment to a social collective and to a relatively slow pace of events (cf. Hatch & Grey 2000). That is, although the global academics share several features with the global businesspersons, differences between a 'scientist' and a 'practitioner' may appear as stronger than the similarities between the two groups, and this may momentarily trigger worry among 'us' regarding the gap between the real and the ideal. However, it is important to note that behind these variations in occupational beliefs there is a more fundamental anxiety over being slower than others and in that sense, being somehow incomplete and impure in the our late modern world of acceleration and instantaneity (Box 5).

> **E-gate makes me look slow and clumsy**
> It is early May and a couple of weeks has elapsed since my last flight. I arrive at the gate a bit late, thinking the queue is gone and I can get onto the plane quickly. However, the gate has just opened, due to a delay that I hear later from the pilot. So, there is a long queue, or actually two queues, one for each of the clerks who check and collect our tickets. The e-gates have been standing next to the more conventional manned ticket control stations, but they have not been operational. As I join the queue, a man that comes after me, passes the queue and heads for the e-gate. I first think this is just a desperate attempt to get ahead of us by pretending not to know how the queue works. However, it soon turns out that the man is serious; he tries to wave his little card at the gate to get it to open. It seems this does not work, and the female clerk closer to the e-gate notices the man trying to introduce his smart card to the machine. The clerk comes, takes the card and places it next to one of the sides of the inner part of the gate. The move helps, and there is action on the screen of the gate. The system identifies the passenger and opens the gate so that the man can walk through, and continue directly to the plane. The rest of us wait several minutes before getting into the crowded compartment. NatAir's personnel and the in-flight magazine have promised that as soon as the experimentation phase is over and the frequent flyer cards are renewed into smart cards, anyone can use the e-gate to board the plane in all domestic and in some selected international routes. I feel slow waiting for the clerk to wipe my old card and promise myself to get one of these new cards soon.

Box 5.

Conclusions

In this chapter I have discussed speed as an effect created in the socio-cultural processes and networks of frequent flying and business traveling. Informed by Bauman's (2000, 1998) analysis of liquid capitalism, the study concentrated on the mutual constitution of global mobility and local immobility. Alongside Bauman, resources from actor-network theory (Law 1992), especially the ideas related to the tactics of heterogeneous engineering, were used. I have looked at the ways in which the 'fast professional' is manufactured as an effect of cultural and material ordering, discussed the various critical 'others' in the build-up of the network, and emphasized the fragility of the set-up via exploring its tendency to crack and confuse. The empirical background against which these themes were discussed was my personal experience as a long distance commuter, extended with some ethnographic and documentary material on the organizational and technological arrangements around frequent flying.

Throughout, the argument has been that the mobile professional or manager is relatively powerless in the face of the considerable investments required to make his or her easy movement possible. The point made is that intensive flying as such is no guarantee that the traveler inhabits the world of flow and instantaneity. Instead, frequent flying is to be made 'easy' by relegating all the laborious, time-consuming and heavy elements of the accomplishment to the backstage, a task which demands effort and clever strategizing. Though ordering is never complete, it seems to create tentative closures that sustain a relatively well-formed elite subjectivity, as the case suggests.

Yet, despite the emerging conclusion that resistance to speed is eventually won, I want to end up with a note that pushes the debate back to the ethical. Exploring business traveling has led to the questions around the formation of a global professional within the field of paid work and Western culture. However, the wider discourse of globalization circulating in politics and transnational institutions affects not only the privileged members of the professional organizations and business corporations, but also those more radically left out from the progress of international economy and technological modernism. These ramifications of the hierarchy between the global elite and the local majority go beyond the immediate concerns of organization studies, to the worldwide distribution of poverty, criminalization of the marginal groups and to the continuing colonialism in science and culture (Bauman 1998; Mir et al 2002). Touching upon these issues brings out, I would argue, the question of how to challenge and change the evolving global order as well as demands a more thoroughgoing deconstruction of our role in reproducing or challenging the new asymmetries. I hope these issues can be developed further in forthcoming studies investigating frequent flying as an organizational and cultural phenomenon.

Acknowledgement: I would like to acknowledge the financial support of the Foundation of Economic Education and Wihuri Foundation.

References

Alvesson, M. & Deetz, S. (2000) *Doing critical management research*. London: Sage.

Bauman, Z. (1998) *Globalization*. Cambridge: Polity Press.

Bauman, Z. (2000) *Liquid Modernity*. Cambridge: Polity Press.

Brewster, C. (1999) *International commuting*. Cranfield: Cranfield School of Management.

Brown, S. (1999) Electronic networks and subjectivity. In: Gordo-Lopez, A. & Parker, I. (eds.) *Cyberpsychology*. London: Routledge.

Calas, M. & Smirchich, L. (1999) Past Postmodernism?, *Academy of Management Review*, 24(4): 649–71.

Callon, M & Law, J. (1995) Agency and the hybrid collectif. *South Atlantic Quarterly*, 94/2: 481–507.

Callon, M. (1986) Some Elements of a Sociology of Translation: Domestication of the Scallops and the Fishermen of Saint Brieuc Bay. In J. Law (Ed.) *Power, Action and Belief: a new Sociology of Knowledge? Sociological Review Monograph*. London, Routledge and Kegan Paul. **32**: 196–233.

Callon, M. (1998) *The Laws of the Markets*. London: Blackwell.

Clegg, S. (1989) *Frameworks of power*. London: Sage.

Foucault, M. (1979) *Discipline and Punish: The birth of the prison*. Harmondsworth: Penguin.

Foucault, M. (1982) Subject and power. In: Rabinow, P. and Dreyfus, H. *Michel Foucault: Beyond Structuralism and Hermeneutics*. Chicago: The University of Chicago Press.

Harvey (1989) *The condition of postmodernity*. Cambridge: Blackwell.

Hatch, M.J. & Grey, C. Why we do what we do? On the necessary antagonism of management education. In: *Proceedings of the 2nd International Conference on 'Emergent Fields in Management: Connecting Learning and Critique'*, 19–21.7.2000. University of Lancaster & University of Cambridge. pp. 195–222. 2000.

Kondo, D. (1990) *Crafting selves*. Chicago: Chicago University Press.

Latour, B. (1991) Technology is society made durable. In: Law, J. (ed.) *A sociology of monsters. Essays on power, technology and domination*. London: Routledge.

Law, J. (1994) *Organizing Modernity*. London: Blackwell.

Law, J. (1992) Notes on the Theory of the Actor Network: Ordering, Strategy and Heterogeneity. *Systems Practice*, 5(4): 379–393.

Law, J. (1996) *The manager and his powers*. A paper presented to the Mediaset Convention, Venice, 12th November, 1996; published by the Department of Sociology at Lancaster University at: http://www.lancaster.a.uk/sociology/stslaw1.html (accessed 30.11.2001).

Meriläinen, S. & Katila, S. (2002) Self in research. In: Aaltio-Marjosola, I. & Mills, A. (eds) *Gender, Identity and the Culture of Organizations*. London: Routledge.

Mir, R.A., Mir, A. & Upadhyaya, P. (2003) Toward a postcolonial reading of organizational control. In: Prasad, A. (ed.) *Postcolonial theory and organizational analysis*. London: Routledge.

Stablein, R. (1996) Data in organization studies. In: Clegg, S. & Hardy, C. (eds.) *Handbook of Organization Studies*. London: Sage.

Van Maanen, J. (1991) The smile factory: work at Disneyland. In Frost, P. et al (eds.) *Reframing organizational culture*. London: Sage.

Watson, T. (1994) *In search of management*. London: Routledge.

SECTION II

The Speed of Organizational Technology

Accelerating Organisations through Representational Infrastructures: The Possibilities for Power and Resistance

Scott Lawley

Acknowledgements

Thanks to Gary Brown and Peter Stokes for comments on earlier drafts of this chapter and to the editors and the anonymous reviewer for comments on later drafts. Thanks to Gibson Burrell and Stephen Linstead for bringing to my attention particular concepts used within the chapter.

1. Introduction

In this chapter, I examine representation as a necessary and constituent process in the attainment of organisational power, but also as a process which simultaneously creates the site for resistance against such power. Following poststructuralist and actor-network conceptions of the nature of reality as ephemeral and travelling at 'infinite speed' (Lee, 1998), I view technologies of representation (Cooper, 1993) as being a source of organisational power by their slowing down of reality in order to make it manageable.

The use of contemporary computer and information technology to process such representations is then examined, noting that whilst representation *slows* down reality, the *acceleration* of such representations through computer networks is a source of increased organisational power. This follows Virilio's (1986) emphasis on the importance of instruments of speed for social power. However, acceleration up to the level of the processing speed of computers can bring about the problems that it was meant to overcome, with information overload, infinite processing speed and complex and unnavigable global networks placing its representations beyond human grasp and thus beyond their appropriation for organisational power. Such problems of representation resonate with the various works of Baudrillard on hyperreality and social passivity.

However, I suggest that this type of analysis places too much emphasis on the representations of reality themselves and ignores the fact that the infrastructures through which they are mediated are embedded within existing social structures (Sassen, 2000, 2002). Through what I describe as processes of 'hosting' and 'portality', conceptualised in terms of the metaphor of the Janus-face, I explain the nature of organisational power and resistance against such power as processed through representational infrastructures where organisational representations are accelerated potentially to an 'infinite speed'.

2. Infinite speed and the impossibility of representing the organisation

Speed – movement so fast it evades measurement and apprehension – is at the core of a set of process philosophies of organisation which I take as the starting point for this investigation. Common to these views is a rejection of the primacy given to social structures, such as to a 'thing' called an organisation. Such a structure, it is suggested, is an ontological illusion or reification which masks a continuous process of movement and disorder – to present reality as a fixed structure is merely to abstract a snapshot of this process. Constant movement means that reality continually evades its own representation or, as Lee (1998: 50) puts it: 'The chase, no matter how speedy, will never catch up with its quarry.'

This idea of constant, infinite movement which leaves reality beyond capture is evident in Cooper's (1990) poststructuralist approach to the concept of organisation, which concentrates on the drawing of the boundary which defines and delineates an organiation. Cooper draws upon Jacques Derrida's (1982) concept of *différance,* which encapsulates the idea that everything is inherently complex and undecidable, and to understand something in one way – to represent it – requires an act which suppresses other possible representations. Cooper illustrates this with the following diagram:

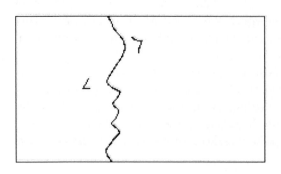

Figure 1: Différance illustrated (Cooper, 1990: 173).

To perceive, or make present, one of the faces in the diagram requires the deferral of perception of the other, and vice versa. The two faces *differ*, and to perceive one requires the *defer*ral of the other. These two aspects of differing and deferring encapsulate the idea of *différance*. The overall structure is undecidable – by performing a definite act of making the structure decidable – by perceiving one of the faces in the present – the other possible perception of it is marginalised temporarily (Cooper, 1990: 173–174). The complex nature of reality and its constant movement at an infinite speed thus has to be artificially bounded and frozen to permit the perception of a structure.

This line of reasoning problematises the notion of an organisation as a stable, ontological entity. Instead, this stability is an illusion that we create in order to compensate for the inability of our minds to grasp the overall complex, dynamic and undecidable nature of reality:

> "The idea of a specific organisation or institution is no more than a positioning strategy that we use to locate the slippery contents of our conceptual mindscapes. Seen against the complex, mobile mix of social reality, the image of a specific organisation... is no more than a provisional placement or transient impression."
>
> (Cooper, 2001: 327)

Chia (1995) expands on Cooper's analysis, stating that the ontology which privileges such entities as 'organisations' misses their ephemeral quality. Emergent interactions and patterns are ignored as we perceive in terms of an 'ontology of being'. For Chia, it is by thinking in terms of static entities – freezing the ephemerality of the organisation – that such entities become reified and take on a life of their own – our abstraction is mistaken for a concrete reality. Instead, we should think in terms of such things as *becomings* rather than as beings. Taken-for-granted entities such as organisations, structures and cultures should be examined to see how they acquire their ontological status – to unmask the heterogeneous workings behind them. This type of analysis, which Chia describes as 'postmodern thinking' is thus about the emergence of organisation, rather than organisation being an actual thing. For Chia, organisation is something which is never complete, but always in a process of becoming, or emergence. There is a process of constant movement which privileging something as an ontological entity ignores – organisation is a precarious ordering taking place in a perpetual present.

This idea of constant movement in a perpetual present, of an assemblage of constantly-shifting relationships where there is always an ambiguous, irresolvable 'in-between', is something in terms of which Cooper (1998) claims we are not tuned to think. Systems, such as organisations, should be understood in terms of a constant remaking of connections between parts rather than as static entities:

"Systems are no longer to be viewed as integrated structures. The human body, for example, is never just an organic whole but a *collection of parts* in the continuous pursuit of *re-collecting* itself. It is this idea of collection-dispersion-recollection that lies at the heart of *assemblage*. Assemblage, therefore, must be understood as partial, dispersed, fragile, tentative. Assemblage is simultaneously *a part of* and *apart from*."

(Cooper, 1998: 110. Original emphasis)

Chia's 'constant becoming' and Cooper's 'assemblage' draw upon the ontological concerns of Gilles Deleuze where, for example, the constant becoming of assemblage is 'the minimum real unit of the world' (Deleuze and Parnet, 2002: 51) and where the relationship between structure and reality is cast in terms of the centralised 'root-tree' structure freezing the complex and ephemeral nature of reality as conceptualised by the 'rhizome' (Deleuze and Guattari, 1987). There are also sympathies and similarities here with analyses from actor-network theories which examine the heterogeneous elements within society, both technical and social, which combine and act together. Where such networks stabilise, they become 'punctualised', or 'black boxed'. The representational façade created by such an entity, an organisation for example, masks the complexity of the heterogeneous elements within the actor-network behind it. The ontological status afforded to social entities is thus a short-cut for a much more complex heterogeneous ordering of technical and social artefacts (Law, 1992).

The analysis in this section posits a complex relationship between reality and representation. There is an implicit acknowledgement that some form of reality exists, but its existence only in a perpetual present places it beyond representational capture. Reality involves social action and artefacts – Cooper's partial connections for example – but to present this as a structure, such as an organisation, freezes its inherent ephemerality. As such, Lee argues that the relationship between reality and representation is similar to a person moving towards the horizon – it is always there, but as much or as quickly one moves towards it, it is always beyond reach – this area beyond representation has 'infinite speed' (Lee, 1998: 41).

3. Reality, representation and organisational power

I would like to move beyond the argument that reality, moving at infinite speed, is simply beyond representation. In terms of organisational research and analysis, there is a danger in adhering strictly to this view in that any attempt to discuss organisational issues results in an ontological shooting down of our very subject matter. We risk flying in 'ever-decreasing circles' (Power, 1990) where a theoretical perception of the inherent disorder of reality prevents a discussion of our own perception of reality – one where structures such as organisations do exist and exert power.

However, it would be unfair to suggest that the authors in the previous section adhere to an idea that organisational structures have no place in some sort of perceived reality. The reality moving at infinite speed is beyond human perception, and thus representation is needed for reasons of 'cognitive economy' (Tsoukas, 1992: 454). Social power may be gained through control over which, from an infinite number of representations, 'sticks' above all others. In other words, in which of many ways is reality 'frozen'?; or how are heterogeneous societal elements mobilised in order to close the black box and mask the constant movement and complexity of reality? Whilst representation may not allow for verisimilitude in representing reality, it is through such representation that order and stability may be produced. This act of power over representation is described by Lee (1998) as a 'slowing' of infinite time.

In his analysis of organisational structure as 'undecidable' and moving constantly back and forth between two faces it is to the actual drawing of the boundary that Cooper (1990) suggests we turn our attention – the act of representational power that makes one particular structuring visible at the expense of others. This act of power, however, is merely a temporary ordering in the present at the expense of other ways of perceiving a structure from the same overall field of 'undecidability'.

In later work, Cooper expands on the techniques used by organisations to achieve this ordering, especially through the use of technologies to effect representation. For Cooper (1993) technology is used by humans to compensate for their inherent weaknesses, and this may include the inability to apprehend reality in its ephemeral form. Cooper (1992) makes a direct link between organisations and representation when he describes the process of *formal* organisation as representation. It is through the formalised representation of the complexities of organisations that management and organisation are made possible and facilitated. For Cooper (*ibid*) representation works as a tool of management by turning an absence into a presence (in the present). Some absent reality is brought to our senses, or re-*present*-ed to them. The absence may be due to geography (something is too far away), time (something has already happened) or complexity (something is too intricate or complex for our immediate perception). Through representational technologies, that which is absent and unmanageable becomes present and it becomes manageable, both cognitively and practically.

Technology here does not necessarily refer to the latest mechanical or microelectronic innovations, but to any means of formalising organisational processes to achieve this transformation of absence into presence – processes of representation that record, classify and calculate aspects of the organisation, making its complexity more manageable. Technologies of representation are thus evident in processes of rationalisation of the work process such as scientific management, bureaucracy and accounting. Other commentators have described such processes of representation as being seminal to, or part of the development of these contemporary management practices. Morgan (1990), for example, highlights the development of cost accounting techniques by Josiah Wedgwood in the 1770s, a process which made visible (or made present) many of the previously opaque workings of the organisation. Hoskin and Macve (1988) suggest that the grading practices of the early 19th Century West Point Military Academy created 'truly calculable men', more amenable to ordering and control.

This historical perspective allows us to understand representational technology as an abstraction of organisational reality into an informational form which makes it more manageable. In our case, it is used as a means of slowing down and freezing the infinite speed of reality to then acheive stability and increase organisational power. Organisations are:

> "... now themselves viewed as *epiphenomena* of implicit assemblages of organisational actions and interactions. As a consequence, postmodern organizational analysis takes a step back to examine the precarious local orchestration of material, technical and social relationships which give rise to relatively stabilised configurations that we then assume to be discrete social entities and/or events."

> (Chia, 1995: 601. Original emphasis)

In these cases, there is a slowing down of the infinite speed of reality through the use of representational technologies, and as such Lee (1998) suggests that this creates 'local, partial and temporal' realities. Such realities, however, emanate from what Lee describes as a 'start' or a 'trace' – as such they are developed from an artificial abstraction of reality.

For Baudrillard (1994), such a frozen and abstracted reality, which is then used as a reference point for future reality can only be an ersatz reality, or a hyperreality. Representational technologies create hyperreal phenomena by breaking down reality into smaller (more manageable?) parts and recreating it from an artificial nucleus of these parts which then comes to be seen as constitutive of reality itself. This technique has been developed principally in the areas of genetics and information theory, where the search is for the smallest indivisible cell, or where reality is broken down into its smallest informational units – binary digits (Gane, 1991: 97–98). According to Baudrillard, it is this recreation of reality through *digitality* that eventually becomes the reference point for reality. The representations which Baudrillard suggests contribute to hyperreality resonate with the very same techniques that I have suggested are a part of the representational activities of organisations in slowing down the infinite speed of reality, *i.e.* abstraction, classification, grading etc.

So, whilst reality can be 'slowed down' through representation, it cannot be represented – only a second-order, tainted 'hyperreality' is amenable to representation. But, at the same time, such a slowing down of reality is used to increase organisational power – to affect, order and direct reality for people. Perhaps we need to look more closely at what we mean by 'reality' in order to understand its relationship to its own representation.

In describing the nature of reality, the infinitely moving essence beyond representation, there are authors who acknowledge that reality is socially located – in 'things', 'parts', 'wholes' and 'heterogeneous elements' for example – yet at the same time they resort to metaphor and analogy to try and describe this essence. Thus Latour (1997: 2) describes a society made up of 'filaments' which are 'fibrous, thread-like, wiry, string, ropy and capillary in nature', or Cooper (1998) borrows Deleuze and Guattari's (1987) botanical concept of the 'rhizome'. When it comes to describing the *essence* of reality, we seem as equally unable to pin it down as with the use of reified structures.

However, if we stick with the idea of reality being socially located then there is much more intertwined relationship between that reality and its representation – one which takes place at infinite speed, but does not discount all potential discussion of reality. In representing reality, the inherently complex is abstracted from in order to *further direct human action*. So whilst representation might not be able to apprehend reality, *its effects direct the reality that is felt by people in a perpetual present*. Reality is enacted and created simultaneously. In our attempt to create reality we are already representing it. For Mol (1999: 75), reality is something that is *done*, but cannot be observed.

This is where theories of representation and infinite speed are of most use. Whilst we cannot apprehend reality, we can describe its ongoing construction. And this construction is through the use of representation and representational technologies. Chia (1995: 597) suggests that we should turn our attention in organisations to the 'micro-practices of division, spacing, framing, hierarchies of arrangements, edge and margins, sectioning, etc. which collectively as local assemblages of organisings produce the phenomena of organisation', in other words, processes of representation. Thus, a railway timetable can tell us more about a railway organisation than an organisation chart – it explains how the organisation extends its networks to organise space and time – and trains within them (Wise, 1997: 57). As such:

> "…these 'assemblages of organizings' enable the remote, obdurate and intractable features of the world to be rendered more accessible, pliable and wieldable and hence more amenable to human intervention."
> (Chia, 1995: 600)

Representational technologies thus mobilise elements within heterogeneous networks, or assemblages. They direct what is done through space and time. Although the elements that they direct may be dispersed temporally and geographically, in actor-network parlance they are close together in terms of their ability to affect each other, and as such result in increased power. But if these technologies affect what happens in space and time, they affect what is *done*. And if what is done *is* reality (according to Mol), then whilst such technologies may be abstracted from reality, at the same time they constitute it. As Kallinikos (1992: 460) states, representation 'imposes its own organisation on the world'.

Representation, then, is at the very heart of the creation of reality rather than being a means of getting an abstracted view of that reality. It is a complex, intertwined relationship where representation cannot give us an accurate view of reality, but contributes to the creation of that pure essence of reality that it can never capture.

With this view, we may criticise ideas such as Baudrillard's hyperreality for giving ontological prominence to a 'reality' from which a 'hyperreality' floats away. Instead, both are produced in a perpetual present as a result of the very same representational processes. For Virilio (1997, quoted in Kellner, 1999), it is a mistake to talk about reality and hyperreality as separate entities – instead we should see hyperreality as a more powerful facet of reality. In this respect, the more power one has over representational technologies which feed into a concept of hyperreality, the more one can affect reality too.

And so it is through the use of representational technologies – the attempt to represent an unrepresentable reality – that organisations in turn have an effect upon that reality – an exercise of power. Even if we cannot apprehend that reality theoretically, we can accept a view that the effects of reality and its representation can be felt within society – we have spoken about representation being used, for example, to direct human action and this will have real, perceived effects for those people subject to it. There is a reality where ethical, moral and human issues exist, even if we may not have theoretical means to appropriate an exact representation of them:

> "In a sense this position scarcely needs defending, since it accords so readily with our everyday working assumptions about the existence of an objective world 'out there', a reality certain of whose features we may not yet (or ever) be able to cognize, yet whose sum total of objects, occurrences and events is none the less real for all that."
>
> (Norris, 1992: 176)

Hacking's (1983) notion of Real-Representation-Reality (quoted in du Gay, 1996: 73) makes a similar point. Here, the reality that we can apprehend will never be a perfect representation – it is a 'lower order concept' given to us by representations of the 'Real', a concept impossible to apprehend in full. But whilst it cannot be apprehended in full, it still *exists* and has effects in *real* terms, effects that can be felt and observed. So whilst, theoretically, we can never represent a 'true' and full reality, this is not to suggest that it does not exist and have real effects upon people and their lives.

It is thus through the slowing down of the infinite speed of reality, through technologies of representation, that organisations gain power. Organisational power here has two interlinked facets. First, there is the everyday view of power – the ability to affect the felt reality for people. Second, there is an increase in this first level of power through a greater command of representational technologies – the ability to process more and more representations of reality, to mobilise more elements within actor-networks. It is this second aspect of power which is greatly enhanced by contemporary electronic technologies.

4. Information technology: accelerating representations, increasing power

Paul Virilio's 'dromocratic society' (Virilio, 1986) highlights a link between speed and power within society. In particular, he suggests that power derive from control over those technologies which are able to increase speed:

> "Virilio's dromology focuses on those instruments that accelerate and intensify speed and that augment the wealth and power of those groups who control them. In his vision, it is groups like the military, the state and the *corporation* which control speed and become dominant societal powers."
> (Kellner, 1999: 105–106. My emphasis).

Electronic, digital technology is an instrument which accelerates and intensifies the speed of the representational technologies which, as was demonstrated in the previous section, increase organisational power. Such technology increases the processing speed of such technologies both within the organisation and beyond it through (potentially) global networks.

In this sense, the electronic coding and manipulation of organisational representations can be understood as part of a system of control in formal organisations (Cooper, 1992); as an intensification of control through the non-human and more efficient processing of atomised, abstracted organisational knowledge and processes (following Ritzer, 1996); or maybe as part of an increase in organisational activity, pushing out the boundary of what is manageable (Jeffcut and Thomas, 1998).

Blackler (1995) provides a metaphor of organisations being simultaneously 'imploded' into electronic codes and 'exploded' outwards into global networks. The image is of the organisation being constituted by electronic technological representations and at the same time circulating these representations around an electronic network which extends geographically beyond the physical presence of the organisation. Blackler notes that information technology disrupts existing working practices – the coding of knowledge, especially by electronic technologies, affects the skills, intensity and routine of work within the organisation. Also, through networking, organisations can also 'operate relatively independently from geographical location, thereby blurring the boundaries between one organisation and another' (Blackler, 1995: 1033).

So, electronically mediated representations might increase the power and control of an organisation, both over its workforce and within society, an increase in power and control which can be summarised in three main areas. First, there might be an increased control and intensification of the work process (e.g. Baldry *et al*, 1998) or a digitisation of the work process to the point where human tasks are made redundant. Second, the geographical 'reach' of an organisation is increased as certain tasks may be performed anywhere where a network connection is available. Whilst this allows increased mobile or home working for workers, it also allows for 'teleclienting' where customers or clients can perform such tasks from home (e.g. shopping, banking transactions etc). This increases the geographical location of the organisation's activities and at the same time makes further employee tasks redundant as clients perform tasks for themselves in a direct connection with the organisation's database of representations. Third, the organisation may accumulate and manipulate vast quantities of knowledge and information. In a Tayloristic sense, further knowledge and skill of the work process moves from the worker to the planning function of management. At a societal level, database entries are created whenever an electronic transaction takes place, indeed supplementary information may also be gathered (by means of supermarket loyalty cards, for example). The portability and instant manipulability of these databases within global electronic networks leads to a vast knowledge market, especially when new information is created from the integration and comparison of separate databases into so-called 'relational' databases (Poster, 1995).

These exercises of organisational power are not conceptually new – they simply extend the uses of representational technology which began as soon as managers started to use systems of calculation, classification and grading to manage complexity, as seen at West Point and at Wedgwood. However, we arrive at a somewhat paradoxical situation. This historical process of achieving organisational power was analysed in the previous section as a slowing down of the 'infinite speed' of reality through its representation. At the same time, this process of slowing down is made more effective and power is intensified by an acceleration of such representations through electronic technology and infrastructures such as digital networks.

Organisational power comes from a *slowing down* of reality by abstracting it and a simultaneous *acceleration* of that abstracted reality.

Given the increasing speed of such representational technologies and networks, is there a possibility that the process of slowing down reality may come full circle to an infinite speed of its own representation, once again becoming unmanageable and unrepresentable?

5. The consequences of reaching light speed

Does the processing ability of computer technology, especially with respect to organisational representations, represent a return to 'infinite speed' and its associated inability to apprehend an ephemeral reality for the purposes of effecting organisation and control?

Certainly the potential speed of digital transmission can be measured – it is, for Virilio (1995) a vehicle which allows movement at 'light speed'. But, of course, the speed of light is a speed to which we can give a figure, a measurement of approximately 300,000 kilometres per second. Mathematically, this is different to infinite speed, which cannot be given a figure. However, in that light speed brings us to the 'upper limit of the physical universe' (McQuire, 1999: 145) then maybe we can judge its effects as being analogous to infinite speed in terms of human ability (or the lack theoreof) to apprehend, represent and further direct reality.[1]

A hypothetical example of this is given by Boland and Schultze (1996) who highlight the limits of electronic representational technologies within organisations as they approach light speed. The representational technology that they describe is Activity-Based Costing, an attempt to effect cost accounting by allocating as many organisational costs as possible to the activities that generate them – to make more accurate the process of individual accountability for costs.

Boland and Schultze (1996: 326–7) paint an imaginary scenario where the costs of executive time are allocated to the product to which they are giving their personal attention at a particular time. This is done by use of an 'executive jacket' – a gadget filled jacket with cameras that can trace through bar codes, the exact product towards which an executive is dedicating their time at any one moment and allocate costs to that product accordingly.

Ultimately, the executives request a real-time display of costs so that the changing costs can be tracked. The irony is that by even looking at the

---

[1] Indeed, we could question whether or not light speed is also an unattainable limit point in terms of electronic networks, but the point I am making is that even the speed of data transfer of home broadband connections and home computer systems, yet alone more powerful organisational systems, allows for a volume, complexity and dynamism of representations beyond human cognitive ability.

display of costs for a particular product, the executive increases those very costs as the cost of the time that they spend concentrating on that product is allocated immediately to that very product. A type of uncertainty principle (Heisenberg, 1930) comes into effect as the act of observing influences the phenomenon under observation:

> "By shrinking the distance in space and time between cost incurrence and its representation to the actors, the edges of action are sharpened leaving little room for people to talk, negotiate and manoeuvre. With the Executive Jacket, managers look into the computer display and see a mirror image of themselves. Action and the accounting of that action become instantaneous..."
> (Boland and Schultze, 1996: 327)

So, electronic representations can speed up the process of representation and the handling and manipulation of that representational data, in the process making visible more absent realities within the organisation – in this case an allocation of costs to products. Boland and Schultze provide a glimpse as to what the potential limits of such a use of representations are – the point at which the use of hyperreal models and abstractions makes myriad absent realities visible instantaneously such that in actual fact nothing is visible for more than a fleeting instant.

This would seem to be a return to square one – the very same vision of an ephemeral, fleeting reality that representation aims to slow down from its infinite speed for purposes of power and control over that reality. Once again, such means of effecting power and control escape our grasp. In terms of human experience (or inability to experience reality), 'infinite speed' and 'light speed' are the same, perhaps neatly summed up by Lash and Urry's (1994) concept of 'instantaneous time'. Whilst organisation is not technically taking place at 'infinite speed' it is, in Lash and Urry's (1994: 242) terms, effected through computer equipment which processes information in 'nanoseconds' at a speed 'beyond the realm of human consciousness' which 'cannot be experienced or observed'. From a human perspective, the representation of reality becomes impossible as the acceleration of representations through electronic networks moves to Virilio's 'light speed'.

In this respect, Boland and Schultze's hypothetical model highlights *information* technology moving at a speed so fast that it produces *information* that is of no human value – the acceleration of the representational technologies effaces any meaning value that they may produce. This atomisation of information and transmission through global networks produces, for Baudrillard, a similar lack of meaning value:

> "Every set of phenomena, whether cultural totality or sequence of events, has to be fragmented, disjointed, so that it can be sent down the circuits; every kind of language has to be resolved into a binary formulation so that it can circulate not, any longer, in our memories, but in the luminous, electronic

102

memory of the computers. No human language can withstand the speed of light. No event can withstand being beamed across the whole planet. No meaning can withstand acceleration."

(Baudrillard, 1992: 2)

Returning to Blackler's implosion/explosion metaphor, Boland and Schultze have highlighted the limits of the implosion of organisations into electronic code and Baudrillard highlights the limitations of this explosion into global networks. For Baudrillard, hyperreality emerges from the atomisation of reality into its smallest informational unit – the '0/1' binary digit or the implosion of the organisation into code. But another implosion takes place – that of any meaning attributable to such informational units, as these hyperreal abstractions saturate global networks, their sheer volume and interaction effacing meaning value.

In describing the Beaubourg Centre in Paris, Baudrillard (1994) highlights the paradox inherent in its attempts to create meaning within society. Set up to promote mass culture, it is the very physical presence of the masses within the walls of the gallery which denies access to that very culture. The infrastructure of the gallery is overstretched, preventing access to the culture that it aims to promote – the system is 'saturated' such that meaning disappears in an act of 'implosive violence' (Baudrillard, 1994: 71–72).

A similar fate befalls information when it is circulated through global networks. The massification of such information, already hyperrealised into digital representations, leads to an increase in the volume of information but a decrease or implosion in meaning. This is something that we may describe as information overload – we are sated in the sheer volume of information such that we do not know where to begin – there is so much swamping us that we are unable to make any coherent meaning out of it. This exponential growth in information:

> "…now expands to such an extent that it no longer has anything to do with gaining knowledge. Information's immense potential will never be redeemed and it will never be able to achieve its finality… [S]ince proliferating information is larger than the needs and capacities of any individual, and of the human species in general, it has no other meaning but that of binding humankind to a destiny of cerebral automation and mental underdevelopment."
>
> (Baudrillard, 1996: 2)

In this section I have examined the view that the consequences of accelerating organisational representations to light speed lead us once again to the inability to capture and represent reality that necessitated these representations in the first place. Light speed again places the representation of reality beyond human capability, the creation of meaning that would further direct human action is lost. This happens in two ways. First, the sheer speed of processing representations effaces the gap – the slowing down of 'infinite speed' – in which representation in the form of human cognition may take place. Second, the ability to circulate such representations globally leads to a loss, or implosion, of meaning through the inability to navigate and create meaning from the sheer volume of representations moving through global networks at light speed.

The paradoxical relationship between the slowing down of reality through its representation, and the acceleration of that representation to improve its efficacy, has come full circle. Does this then mean that instantaneous computer speed has gone beyond its own usefulness in terms of organisational power?

6. Highways and assemblages

Experience tells us that in a globally-networked society where organisational representations are transmitted instantaneously, there are organisations which use such networks to grow, exert power and extend their influence. Indeed, the Amazons and E-Bays of this world have grown and extended their influence purely within such an electronic medium. How does this sit with the idea that representational technology has reached 'light speed,' losing its power of representation and thus its ability to further direct human action?

An important distinction needs to be made here. Where Lee has spoken of 'infinite speed'; Chia of a constant state of 'becoming'; and Cooper of inherent 'undecidability', they are describing the nature of reality itself – the very reason for which acts of representation, or the slowing down of such reality, are needed. In describing the move back up to light speed we are talking about the acceleration to infinite speed of the *representations* and not of the reality itself.

Whilst I have explored a complex relationship between reality and how it is directed as a result of its representation, we should not confuse and conflate the two terms. There is a reality, however inapprehendable, within which organisational representations exist. The problem occurs if we see ideas such as Baudrillard's hyperreality and Blackler's implosion and explosion as being descriptive of reality rather than of the status of representational code within reality. The organisation is more than a set of zeroes and ones, even if more and more of its reality is coded that way. In this respect we can take note of Bauman's (1992) analysis of Baudrillard in which he concludes:

> "It becomes a philosopher and an analyst of his time to go out and use his feet now and again. Strolling still has its uses."
>
> (Bauman, 1992: 155)

Whilst we may not be able literally to 'stroll' through the terrain of digital organisational representations, we may look at aspects of their use and efficacy that go beyond reducing our analysis to an instantaneous flooding of zeroes and ones.

Returning to Virilio (1986), he has stated that it is *speed* rather than *space* which is at the heart of societal power – a move from geo-politics to chrono-politics. Command over the *infrastructures* of speed – cars, highways, railways etc – leads to power. Given its ability to work at light speed, Virilio describes computer technology as the 'last vehicle' (quoted in McQuire, 1999: 144). Now, electronic representations are mediated globally through a series of infrastructures. They do not simply run free and colonise the whole of reality, they are mediated by cables at the most basic level and through other organised infrastructures at hardware and software levels. They are to digital code what the highway is to the car or the track is to the train. It is to these infrastructures, and how they allow electronic representations to still facilitate organisational power despite their infinite speed, that I now turn.

The highway metaphor is a tempting one to use in describing the mediation of the flow of electronic data globally, especially when coupled with Virilio's description of the computer as the last vehicle. Indeed, the 'information superhighway' is a term often used to describe the Internet. For Nunes (1995), however, this highway metaphor has its limits and is, in fact, incorrect in the way that it describes the actual journey of electronic data globally. Thinking in terms of a 'highway' presents far too *linear* a metaphor for a much more complex, networked, systemic process (cf. Burrell, 1998, on the damage that linear conceptualisations can do unto a more complex reality).

Let us take a hypothetical organisation, a supermarket, and look at some realistic examples of events that may take place simultaneously or at different times during the course of a working day – events which involve the organisation's own database of electronic representations and the interaction of that database with the networks of other organisations.

- *Event 1* The central stock database is updated in real-time as products are scanned through the checkout. Goods are re-ordered automatically on a daily basis. This is done by communicating with the computer systems of suppliers.
- *Event 2* A customer pays using a debit card which is swiped through the checkout. The supermarket's computers link with those of the bank, which checks its database entry for the customer and adjusts the records accordingly. The checkout operator may even give the customer cash from their bank account, thus acting temporarily as a bank teller. Indebtedness between the banks, supermarkets etc is settled through the interaction of computers through clearing networks with figures on databases adjusted accordingly – no physical money changes hands.

- *Event 3* The same customer hands over a loyalty card which is swiped through the checkout. This is added to a database which is used by the supermarket to manipulate the data for marketing purposes. It may also interact, through networks, with other databases to build up valuable cross-referenced marketing information, so-called relational databases (Poster, 1995).
- *Event 4* A customer orders their shopping through the Internet. The link from their home to the organisation's database is mediated through several levels (the customer's telephone line and Internet Service Provider, the national telephone network etc), but in terms of a stream of zeroes and ones moving along wires, the customer's home and the organisation are, for the duration of the transaction, connected.
- *Event 5* At the same time, one of the organisation's executives is working on a laptop computer connected to a mobile telephony device whilst sat on a train. They require real-time sales figures, so they dial into the organisation's central database to retrieve these on their own screen. Given their hierarchical status within the organisation, they have a password which enables them to instruct several transactions to be performed. Just like the customer, this worker is briefly connected to the organisation for the duration of this activity.

The organisation increases its range of operation by continually joining with other digital networks to process transactions, receive orders etc. Indeed, at one point the organisation is actually playing the role of another organisation – a bank. The roles and boundaries of the organisation become increasingly blurred. The connections made to other organisations' networks are not permanent but temporary and ever-changing. But, in terms of actor-network theory, they are at the point of connection linked together, one and the same, enrolled in the same network. Our conditioned manner of thinking is in terms of geographical proximity, but for Latour (1997: 4) closeness is defined in terms of how far away things are from each other in terms of an actor-network. Two people separated by a large geographical space are thus close together in network terms if they are having a telephone conversation. Spatiality is thus held by virtue to the relation of one element to others in a series of links, not by their position in three dimensional space (Law, 1999: 6). So, the customer at home, the executive on the train, the bank and supplier in another town, all at some point become part of the same network despite their geographical distance.

This presents a different picture of the organisation to that of the highway metaphor. Instead, we see something akin to a digital version of Cooper's (1998) concept of assemblage, where partial connections are constantly being made and remade. The organisation becomes a continually-shifting network of digital flows.

In this respect, Cubitt (2001: 129–30) uses similar Deleuzian language to Cooper (1998) in describing the contemporary organisation as a 'shifting, headless rhizome of connections'. De Cock *et al* (2001) examine the rhetoric of new economy advertising and note the emphasis on organisations gaining power through speed and global connectivity. Munro (2000), following Castells (1996), suggests that organisational power derives, in part, from the control of networks of flows of digital code. Jeffcutt and Thomas (1998) note the 'multi-faceted' nature of contemporary organisations which exist within 'flows and webs' of digital code. As such:

> "...our attention is directed towards organising as a constituent of, and a contribution to, the implosions of boundary and form effected by the complex flows and relativisations of an information society. In other words, organisation becomes an unfolding process of tension between order and disorder in unstable flows which both pluralise and cross-connect artefacts and subjects, in, so to speak, a worldwide web."
> (Jeffcutt and Thomas, 1998: 68–69)

We have been given a picture of organisational complexity, one which Jeffcutt and Thomas (1998) suggest we do not appreciate given our innate desire for ordered structures. Given the scale, speed and ephemerality of these networks of electronic representational data, there are certainly the possibilities for scenarios as described earlier by Baudrillard, where the sheer mass of information and means of navigating though it drowns out any possible meaning from it; or by Boland and Schultze, where the instantaneity with which such information can be manipulated leaves its representation beyond capture.

But again we are in danger of taking the electronic flows of code as concept representative of organisational reality. Whilst Cooper's notion of assemblage is a useful metaphor with which to describe the interaction between global digital networks, it would be wrong to fully transpose Copper's appreciation of human-technology interaction onto just this one aspect of organisational representation.

Instead, I would like to examine how the infrastructures which mediate these representations are managed from a position of inapprehendable complexity to one where organisations may exert and wield power. Where it is possible to get carried away with an analysis of digital networks and 'cyberspace', Sassen (2000, 2002) notes that such networks are still embedded within existing social structures. This is contrary to views, such as those of Baudrillard, which would see the representations effacing social reality. It is through these social structures that organisational power may be gained, or access to such power denied.

7. Exclusion and power in representational infrastructures

I have moved through a number of stages in this examination of the relationships between organisations, reality, representation and speed:

- Reality moves at 'infinite speed' beyond representational capture.
- This 'infinite speed' is 'slowed down' through processes of technological representation to make the further management of organisational reality and thus organisational power possible.
- This process of slowing down, and thus organisational power, is facilitated paradoxically by 'speeding up' the mediation of these representations.
- Computer technology returns the representations to a perceptual equivalent of infinite speed within a complex global network.

Whilst the final stage appears to have brought us full circle, we should not confuse the infinite speed of reality with the infinite speed of its representation. However, if data were moving globally through networks at light speed, then similar problems for organisations may occur – the grasp on power is lost if reality evades more than a fleeting representation or if the saturation of representations is so great that they become meaningless.

This data 'free-for-all,' and its potential weakening effect on power, is sometimes used in utopian conceptions of the Internet as a democratic forum where there is access to all information and any person or organisation may be represented within. For Sassen (2002: 367), however, this utopian reading cannot be taken as an 'inevitable feature' of representational infrastructures. Against the potential the Internet provides for increased democratic participation, 'recurrent attempts to control its data and steer its data flows have been made' (Röhle, 2003: 404).

Thinking back to the supermarket example, the need for such control of data flow in order to retain power is evident on two counts. First, if there were a 'free-for-all' of access and data, then sensitive data could be accessed (peoples' bank details, company accounts, in fact anything which can be coded into electronic representations and communicated through interfacing with other networks.) Second, if all people, organisations etc have equal access to the Internet, then how would people such as customers be able to navigate and find the one organisation – the supermarket – amongst countless others? How could an organisation exert power when its ultimate representation is drowned out by the multitude of others?

From these issues of privacy against the need for continual access to increase organisational power, and of the need to be 'seen' amongst the multitude of digital representations within global networks, emerge the infrastructural tactics which provide for organisational power, but at the same time which highlight the possibilities for resistance. Sassen (2000) has already highlighted that existing social structures play a part in these infrastructures – that we need to see beyond mere flows of electronic representations of reality. She describes an 'embeddedness' of digital networks:

> "In addition to being embedded in some of the technical features of the hardware and software, digital space ... is partly embedded in actual societal structures and power dynamics. Its topography weaves in and out of non-electronic space."
> (Sassen, 2000: 28)

This quote highlights three levels of infrastructure within which we can examine the development of organisational power through electronic networks: the hardware, the software and societal structures. I shall now examine some examples of this power, which I argue works on a basis of inclusion within and exclusion from such infrastructures.

In terms of hardware, the position of flows of electronic representations is put firmly into perspective when we realise, as discussed previously, that they have to travel through cables and physical hardware. If such a basic infrastructure doesn't exist then access to this representational world is closed off. This is pertinent to discussion of a so-called 'digital divide' between an infrastructurally-rich developed world and a developing world which has little access to such infrastructures (see, for example, Munro, 2000 and Sassen, 2002). We may see it also in the case of national regimes that may wish to restrict their population's access to the Internet by means of severing infrastructure within their own physical territory[2]. There is a possibility of exclusion from the hardware of global networks, and existing societal arrangements – economics, politics, territory etc – may be a contributory factor in the power relations affecting such an exclusion.

Access to hardware is not enough in itself to freely connect with global networks. There are a series of intermediaries from the end user to these networks – internet service providers (ISPs), telecommunication companies etc. They are able to exclude from access on a variety of bases – the amount they charge for access, potentially illegal or libellous use of networks or even that the proposed use of networks goes against the taste or values of the intermediary. For Braman and Roberts (2003) it is the 'terms of service' and 'acceptable use policies' of ISPs, to which users must sign-up, which effectively become the law of the internet. Again, we see social factors play-

---

[2] For example, *The Guardian* (15th February, 2005) reports how the Chinese government not only blocks access to pornographic or subversive websites, but has also closed internet cafes near to schools, thus preventing children from access to the infrastructure to access such material in the first place.

ing a part in the exclusionary power of digital infrastructures – commerce, law and socio-cultural sensibilities.

Once connected to global digital networks, access to the electronic representations circulating within is still not a free-for-all – the software which mediates such representations also has exclusionary functions built in. As discussed, organisations will want to restrict access to data or keep portions of it private and to these ends 'firewall' technologies provide a protective boundary around an organisation's data whilst password systems allow multiple levels of access to that data depending on the user's status (e.g. individual customer or chief executive of the bank). There is a balance to be achieved if the organisation is to function and increase its activities in network terms, a balance between excluding general access but allowing individualised access to certain portions of data.

Sassen (2000: 20) notes that the main recent developments in Internet technology have been 'firewalled intranets for firms and firewalled tunnels for firm-to-firm connections'. The image is of a 'privatisation' of the 'public space' of the Internet – an exclusion from general access. In our supermarket example, we would expect such software protecting the transactions between the bank and supermarket; between the supermarket and its suppliers; between the supermarket and marketing firms with which it shares its loyalty card information and around all of the banks in the clearing network which settles indebtedness.

Privatised, exclusionary enclaves of the Internet are prevalent – from a password protecting a small community discussion forum to the massive international financial networks which transact billions of pounds worth of currency daily. As such, we see embedded in cyberspace the social and commercial desires for privacy and security – a parallel of the '… growing, and more intense, deployment of border-controls' that Franzén (2001) suggests exist in urban (i.e. real?) space.

Unlike real space, however, cyberspace is potentially infinite in its capacity. If we have access to the networks then we can all set up our own (maybe privatised) presence within them. However, the Baudrillardian view of representational saturation comes into play here – we return to the problem stated earlier in the section of how an organisation would achieve representational visibility amongst such a saturated terrain and thus how it could operate and increase its power. Just as power comes from the ability to exclude from hardware and software aspects of digital networks, so it comes from the ability to impose navigational aids – to include and exclude from the 'route map' of such networks.

Search engines and so-called 'portal-sites' fulfil this task to an extent by directing users in certain directions depending on certain search terms. Inclusion in their directory or database gives a better chance of being discovered than exclusion from it. As such, through their ability to include and exclude, search engines have the power to make sites 'disappear' (Introna and Nissenbaum, 2000: 180). This is not the only means of imposing navigation upon the Internet however. Again we can look at existing social arrangements and see that brands, already existing in 'real' space, can increase representational prominence in cyberspace over and above non-established start-ups. Indeed, following Klein's (2000) analysis of the role of brands and multinationals within society, we are seeing a parallel colonisation of the hardware, software and brand infrastructures by large multinationals (AOL, Microsoft, Yahoo to name but three).

The social aspects of exclusion extend beyond the influence of existing social institutions, such as law, government and corporations, upon digital infrastructures. As we have seen with the digital divide, social inequalities can be mirrored in such infrastructures and Sassen (2002) suggests that this extends to other societal inequalities such as those of gender.

Gotved (2002) looks at such social structuring at the level of on-line communities, which we have seen already use exclusionary techniques such as passwords. There are, however, other boundaries to be maintained within such communities, those based around social factors of norms and values and 'local interpretations' of acceptable on-line community behaviour. Such group dynamics play a part in the 'symbolic maintenance' of community borders:

"The establishment of social borderlines (the inside versus the outside and the possibility of membership versus exclusion) is a constant negotiation between those who feel like leaders and, together with newbies, those who are not interested. The regulars thus have considerable influence, and different strategies may be invented to demarcate the social space and punish those who do not respect the definitions of proper behaviour. Still, the social space is hard to define, even for the members – it is the totality of interactions, interpretations, imaginations, expectations and demarcations."

(Gotved, 2002: 410)

This tour of the infrastructures of global networks, and the various facets of power within them, is brief and by no means complete. It does, however, indicate how power resides in the exclusionary abilities of such infrastructures, and how this exclusionary ability resides partially within existing societal entities and behaviours. These exclusionary mechanisms are manifold, located at different levels on the hardware, software and societal aspects of representational infrastructures. At the previous quote indicates, these mechanisms can also be complex and difficult to define. I suggest that this exclusionary power can be seen in terms of the metaphor of the Janus-face, and conceptualised in terms of intertwined processes of *hosting* and *portality*.

8. Hosting, portality and the Janus-face

Power, in terms of organisational network extension, derives from the ability to be represented, or hosted within digital networks. Ownership of, or influence over such infrastructures, whether at hardware, software or social level thus offers the power of *hosting*, and simultaneously the power of non-hosting, that is to say exclusion from such infrastructures (cf. Derrida's (1997) etymological association of the words 'host' and 'hostility'). So, the hosting infrastructure could be the physical cables, the privatised digital space, a more intangible brand name, or the structures through which an online social community operates.

Hosting gives the ability to control movement through such infrastructures, and movement is necessary if interaction and network extension is to take place. This control of movement, of the interfacing of networks, comes with the power of hosting and is a strategy I have called *portality*. Technologies such as firewalls and passwords which allow multiple levels of access to a private area of the Internet, and brands and associated portal sites which map out certain routes through the Internet making them more salient than others, are both examples of portality.

Strategies of hosting and portality move us away from the two problems for organisational power within digital networks moving at light speed. They allow for exclusion from areas of digital space, rather than all data being freely available. And, they allow for navigation to be imposed upon digital space where previously there may have existed an impenetrable saturation of representations.

I began this investigation with process (i.e post-structuralist and actor-network) conceptions of 'reality'. As something inherently inapprehendable and ephemeral, reality can only be represented in an artificially-frozen form and to do this is an act of power which excludes other, infinite possible means of representing that reality. At the end of the investigation, we again see power being achieved by processes of exclusion. The process perspective was exemplified by Cooper's two faces from figure 1, an undecidable figure made decidable by structuring, boundary-drawing and exclusion. I suggest that, in the case of hosting and portality within representational infrastructures, this structuring, boundary-drawing and exclusion can be illustrated by reversing Cooper's two faces to create the Janus-face (figure 2). In Roman mythology, Janus is the spirit of the door, entrance or gateway (Burchett, 1918) – in effect a spirit of portality. Looking simultaneously inwards and outwards, Janus guards that which lies within and keeps out that which is deemed bad. So, as well as being a spirit of portality, Janus also exemplifies the exclusionary powers of hosting.

Figure 2: The Janus-face.

In terms of organisational representations and infrastructures, this high-lights the value of the representational infrastructure in terms of the data it contains and thus its need for protection, but also the need to engage and interface such representations in order to build networks and maintain and increase organisational power. Janus is at once watching over the host representational infrastructure whilst acting as a portal controlling the movement of such representations, providing a secure and manageable link between the two facets of Blackler's imploded and simultaneously exploded organisation. It is no surprise, then, that Janus has been used as a name for Internet firewall technologies.[3]

The Janus face is not so much an immediate reversal of Cooper's faces, rather it is a metaphor for control over technologies of representation as circulated within representational infrastructures. As such it is a couple of stages removed from the undecidability of reality itself, as encapsulated by Cooper's faces. Cooper highlights the importance and power of drawing the boundary and making the undecidable decidable, through the use of technologies of representation. In this chapter, however, I have highlighted how such technologies of representation, whilst frozen and manageable structurings of reality, may again return us to a position akin to undecidability when they are accelerated through representational infrastructures. It is the processes of hosting and portality, of inclusion and exclusion, which draw the boundaries here, and it is here that the reversed Janus-face exerts its power. The Janus figure is thus a metaphorical illustration of the processes of 'slowing down' light speed within representational infrastructures. Hosting and portality are the socially-embedded strategies of power through which an

---

[3] See, for example, http://www.cs.berkeley.edu/~daw/janus/

inherent undecidability – in terms of the felt reality of organisational representations – is made decidable, and which allow for further power to be effected over that reality.

This, however, is not a monolithic power over representational infrastructures. There is not one Janus, but many Januses operating at multiple locations and boundaries within represenational infrastructures. These we have seen operating as boundary markers within the technology itself – firewalls and passwords, for example – but also at multiple social levels within representational infrastructures. Just as a password has the power to exclude, so do the norms and shared language of an online community. Power within representational infrastructures, then, is distributed throughout their networks, and found in numerous tangible and intangible instances of hosting and portality. Power can be seen at various levels of scale, from government restricting access to a whole nation, to exclusion from the smallest scale online community. These multiple locations of power have led to representational infrastructures being analysed in Foucauldian terms (e.g. Munro, 2000; Röhle, 2003) where power is not centrally located, but operates through a mesh of interactions – multiple structurings of reality in different locations.

This Foucauldian analysis of power gives another insight into the importance of hosting and portality in the maintenance of organisational power. Munro (2000: 686), following Foucault, suggests that the nature of power can be understood by examining resistance to such power. Munro (ibid) suggests that examples of such resistance in a network society include computer hacking and viruses. We could add such things as 'denial of service' attacks where a computer is repeatedly accessed such that it is overloaded and crashes. This is the type of resistance that the Janus-faced processes of hosting and portality try to guard against.

The resistance here is aimed at stopping the flow of electronic representations, the means of network extension and connectivity for an organisation, or indeed destroying those very representations within the organisation, i.e. wiping and corrupting its data. If successful, the organisation cannot operate through digital networks and its power is diminished. It is through strengthening host and portal infrastructures and mechanisms against such attacks that power may be regained. The host infrastructure and the portal technologies that include within and exclude from that infrastructure are thus a contemporary battleground for organisational power and resistance, the aim being to defend or attack the representations and the networks though which they flow.

The balance that hosting and portality need to achieve – between allowing flow through representational infrastructures such that organisations can operate and extend their power, and protecting this flow against potential resistance, is encapsulated in Boase and Wellman's (2001: 39–40) analysis of the similarities between computer and human viruses. In both cases it is frequent contact or connectivity which increases the chance of infection, but unlike humans, physical proximity is not necessary[4]. We could say that is the proximity of representations in infrastructural terms which poses the danger for viruses to be transmitted at 'hyperspeed' (ibid: 40). But this constant proximity is also necessary for organisations to function within representational infrastructures, through flows of representations.

Conceptually, the process is no different to the use of technologies of representation as described at the start of the paper, albeit now mediated through representational infrastructures. And resistance is possible because re-*present*-ation is something that, whilst inapprehendable in the *present*, takes place in a perpetual *present* in order to further direct reality. It is a process that needs to be maintained constantly – an act of power to continually suppress other possible means of representation. And thus it is to the technologies and infrastructures that effect such a perpetual representation that resistance against organisational power might take place.

The Janus figure represents the taming of accelerated representations within representational infrastructures at multiple levels. As such, it shows the instances of structuring and boundary maintenance through which power may be exerted. At the same time, it shows the fragility of such power, and its need for constant maintenance within the realm of accelerated representations through the social and material processes of hosting and portality. Accelerating representations to the full potential speed of representational infrastructures does not inevitably lead to an unmanageable free-for-all. However, the acts of power which make representational infrastructures manageable also bring about the sites for potential resistance against them.

References

Baldry, C., Bain, P. and Taylor, P. (1998) 'Bright Satanic Offices: Intensification, Control and Team Taylorism.' Ch. 9 in in P. Thompson and C. Warhurst (eds.) (1998) *Workplaces of the Future* Basingstoke: Macmillan; 163–183.

Baudrillard, J. (1990) *Fatal Strategies* translated by P. Beitchman and W. Niesluchowski; New York: Semiotext(e).

Baudrillard, J. (1992) *The Illusion of the End* translated by C. Turner; Cambridge: Polity Press.

Baudrillard, J. (1994) *Simulacra and Simulation* translated by S.F. Glaser; Ann Arbor: University of Michigan Press.

---

[4] Here we can refer to the analysis from actor-network theory which suggests that, in terms of representational infrastructures, proximity of representations within a network would equate to physical proximity.

Baudrillard, J. (1996) 'Global Debt and Parallel Universe.' *CTheory*; http://www. ctheory.net/text_file?pick=164, published 16/10/1996.

Bauman, Z. (1992) *Intimations of Postmodernity* London: Routledge.

Blackler, F. (1995) 'Knowledge, Knowledge Work and Organizations: An Overview and Interpretation.' *Organization Studies*; 16(6): 1021–1047.

Boase, J. and Wellman, B. (2001) 'A plagues of viruses: Biological, Computer and Marketing.' *Current Sociology*; Vol. 49(6): 39–55.

Boland, R. and Schultze, U. (1996) 'From Work to Activity: Technology and the Narrative of Progress.' in W. Orlikowski, G. Walsham and M. Jones (eds.) (1996) *Information Technology and the Transformation of Work* Amsterdam: Elsevier; 315–330.

Braman, S. and Roberts, S. (2003) 'Advantage ISP: Terms of service as media law.' *New Media and Society*; Vol. 5(3): 422–448.

Burchett, B. (1918) *Janus in Roman life and cult: A study in Roman religions* Menasha, WI: George Banta Publishing Company.

Burrell, G. (1998) 'Linearity, Control and Death.' Ch. 8 in D. Grant, T. Keenoy and C. Oswick (eds.) (1998) *Discourse and Organization* London: Sage; 134–151.

Castells, M. (1996) *The Rise of the Network Society* Oxford: Basil Blackwell.

Chia, R. (1995) 'From Modern to Postmodern Organizational Analysis.' *Organization Studies*; 16(4): 579–604.

Cooper, R. (1990) 'Organization/Disorganization.' Ch. 10 in J. Hassard and D. Pym (eds.) (1990) *The Theory and Philosophy of Organizations: Critical Issues and New Perspectives.* London: Routledge; 167–197.

Cooper, R. (1992) 'Formal Organization as Representation: Remote Control, Displacement and Abbreviation.' Ch. 13 in M. Reed and M. Hughes (eds.) *Rethinking Organization: New Directions in Organization Theory and Analysis* London: Sage; 254–272.

Cooper, R. (1993) 'Technologies of Representation.' In P. Ahonen (ed.) (1993) *Tracing the Semiotic Boundaries of Politics* Berlin: Walter de Gruyter 279–312.

Cooper, R. (1998) 'Assemblage Notes.' Ch. 5 in Chia, R (ed.)(1998) *Organized Worlds: Explorations in technology and organization with Robert Cooper* London: Routledge; 108–130.

Cooper, R. (2001) 'Un-timely mediations: Questing thought.' *Ephemera: Critical dialogues on organization* Volume 1(4): 321–347.

Cubitt, S. (2001) *Simulation and Social Theory* London: Sage.

de Cock, C., Fitchett, J. and Farr, M. (2001) 'Myths of a near future: Advertising the New Economy.' *Ehphemera: Critical Dialogues on Organization* Vol. 1; No. 3: 201–228.

Deleuze, G. and Guattari, F. (1987) *A Thousand Plateaus: Capitalism and Schizophrenia (trans. B. Massumi)* Minneapolis, MN: University of Minnesota Press.

Deleuze, G. and Parnet, C. (2002) *Dialogues II (trans. H. Tomlinson & B. Habberjam)* London: Continuum.

Derrida, J. (1982) *Margins of Philosophy (trans. A. Bass)* Brighton: Harvester Press.

Derrida, J. (1997) *De l'hospitalité* Paris: Calmann-Lévy.

du Gay, P. (1996) *Consumption and Identity at Work* London: Sage.

Franzén, M. (2001) 'Urban order and the preventive restructuring of space: the operation of border controls in micro space.' *The Sociological Review*; Volume 49, Issue 2: 202–218.

Gane, M. (1991) *Baudrillard's Bestiary: Baudrillard and Culture* London: Routledge.

Gotved, S. (2002) 'Spatial Dimensions in Online Communities.' *Space and Culture;* Vol. 5, No. 4: 405–414.

Hacking, I. (1983) *Representing and Intervening* Cambridge: Cambridge University Press.

Heisenberg, W. (1930) *The Physical Principles of Quantum Theory* Chicago; University of Chicago Press.

Hoskin, K. and Macve, R. (1988) 'The Genesis of Accountability: The West Point Connection.' *Accounting, Organizations and Society;* 13, 1.

Introna, L. and Nissenbaum, H. (2000) 'Shaping the Web: Why the Politics of Search Engines Matters.' *The Information Society;* 16: 169–185.

Jeffcut, P. and Thomas, M. (1998) 'Order, disorder and the unmanageability of boundaries in organized life.' Ch. 3 in R. Chia (ed.) (1998) *In the Realm of Organization: Essays for Robert Cooper* London: Routledge.

Kallinikos, J. (1992) 'Digital Songs: Aspects of Contemporary Work and Life.' *Systems Practice;* 1992; 457–472.

Kellner, D. (1999) 'Virilio, War and Technology: Some Critical Reflections.' *Theory, Culture and Society;* Vol. 16 (5–6): 103–125.

Klein, N. (2000) *No Logo* London: Flamingo.

Lash, S. and Urry, J. (1994) *Economies of Signs and Space* London: Sage.

Latour, B. (1997) 'On Actor-network theory; A few clarifications.' *http://www.keele. ac.uk/depts/stt.*

Law, J. (1992) 'Notes on the Theory of the Actor-Network: Ordering, Strategy and Heterogeneity.' *Systems Practice;* Vol. 5, No. 4: 379–393.

Law, J. (1999) 'After ANT: Complexity, Naming and Topology.' in J. Law and J. Hassard (eds.) (1999) *Actor Network Theory and After* Oxford: Blackwell; 1–14.

Lee, N. (1998) 'Two speeds: How are real stabilities possible?' Ch. 2 in Chia, R. (ed.)(1998) *Organized Worlds: Explorations in technology and organization with Robert Cooper* London: Routledge; 39–66.

McQuire, S. (1999) 'Blinded by the (Speed of) Light.' *Theory, Culture and Society;* Vol. 16 (5–6): 143–159.

Mol, A. (1999) 'Ontological Politics. A Word and Some Questions.' in J. Law and J. Hassard (eds.) (1999) *Actor Network Theory and After* Oxford: Blackwell; 74–89.

Morgan, G. (1990) *Organizations in Society* Basingstoke: Macmillan.

Munro, I. (2000) 'Non-disciplinary Power and the Network Society.' *Organization;* 7(4): 679–695.

Norris, C. (1992) *Uncritical Theory: Postmodernism, Intellectuals and the Gulf War* London: Lawrence and Wishart.

Nunes, M. (1995) 'Baudrillard in Cyberspace: Internet, Virtuality and Postmodernity.' *Style;* Vol. 29: 314–327.

Poster, M. (1995) *The Second Media Age* Cambridge, UK: Polity Press.

Power, M. (1990) 'Modernism, Postmodernism and Organization.' in J. Hassard and D. Pym (eds.) (1990) *The Theory and Philosophy of Organizations: Critical Issues and New Perspectives.* London: Routledge; 109–124.

Röhle, T. (2003) 'Power, reason and closure: Critical perspectives on new media theory.' *New Media and Society;* Vol. 7 (3): 403–422.

Ritzer, G. (1996) *The McDonaldization of Society: An Investigation into the Changing Character of Contemporary Social Life* (Revised Edition) Thousand Oaks, CA: Pine Forge Press.

Sassen, S. (2000) 'Digital Networks and the State: Some Governance Questions.' *Theory, Culture and Society*; Vol. 17(4): 19–33.

Sassen, S. (2002) 'Towards a Sociology of Information Technology.' *Current Sociology*; Vol. 50 (3): 365–388.

The Guardian (2005) 'China shuts internet cafes.' 15th February, 2005.

Tsoukas, H. (1992) 'Ways of Seeing: Topographic and Network Representations in Organization Theory.' *Systems Practice*; 1992: 441–454.

Virilio, P. (1986) *Speed and Politics* New York: Semiotext(e).

Virilio, P. (1995) 'Speed and Information: Cyberspace Alarm!' *CTheory* http://www.ctheory.net/text_file.asp?pick=72 published 27/8/1995.

Virilio, P. (1997) 'Cyberwar, God and Television: An Interview with Paul Virilio.' In *Digital Delirium* New York: St. Martin's Press; 41–48.

Wise, J.M. (1997) *Exploring Technology and Social Space* London: Sage.

Chapter 6

Hot-Nesting: A Visual Exploration of the Personalization of Work Space in a Hot-Desking Environment

Samantha Warren

Introduction

"People and their physical environments exert mutual influence, and together form interdependent systems" (Sundstrom 1986). Yet as Davis (1984: 271) comments: "the internal physical environment within offices has been given very little attention and is one of the most vaguely understood aspects of management and organizational behaviour". Since the Hawthorne Studies established social interaction as more important for productivity than environmental factors (Sundstrom 1986), the material and physical surroundings that work is conducted in, with and through have taken a back seat to people-centred interactionist theories of human behaviour at work – Herzberg's classification of the physical environment as a mere 'hygiene factor' being a case in point (Davis 1984). However, since the mid-seventies there has been a slow but steadily growing interest in the influence of the physical environment mainly from the field of environmental psychology (Steele 1973; Sundstrom 1986; Davis 1984), an interest which has gathered momentum – 'speeded up' – over the past decade. The rapid development and introduction of new forms of communication technology, such as the Internet, e-mail, mobile phones and wireless application protocol, as well as the increasing portability of powerful computing equipment are changing the ways we are able to work – and changing the requirements of the environments we work in. As Nathan & Doyle (2002: 1) tell us:

> "In fact the years since the early 1990s have seen something of a golden age in office design. On the back of economic expansion, the ICT revolution and the dotcom boom, designers and architects have constructed a wave of exciting, innovative spaces... Moving into a new HQ, or facelifting the old one, is now a recognised technique for changing corporate image and energising organisational culture."

This paper, therefore, represents a contribution to the theme of this collection: 'speed' in three ways. Firstly, business and organization have got faster, creating an expectation of immediacy among customers. As is discussed below in the context of this particular study, speed is a central concern for Dept. X; staff were located on clients' premises for reasons of 'convenience', or in other words to speed up interaction between Dept. X and their clients, to get the job done faster. Within Dept. X's own office, the designers, some of whom are the respondents for this research, were moved from their own workspaces to physically sit alongside teams of other 'uprooted' people all working on the same project at that particular time. Consequently, within this technological environment, seating patterns and workspaces were envisaged by management as 'fluid', with people moving speedily between their tasks.

This points to the second element of speed and, moreover, one which was incongruous with many of these respondents' desires and wishes surrounding their working realities; that of the notion of 'hot-desking'. Moving people between 'impersonal' desks for reasons of greater efficiency and speed of task completion is as much at the heart of the organizational rationale for hot-desking as the desire to reduce costs and use space more efficiently – for after all time is, we are told, money. So speed is an underpinning factor in the changing nature of organizational space.

Finally, this kind of efficiency and speed was something that the respondents to a large extent wished to resist. Generally speaking, as I elucidate in more depth in the rest of the paper, respondents talked of stability, being static, 'putting down roots' and carving out little pieces of organizational space that they belonged to, that they could call their own – places where the inexorable pursuit of speed might be slowed for a while. These spaces allowed them to reflect, to reclaim some of themselves in their busy working lives and furthermore, enabled them to feel that they belonged to a community which had a past, present and a future – something which they felt took time and stability to build and is clearly at odds with the organizational drive for ever faster efficiencies. This theme of speed is threaded through the discussion that follows, beginning with an overview of the concept of hot-desking. I then move to discuss the context, aims and methodology of the study before turning to explore and theorise three themes that I consider to have emerged from the data.

Hot-desking: a quick overview

Much has been made of the organizational benefits of manipulating office space. Designing spaces to aid creativity, facilitate communication and team working it is argued can boost productivity and staff morale, whilst encouraging or allowing staff to work remotely from home, clients' premises or even their cars means that organizations can reap the benefits of significant cost savings by moving to smaller premises or by redesigning existing offices. With the cost of providing a personal desk estimated to be £6000 a year and the average desk unoccupied for 55% of working hours (Nathan & Doyle 2002), empty desks and offices arguably represent a significant waste of money; "As employees become more mobile, companies are realizing that dedicating floorspace to the service of a person who is not always there to occupy it is a waste of resources" (*Management Development Review* 1997: 145). Consequently, one of the most significant contemporary trends in workplace design is the concept of 'hot-desking'. Originating from a naval term for shared bunks onboard ship, 'hot-desking' is the term used to describe the "sharing of a desk/ seat/ workstation arrangement by more than one member of staff" (Daniels 1994: 7). As outlined above, technological advances mean that much work can be carried out without the need for staff to come into the office every day. Similarly, for consultants and sales people, as for a significant number of the respondents in this study, work is often carried out on the client's premises. Large corporations including IBM, Digital Equipment, British Telecom, British Airways, Andersen Consulting, Ernst & Young, Pearl Assurance, British Gas and Fujitsu-ICL Systems (Ashworth 1997; Gillies 1998; Goodwin 2000; Hoare 1999; Murphy 1995) have all introduced hot-desking schemes in an attempt to reduce accommodation overheads by up to a third (Conroy 2000).

Moreover, it's not just large private companies, who are keen to reap the benefits of innovative approaches to space utilization. Recent postings on the Flexibility Forum (www.flexibility.co.uk/forum) show several enquiries from people in local health, education and government looking for help and advice on how to implement hot desking in their offices too. As the opening line of a 1997 article in *Management Development Review* astutely predicts, "the ancient custom of providing one desk for each employee may soon be as out of date as the typewriter".

From an organizational perspective, hot-desking seems to be an ideal answer to the inevitably empty (expensive) desks and offices resulting from staff who are working remotely either from home, customers' premises or elsewhere. When staff do decide to work from the office, on arrival they collect their personal files and paraphernalia which are usually stored in a mobile 'cart' (a set of drawers on wheels) and sit down at the nearest available desk. From here, laptop computers can be quickly connected to the organization's computer network and calls can be diverted to the day's telephone extension. Booking systems can be used to make sure that there are always enough desks for people who want to use them at any given time (known as 'office-hoteling') and the organization can enjoy maximum space utilization with all the associated cost savings. In fact, until recently, the majority of management (practitioner) literature seemed to extol the virtue of hot-desking almost unanimously, seeing only inefficient organization, poor levels of support service provision and inadequate technology as the potential pitfalls (see for instance Ashworth 1997; Daniels 1994; Conroy 2000; Goodwin 2000; Hoare 1999 and Management Development Review 1997).

However, initiatives that save businesses money are often overly focused on the organization – disregarding the impact on individual employees. This is also a predominant feature of much of the academic literature concerning the physical working environment, as Scheiberg (1990: 330) tells us:

> "…most are concerned not with the individual and his or her emotional and aesthetic needs, but rather with the workplace as status symbol, as an arena for formal and informal interaction, or as something to be defined and designed from above."

This study aims to contribute to the task of redressing this balance in the light of a recent Industrial Society report which found that only half of those who hot-desk prefer it to their old personal fixed desk. This figure drops to only 15% among secretarial and clerical staff (Saunders 2002). What might be the reasons for the un-popularity of hot-desking? Why are employees dissatisfied with the flexibility that hot-desking affords? As Nathan & Doyle (2002: 21) note, "[hot-desking] may be all the rage, but not with employees". One criticism of flexible working practices in general is that some employees simply may not be able or willing to work from home – quite apart from practical issues such as space and family issues – the sanctity of the home as a haven from (paid) work and the social contact that the office environment enables are major issues in the resistance against remote working and hot-desking that recent figures appear to show (Nathan & Doyle 2002). Likewise, as Murphy (1995) comments, office space has long been part of the traditional trappings of organizational status. The size and position of the office itself, the type of furniture and objects within it and even the depth of the pile on the carpet are often symbolic indicators of the occupant's position in the company (Gagliardi 1986; Sommer & Steiner 1988; Steele 1973; Strati 1999; Sundstrom 1986). Hot-desking's transformation of symbolic office spaces into anonymous work areas (Eadie 2000) removes these hard won marks of success that, especially in more traditional organizations, some may find hard to relinquish in the name of productivity. Relatedly, some writers have argued that personal desks and offices function as 'territories' marked and defended with personal belongings, regulating social interactions with others, as well as providing a sense of individuality and control within the organization (Altman 1975; Sundstrom 1986; Wells 2000). As Eadie (2000: 541) notes: "[hot desking] may be efficient, but it is not natural. Office workers like a corner to call their own, where they put photos, pot plants, cuddly toys and their chipped, stained, but special, coffee mug" – a theme strongly echoed in the data I present below.

The study – aims and methodology

The aim of this chapter then, is to qualitatively explore issues surrounding personal space in a hot-desking environment. A self selecting sample of sixteen employees in the web-design department of a large IT firm (Dept. X), based in a rural location in the south of England were asked to photograph their desks using a digital camera. The sample comprised twelve men and four women, of whom seven were graphic designers, six were programmers, two (both female) were support staff and one was a project producer[1]. During 'guided conversations' (Patton 1990) they were then asked to talk about the importance they placed on the personalization of their organizational space, by 'talking me round' the objects and artefacts shown in the photographs. The significance of personal artefacts and paraphernalia in the workplace and the meanings of the objects that the respondents chose to display on and around their desks were discussed in the light of the organization's 'hot-desking' policy which the majority of staff were opposed to in practice, although they could understand the rationale behind its introduction. The manager of Dept. X explained to me that hot-desking had been introduced partly for reasons of cost efficiency and partly because she believed the continual stimulus of regularly moving to a new environment helped her staff to be more innovative and prevented them 'stagnating'. She also felt that enabling project teams to work together in one location aided team-working and ultimately provided a better service for the client.

The conversations were not carried out at the respondents' desks for practical reasons such as privacy and the difficulty of tape recording voice clearly in a busy office environment where music was often playing. Photography therefore offered a valuable means of capturing the visual data 'contained' in the respondent's work space. This method of using images to stimulate discussion is widely used in marketing research (Emmison and Smith 2000) but few organizational researchers have used 'photo-elicitation' techniques (Wagner 1979) as an aid to gathering qualitative data. In my experience during this study, I found that using photography added another dimension to the research process. Respondents seemed to feel a sense of ownership of the photographs – they chose how they framed the shot, and they retained control over what was and was not included in the photograph. The images were viewed on a laptop computer which the respondents' often chose to operate, and I feel this helped diminish the power dynamic that often exists between the active researcher who is seen as 'doing research on' passive respondents (see also Warren 2005b). As Sarah Pink (2001) and Dona Schwartz (1994) both note, using photographs taken by respondents or of respondents can be a method requiring collaboration between researcher and researched lead-

---

[1] Respondents are identified anonymously using a three digit code explained in Appendix 1.

ing to a greater sense of involvement with the participants, in my opinion, enhancing relationships with the respondents leading to richer data. Rob Walker and Janine Weidel (1985: 212) call this process of stimulation "the can opener effect" suggesting that data is generated **through** the image as well as the captured **by** it. Thus meaning is actively constructed through the dialogue surrounding the image, rather than 'extracted' from either the image or the respondent. As Pink (2001: 68) elucidates:

> "In a photographic interview, therefore, ethnographer and informant will be able to discuss their different understandings of images, thus collaborating to determine each other's views."

Some view this collaborative relationship between researcher and respondent as problematic, since the researcher is to some extent influencing what the respondent chooses to reveal about him or herself. However, the stance I am taking here is that researchers will always influence the data they gather at all stages of the process – from the very intention to research a topic (Gummesson 1999) through to the interpretation of the data and presentation of findings, as Simon Gottschalk (1998: 212) neatly puts it, "site affects sight affects cite." Furthermore, it is my belief that collaboration aids the collection of plausible data in a qualitative context since it is conducive to forming a greater rapport between researcher and respondent, something writers in the ethnographic tradition have long advocated as vital for high quality qualitative research (Hammersley and Atkinson 1995; Coffey 1999).

As well as serving as 'prompts' for discussion, the subjects, objects and events pictured in the photographs added a visual dimension to the respondents' spoken descriptions during the research process. In showing me their photographs, respondents did not need to explain the aesthetics of their desks in great detail – they were literally able to show me. Of course, they would have been able to do this if the interviews had been carried out at their desks – a strategy used by Wells (2000), but as I explain above in this case, this would have been problematic for practical reasons. However, this visual element **can** be used to aid my dissemination of the data here in a way the physical materiality of the respondents actual desks cannot.

Most qualitative researchers (particularly within the ethnographic tradition) agree to some extent that the 'validity' of qualitative data stems from its plausibility to the reader and the participants in the research (Sanger 1996). One of the ways Geertz (1973) has suggested this plausibility might be conveyed is through what he terms 'thick description' – an evocatively detailed account of context as well as the 'facts'. Other writers go beyond this, advocating a literary approach to dissemination, akin to those employed in the writing of fictional novels (Banks and Banks 1998; Czarniawska

1999; Linstead 1994; Mitchell and Charmaz 1996). However, as Barbara Czarniawska (1999: 26) succinctly puts it because "words cannot be compared to worlds" the assumption that photographs bear some resemblance to reality – even if that reality is selectively framed – makes them potentially valuable in the 'thick descriptive' process. Whilst I wish to avoid suggesting that the photographs I include are 'evidence' of the arguments I put forward in any realist sense, the fact that they were taken by the respondents hopefully renders them at least relevant to the realities of those respondents. The relative merits of images and text as 'truth' is a healthy and vibrant debate in academic scholarship. Although I have by no means done it justice here, suffice to say that my perspective on the role of images in research follows Mitchell's (1994: 89) notion of an 'image-text'. Within this framework, both words and images are synthesised in the description without either being reduced to, or being placed as superior over, the other. It is for this reason that I include photographs in the chapter (where relevant) to convey a more 'sensually complete' account of the data I present[2].

The study – context and contribution

This study is part of a wider study into the manipulation of workplace aesthetics in the department (Warren 2005a). This is in itself an example of the growing trend towards 'wild and wacky' organizational environments, the so-called "golden age of office design" that Nathan & Doyle (2002: 1) describe above. Offices and work areas are deliberately designed to be playful, stimulating, surprising and unusual places to be in. Following Bauman (1998) I use the term 'aestheticization' to describe this organizational manipulation of sensory and emotional stimuli in the physical environment for organizational ends (for examples see Eadie 2000; Gillies 1998; Hilper 2000; Nathan and Doyle 2002; Stretton 2000). Dept. X's office space had recently been aestheticized to create an environment which management hoped would more effectively communicate the organization's ability to produce creative and innovative web-site designs for its clients. It was also designed to be an environment to help inspire those who worked within it and stimulate their creativity as well as being a practical solution to the space utilization and flexibility issues I discuss above. Among the items introduced into the environment were toys, including a micro-scooter, lego, table football and a pool table; coloured lighting; oversize sculptures; a bright red brainstorming room filled with foam shapes and the introduction of a hot-desking system where designers, project producers, programmers and clients could all sit together as a team for the duration of a project

---

[2] For a fuller discussion of photography as a research method see Warren 2002 and 2005b.

– before moving onto the next task and a new set of desks, as I have already mentioned above. (Fig 1)

Figure 1: Views of the 'aestheticized' Dept. X.

When I arrived at Dept. X in spring 2001 I was immediately struck by the way the office looked – not for the unusual paraphernalia and sculptures that were scattered around the place, nor the way the space had been designed or decorated – but the fact that the office hardly resembled a hot-desking environment at all. Far from appearing to be an anonymous work space as one might expect, almost every desk showed personalization to some extent, with objects, photographs, pictures and all sorts of interesting personal effects covering most of the desks I could see. I later discovered that the hot-desking policy had been abandoned completely (although not entirely officially), in one area of the department – the design studio – and although the rest of the staff did not have permanent desks there seemed to be a fair degree of stability in the seating arrangements over the three months I was there. I also noticed that there were marked differences in the ways people personalised their desks. Some displayed only a few personal items, whereas in the design studio desks exhibited what Scheiberg (1990: 332) calls *"rampant personalization of space"*. Intrigued by these observations, I decided to explore the dynamics of personal space with some of the respondents taking part in the main study.

Given the small scale nature of this research and its subjective character, the findings I present below are not intended to be generalised to other employees' experiences of hot-desking or personalization. However, as Remenyi et al. (1998:116) note what qualitative research such as this does do is to "lay bare the mecha-

nisms one suspects may be present in other organisations". This indeed seems to be the case with the findings from this research which resonate with conclusions drawn from other studies (both qualitative and quantitative) of personalization and personal space at work.

To summarise then, in this chapter I explore the meanings that personal work spaces have for these respondents and the role that personalization plays in creating and expressing those meanings. In doing so, I present data centred on three themes that emerged from the study:

- **Emotion and Aesthetics** – the respondents' desire to humanize the experience of work through the display of personal material objects infused with affective and aesthetic meaning;
- **Self-identity** – personalization as an expression of and way to maintain a sense of self at work – even the decision not to personalize space respondents recognised as saying something about 'who they were'; and
- **Belonging** – the role of personalization in fostering, maintaining and encouraging a sense of community within the department – seen by the respondents as vital to their happiness at work and ultimately their productivity.

These themes suggest that personalization and the control of personal space is important to individuals at work and importantly for my purposes here, is at odds with the creation of anonymous hot-desk environments. The data presented below show how personal space is an important element of psychological satisfaction at work – a finding supported by Nathan and Doyle (2002: 24) who found that "flexible workspaces may be making some employees unhappy by denying them their territory".

Furthermore, the themes outlined above lend support for more theoretical treatments of the role of material objects in everyday life within cultural studies, environmental psychology, anthropology and consumer behaviour, as well as in organisation studies itself, in which limited attention only has been paid to these issues. Very few studies have been carried out which explore personalization in the workplace, all of which were carried out in the US. Some of the most notable include Eric Sundstrom (1986: 219–229) who eloquently summarises some of the key issues surrounding the desire to personalize in his chapter on 'symbolic workspace: self-identity and status'; Susan Scheiberg (1990) who carried out a qualitative exploration of the emotional significance of personal decoration of work space; and Meredith Wells' (2000) quantitative investigation into a possible link between personalization and employee and organizational well-being. However despite Wells' (2000: 239) introductory comment that "with the changing nature of offices, employee personalization of office environments takes on special significance" there has been little attempt thus far, in the field of organization studies at least, to link workplace personalization to the broader revolution occurring in office design. A strand of Nathan and Doyle's (2002) fascinating report for The Industrial Society into the "politics and geography of working space" does deal with personalization as a function of territory and ownership in the workplace, but due to its broad focus, is unable to fully explore the meaning and significance of such personalization to the individuals concerned in any depth. By providing an in-depth insight into the meanings personal objects, spaces and decorations have for people in Dept. X, I hope this study will draw together some of the strands of existing research into these phenomena and place them within the framework of contemporary organizational practice. To this end, I weave some of the ideas in this literature through my presentation of the data below.

"I've finally found a home" – emotional and aesthetic dimensions of personalized spaces.

"…it's just things that remind me of people – friends, like the little dolphin up there was given to me by a girl who came to stay with us in Sydney – and New Zealand on my screen-saver because I had such a fantastic time there, and the little Flipper writing was an envelope that a friend had given me with a card inside, you know? The little stamp was another thing from a friend, so it's all little bits and pieces that friends have given me and then obviously with the
photo *of my family* [at her sister's wedding] *'cos it was such a great day. We call it our Dynasty shot, because we used to love watching 'Dynasty' when we were kids and we really used to love all the characters… 'cos I'm one*

of five and it used to be this Friday night ritual kind of thing, so we had a Dynasty pose for the wedding..."
(F.T.1)

The above quotation and photographs are from the interview transcript of a female technical support officer. I'd asked her to tell me about the things on her desk – which, as her words show, she did with great affection. This respondent's description is typical of the emotionally infused explanations people gave of their personal objects. Concepts like 'familiarity', 'homeliness' and 'comfort' were talked of repeatedly by almost all the respondents as they spoke of their personal paraphernalia in terms of their emotional attachment to them – or more specifically to the significant person or event that these objects reminded them of. Marcus Kwint et al. (1999) use the evocative term 'material memories' to describe objects that have become infused with emotional significance – a significance which transcends the functionality of the object. For the respondents in this study, objects which were described as material memories included gifts from family and friends, drawings made by children, mementoes and souvenirs from social events and in almost all cases, photographs of significant family members, friends and events[3]. As Melanie Wallendorf and Eric Arnould (1988: 537) tell us from their study into the meanings of favourite possessions for American and Nigerian householders: "The meaning of these objects, then, often derives from symbolic person, event and maker attachments rather than from their physical attributes." Indeed, one female customer support officer told me how she didn't like the cuddly toy that appeared to sit proudly on her desk. It had been a present from a friend and when I asked her if looking at it cheered her up she replied,

---

[3] The status of photographs as material objects rather than representations of subjects has been the cause of some debate (Edwards 1999). However, following Barthes, Elizabeth Edwards (1999: 222) argues that *"the image and its referent are laminated together, two leaves that cannot be separated, so are the photograph and its materiality, the image and the object brought into a single coherent form"*. She goes on to state that although photographs are treasured for their link to the subjects they represent, they are also tangible objects which can be *"handled, framed, cut, crumpled, caressed, pinned on a wall, put under a pillow or wept over"*. (ibid: 226) and therefore their materiality is inextricably part of their status as a material memory.

"No – cos I don't actually like cuddly toys! Now you'll think I'm really weird! If I leave it on my desk I don't have to have it in my room, but I couldn't possibly get rid of it cos I am sentimentally attached to it ..." (F.S.1)

This draws parallels with the findings of Susan Schultz Kleine et al. (1995: 345) whose quantitative study of material possession attachment found that people can become strongly attached to objects even though they don't actually like them or consider them to reflect their personalities. The emotional attachment, they argue, comes from "... the meaningfulness of other-gifts ... reflected through deep emotions resulting from the conjoining of giver, receiver and gift" (Schulz Kleine et al. 1995: 354).

The notion of an emotional memory symbolised by or embodied in a material object tells us that such objects form a link to the owner's past. Kwint (1999: 2) suggests that objects act as memories in three ways. Firstly that they furnish recollection – they are incorporated into our remembered personal history, yet as objects they stand as separate from us, so we can quite literally 'look back' at them. Secondly, the very nature of their materiality triggers forgotten or repressed memories of that history when we see, hear, touch, smell or even taste them. This intuitive point brings to mind the memories which come flooding back when one smells a past lover's perfume or hears a long-forgotten song from childhood. Lastly, objects serve as systematically organised records of our past. One only has to think of museum collections or the accumulated contents of a family dresser to realise the truth of this statement. As Kwint goes on to say: "Here [in objects] memory connects with the entire body and the full complexity of the world around" (1999: 4). This 'physical past' as Kwint calls it (ibid.) is integral to our sense of who we are, and as Belk (1988: 148) summarises, the objects that make our past concrete "conveniently store the feelings and memories [that attach us to] our sense of past". Clearly, these feelings and memories are for the most part personal and unique to the individual who owns the object. Although meanings may be shared with significant others, such as family or friends – to an 'outsider' the significance a personal object has for its owner is not transparent **outside of the context it exists within.** In other words, Belk's conceptualisation of objects as 'containers' for storing emotional memories perhaps diminishes the active role that objects play in keeping these memories alive – privileging the human over the non-human

130

elements at play here. I am borrowing ideas here from the branch of socio-logical investigation known as actor-network theory, in which the relations (or networks) that objects and people form through their interactions with one another produce the effect of a finished entity[4]. These ideas appear quite complex but at their most basic rest on the premise that people and things are meaningless when placed in a different context. Thus a personal object is only meaningful as a material memory when placed in relation to its owner within a specific geographical, temporal, cultural and discursive location. If the object moves into another set of relations, its function as a container of memory is defunct. As Wallendorf and Arnould (1995: 537) explain of the reasons people gave for valuing a particular possession,

> "...the reason given for these attachments typically derives from a shared his-tory between the person and the object... this history is not purchased with the object. After years of use, the web of semiotic and symbolic associations spun around the object by which it becomes decommodified and 'singular-ized' for the individual...come to be the reasons for its selection as favorite object."

To illustrate this point, imagine an urban antique shop – its window crammed full of curios and once treasured objects cleared from the houses of the deceased, elderly and infirm. Standing outside the shop we can only guess at the meanings that these objects once had for the people who owned them, but they do not passively **contain** these meanings themselves for us to see. As Wallendorf and Arnould tell us, the memories these objects sup-posedly 'contain' have been produced through the shared history of thing and person. As we look at them, these things have moved into **our** network of relations and what they 'are' has changed. Objects therefore, might be better seen as active elements or 'actors' in the network of relations which come together to produce meaningful effect – in other words, memories. Notwithstanding the above, the fact that objects are entwined in the process of remembering is an intuitive one and one of significant importance for my purposes here.

Although the above discussion is indeed a persuasive account of the emo-tional significance of objects, the term 'memory' perhaps invokes too strong a connotation with historical events to reflect the full range of emotional meanings that the respondents' objects had for them. Whilst many of the objects they showed me were links to times past, there was a strong sense (to me at least) that objects embodied emotions which were much more 'current'. Although the objects which reminded people of their loved ones undoubtedly served on some level as reminders of them whilst in temporary

---

[4] For an introduction to the principles of actor-network theory see Callon 1986, Latour 1999 and Law 1992.

absence, I gained the impression that some respondents used these objects as ways of bringing their 'non-work selves' into the work environment to make it more 'homely' as the following extracts from interview transcripts illustrate:

"...there's no division between your work and personal life really, only what you choose to put there and I don't like to think like that." (M-D-6)

"Um, the red envelope was from a Thai restaurant cos it was Chinese New Year, or whatever and it's got a coin in it and it was for good luck... I thought that was really nice so I kept that." (F-D-1)

"I like having some pictures, I like it to be homely... when you're spending every day at your desk, I like it to feel vaguely homely and stuff so there's pictures of snowboarders [respondent's hobby] *– I've got loads of pictures but there's not enough room to put them all up."* (M-T-1)

These objects had been chosen by the respondents to show me how they tried to make their work environment more pleasurable through the emotional attachments they had outside the organization. Indeed, many respondents explicitly stated how certain objects were displayed purely for their amusement value – objects as diverse as sweet wrappers, children's toys, silly stickers and clippings from magazines. Some respondents actually displayed satirical cartoons, but mostly the objects intended for entertainment were less overt in their messages to 'outsiders'.

A further category of personal objects were chosen and displayed solely for their aesthetic qualities. Perhaps unsurprisingly, these were most commonly found on the desks of the designers – although not exclusively. One male producer had an arrangement of compact discs pinned to the partition above his desk, purely because he liked their shape and the colourful refraction of light they gave.

Other respondents talked of their liking for natural and tactile objects such as stones they had retrieved from the organization's grounds and of course plants – which seemed to give pleasure just by being there, regardless of whether they had been received as gifts or not. There were also many postcards and pages torn from magazines as examples of 'cool' designs pinned up beside desks. Some respondents spoke of these as inspirational and creative aids, but more often they were chosen and displayed because the owner simply 'liked them'.

This last strand of data – the display of objects for aesthetic pleasure – can be seen as a further dimension to Susan Scheiberg's (1990) exploration of personal decoration of workspace. In a delightfully written, but rather functionalist account of personalization, she comes to the conclusion that people "designed their space to help them cope with aspects of their work life directly related to emotions" (1990: 334). Objects were either outlets for emotions which would otherwise not be able to be expressed at work, such as frustration or flamboyancy, or they acted as "specific and concrete stimuli to which the individual will have a predictable emotional response – an emotional response that the individual finds useful for his or her job situation or work style" (ibid.). Although I do not wish to challenge Scheiberg's interpretation of her own data, I do feel, on the basis of the data I present here, that the teleological and instrumental way she suggests people might use their personal displays is too simple an analysis. Whilst I did find evidence to suggest that the respondents in the present case did use their objects as a means of 'escape' or 'rest' from their jobs, or as sources of inspiration, this explanation, along with the arguments put forward in the arguments from Kwint (1999) and Wallendorf and Arnould (1988) that I discuss above, do not go far enough in illuminating those seemingly 'purposeless' objects displayed in personal spaces. Relatedly, Scheiberg also fails to account for the social and socialised dimensions of personalised space – an issue I turn to now.

"Everybody's little space is different" – on identity and desks

"You know people are image conscious on the whole – they do put something up because they want other people to see it, or um, even as a talking point or something – somebody'll come past and say 'Oh!' you know – just like you did – 'Ooh look, Florence' and then of course I can go off on one talking about Florence..." (M-P-2 talking about a photograph of Ponte Vecchio, Florence – material memory of where he used to live and work.)

The discussion of emotion and aesthetics I present above assumes that personalization is an intensely private and individual affair. Although respondents did talk of the very personal meanings their objects had for them – meanings which were largely opaque to other people – the fact that they chose to display those objects publicly is of considerable significance. Why did they choose those particular objects? Why should those particular material memories and emotional-aesthetic cues have been of importance to the individuals concerned and moreover, why did they want others to see them? We have seen how the emotional significance of objects might help individuals create a comfortable environment, more akin to the emotional security and familiarity of home than work, and how they might provide a link to cherished memories. But what of the social interaction surrounding those objects? As the quotation from my data at the beginning of this section shows, objects invite comment. They spark interaction helping people to talk about themselves with others, and in so doing I suggest they may help to establish, build, maintain, negotiate and express a sense of self and identity at work.

As Sundstrom (1986) tells us, for a workspace to act as a means of self-expression, or indicator of identity, firstly, the person must feel they 'own' it and secondly, that the space must be recognisable to others as belonging to that person. The extent to which the people I spoke to in Dept. X felt that they had a personal space was striking. Without exception, they referred to *"my"* desk or *"my"* PC, no matter how transient they felt their occupation to be. This sense of ownership indicates that at some level they identified with the space they currently occupied as an objectified possession – a place that belonged to them.

The idea that objects might play a part in the formation of identity is not new as Mihalyi Csikszentmihalyi and Eugene Rochberg-Halton (1981: 1) tell us:

> "The things with which people interact are not simply tools for survival, or for making survival easier and more comfortable. Things embody goals, make skills manifest, and shape the identities of their users. Man is not only *homo sapiens* or *homo ludens*, he is also *homo faber*, the maker and user of objects, his self to a large extent a reflection of things with which he interacts. Thus objects also make and use their makers and users."

The role of possessions in the creation, communication and maintenance of identity has also been investigated by writers in the field of consumer behaviour (Belk 1988; Wallendorf and Arnould 1988; Schultz Kleine et al. 1995). As Belk (1988: 139) simply states "knowingly or unknowingly, intentionally or unintentionally, we regard our possessions as parts of ourselves". Using a range of empirical and theoretical arguments he grounds his thesis in the assumption that those possessions we invest ourselves in through the effort of our labour[5] become part of us as an *"extended self"* (ibid.). Among others, he gives cross cultural examples as evidence that possessions have always been important to human beings as part of who we 'are' – the ancient practice of being buried with one's possessions (so-called 'grave goods') and the fact that archaeologists regularly infer the behaviours and activities of lost civilizations through the material objects that remain long after the person or people who once owned them have died. Conversely, he gives examples where a loss of possessions has resulted in a diminished sense of self, as in the case of the ritual removal of patients personal effects in Goffman's study of asylums: "The result of this systematic substitution of standardized identity-kits for former possessions is an elimination of uniqueness and a corresponding and often traumatic lessening of the individuals sense of self" (Belk 1988: 142). Following McCarthy, he concludes that "objects act as reminders and confirmers of our identities and… our identities may reside in objects more than they do in individuals" (Belk 1988: 141). Again, Belk alludes here to a conceptualisation of objects as passive receptacles rather than active constructors of identity. However, his proposition firmly integrates objects into a view of 'self' which extends beyond our somatic boundaries, meaning that through the objects we choose to possess, display, value and infuse with meaning, we communicate to ourselves and others who we are – or perhaps more accurately who we want others to see we are. One respondent explicitly recognised this in the way he personalised his desk:

"Its um – there's this whole psychology about what you have on your desk – again it goes back to the perception of 'I'd like to be this person and so I'm going to have this screensaver' and yeah, I think I fit into that group where I want to associate myself with [a particular] *group and most importantly I want everyone else to see that's my mindset and that… basically these are the things I feel comfortable with and please me. That's why they're there."*
(M-D-1)

Similarly, Schultz Kleine et al. (1995), argue that identity is constructed through two dialectical tensions, Firstly, they suggest on the basis of their literature review, that our sense of self comes from the desire to (paradoxically) establish ourselves as autonomous beings whilst retaining a degree of affiliation with significant others and social groups. In terms of our personal possessions, objects which communicate individual achievements or distinctiveness are evidence of our need for autonomy, whereas objects which emphasise connections to others or to past heritage and tradition exemplify

---

[5] Belk notes that possessions are not often physically created by the owner, but purchased by the owner as a consumer with money. Money is thus the symbolic investment of self (through its nature as earned income) in these cases.

our need for affiliation (Schultz Kleine et al. 1995: 328). Secondly, they suggest that the maintenance of self is part of an ongoing resolution of "the dialectical tension between stability (ie: maintaining a facet of identity) and change (ie: acquiring or discarding a facet of identity)..." (1995: 328). Thus, although unlike Belk, they prefer to conceptualise objects as "artefacts of the self" (ibid.) rather than extensions to the self per se, they argue, "possessions create a tangible residue of past, present, and possibly future identity development" (ibid.). If personal objects are indeed an important part of identity development, they argue that an exploration of those objects should produce an individual's "portfolio of attachments – each reflecting different combinations of affiliation, autonomy seeking, and past, present or future temporal orientation" (Schultz Kleine et al. 1995: 329). This is an interesting argument, since the desks in Dept. X undoubtedly displayed objects which clearly fitted these categories. However, despite two of the respondents who spoke of the way they thought their personalised desks 'said' something about who they were (or wanted to be), on the whole my data doesn't really seem to support the argument that individuals use objects as part of a narrative of **personal** identity, or at least not explicitly. Instead, there was more of an implicit strand in the data which hinted at this. Respondents told me how the items they displayed were just things they liked, or felt to be 'cool', which might indicate something about the image of themselves as a person that they wished to give to others, and the groups they aspired to identify with. The following interview extract shows that certain desks were indeed broadly identifiable as belonging to different groups of people:

"... the artwork that people put up and some of the design cut-outs they've put up and you know instantly that its done by a designer – who's cut them out and put them up cos it's just... if that was on a customer support desk, it would be 'what?' but cos it's a designer you think 'cool!'" (M-P-1)

Notwithstanding this respondent's comments, this kind of inference relies heavily on a psychoanalytical interpretation of the self as expressed unconsciously through objects in personal spaces. However, it would be fair to say that it is possible, to a greater or lesser extent, to make inferences about the role and significance of objects in relation to people and their personalities, based on a shared understanding of reality, or "symbolic universe" (Berger and Luckmann 1967). Based on these shared understandings, Steele (1976: 54) tells us that we can *"read statements"* about people based on the way they arrange their personal space and the objects within it and furthermore that "to read something about a person from his immediate setting does not require however, that he had others in mind when he made his choices". Although Steele probably meant here that we decorate our spaces to please ourselves and not overtly to please others, in my opinion, this statement still underplays the importance of social interaction in the dynamic between self and object. According to George Herbert Mead (1934) our development as social beings depends entirely on 'having others in mind'. The stance I am taking here with regard to self-identity is grounded in the social constructivist view that the self develops through interaction with others (Berger and Luckmann 1976) and through the act of taking the role of the 'other' (Mead 1934). This 'other' need not be a specific person, but a 'generalised other' (Mead 1934). I do not intend to fully elucidate these ideas here, suffice to say that through psychologically taking the role of the other we can imagine how they might behave, how we might appear to them, and make (self) adjustments accordingly. Furthermore, as Csikszentmihalyi and Rochberg-Halton (1981) note, Mead included objects as part of the generalised other:

> "Any thing – any object or set of objects, whether animate or inanimate, human or animal, or merely physical – toward which he acts, or responds, socially, is an element in what for him is the generalized other; by taking the attitudes of which toward himself he becomes conscious of himself as an object or individual and thus develops a self or personality." (Mead, cited in Csikszentmihalyi and Rochberg-Halton 1981: 51)

They go on to affirm how using an object in a "culturally appropriate way means to experience that culture directly – becoming part of the medium of signs that constitutes that culture" (ibid.). In the present case, the way objects were used in a "culturally appropriate way" included displaying them as part of a personalised workspace. Furthermore, as Berger and Luckmann tell us, our sense of who we are is continually reinforced and negotiated through our interactions with others, interactions which as we have seen in the respondent's quotation which opens this section of the paper, are often centred on these material elements of ourselves – our clothing, the way we adorn our bodies, our cars, houses, possessions and so on.

These ideas were strongly echoed in my data. Instead of speaking of the way personal objects helped establish an **individual** self-identity, respondents recognised their role in the creation of an affiliative group identity – an identity recognisable to others:

"I think that [personalisation] *says a lot, not necessarily about the individual, but as a collective – that people use them* [personal objects] *as a kind of identity forming thing. And that's cool – I like that. It's definitely more to do with the community 'cos I can't remember any one particular desk, what is pinned up, but I can think of many things that are pinned up throughout the design studio. It's that kind of childish innocence belied by a devil-worshipping soul underneath – which is good!"* (M-P-1)

"I like making it my space, and community is important – and that's part of being in a community – having all your familiar items and all the little things around you." (M-D-5)

Thus, although material possessions and personal space are important aids to the creation of **personal** narratives and **self**-identities in the largely private sphere of the home – the arena that the majority of writers on the issue are exploring – in a communal environment such as the open plan office of Dept. X, they seem to be more important to the creation of a group identity and a sense of permanence, belonging and stability. This is perhaps the strongest theme in the data so far and I discuss it further below.

"Putting down roots" – Belonging and Community

Many respondents spoke of the loss of 'community' since the move to Dept. X's new office. The previous office was cramped and over-crowded and had been located in a basement with little natural light. It is perhaps surprising that the employees did not generally view their move to a new, aesthetically designed, light, spacious office more favourably. Although they did seem to prefer the physical aspects of the new environment, most respondents – particularly the designers among whom there seemed to be the strongest sense of community – spoke nostalgically about the past, as this interview extract shows:

"…see this is the big difference, in the dungeon [previous office] *all of the design community used to sit together… and it meant you could put down some roots where you were… we actually had a thing up outside our quad-*

rangle, cos there were like three desks in each corner and there was actually like a little barrier up around it... and it just felt a bit more cosy and like outside we had a thing saying who we were and you couldn't do that now – you wouldn't bother now, cos you don't know where you're going to sit."
(M-D-2)

Other respondents told me that they used to display many more personal items when they had fixed desks in the 'dungeon' and that the lack of personalisation generally within the new office space reflected that people felt a loss of the group identity and community spirit they had before.

To return to Schultz Kleine et al's (1995) dialectic of affiliation vs. autonomy seeking, once again it seems that the attachment to objects in a communal environment is oriented firmly toward the affiliative end of the continuum – toward the establishment, maintenance and display of group identity rather than individuality. This has been noted by Nathan and Doyle (2002) who, following Altman and Low argue that our attachments to work environments come to resemble those which we feel towards our homes given the extent to which work is increasingly seen by many people as a community to which they belong and the length of time usually spent by employees at work. Wallendorf and Arnould (1988: 543) also note that, "rather than serving as substitutes for a social network, favourite objects serve to solidify and represent both one's connections to and differences from others. Thus favourite object attachment does not appear to be an expression of loneliness, but rather an expression of connections to others."

This 'socialising' power of objects (Csikszentmihalyi and Rochberg-Halton 1981) – that is to say the importance of objects in forming group norms – and the extent to which personalisation in Dept. X was a culturally related practice, is further illustrated by the following comments from a project producer, (temporarily sitting in the design-studio). He told me of the 'pressure' he felt to personalise his desk yet also spoke at length about how positive he felt about the fact that the design community had an identity through their prolific displays of personal objects:

"I've never been one for um, photos and cuddly toys at work, I'm there to do a job... now and again I might put a couple of things up but I'm very aware that I'm doing it and it doesn't feel quite – it feels a bit 'officey'[6], feels a bit 'why am I doing this? Am I doing this because everyone else is? And also what statement am I making about myself? I'm a crazy guy cos.... y'know?"
(M-P-1)

---

[6] The comment that personalisation feels a bit 'officey' is an interesting contrast with the predominant feeling among the respondents that displaying personal objects made their desks feel more 'homely'!

At this juncture, it is interesting to note that other writers on the personalization of organizational space do not seem to have found these themes in their data. Instead, there is an emphasis on the establishment of individuality through personal displays as a means of resisting the 'anonymising' discourses of organization. In 1978, a study found that 77% of those surveyed considered it 'very important' to feel like a recognised individual and not a 'cog in a wheel' at work (Sundstrom 1986). One of the ways this individuality might be expressed is by personalising and colonising space (Wells 2000). The idea of colonising personal space as 'territory' is also prevalent in the literature on organizational space as a way to maintain individuality and control at work, despite little evidence that people do in fact act territorially around their space. Irwin Altman (1975) suggests that 'primary territories' at work represent for their occupants a sense of control over something in the organization, even when the employee's 'real' influence is limited. He suggests that personalisation plays a key role in defining territory, something which people in Dept. X did allude to – certain desks were identifiable as belonging to certain people from the objects on them even when the physical location of that desk had changed. Nathan and Doyle's recent research (2002: 24) did find evidence that respondents in their study regarded their desks and certain areas of their office as territories, and in hot-desk environments, "employees [were] bending the rules and developing their own rituals to grab territory back" which effectively involved colonising hot-desks against company rules.

There was evidence that this was occurring to some extent in Dept. X, as the following remarks show:

"It's not quite a total hot-desking place and a lot of people are very protective over their desks as well. If they're away for a day [they say], 'Make sure nobody comes in and messes around with my stuff! [laughs]" (M-P-2)

"I don't think I would put loads of stuff up at work – I don't really feel the need to, although if anybody tried to move me from that desk they would end up with a fight!" (M-T-2)

Indeed the fact that the design-studio had managed to secure quasi-exemption from the policy might be seen to indicate the 'grabbing back' of territory that Nathan and Doyle (2002) found.

However, as I have already mentioned, in this study, although personalised spaces were important to the respondents for emotional, aesthetic, expressive and perhaps territorial reasons, the most prominent reasons given for attachment to personal space were embedded in the wider relationship with the organizational community, and in particular the design community. Even those respondents who did not class themselves as part of this community spoke of an uncomfortable sense of 'homelessness' when they were forced to move desks:

"There are no such things as permanent desks – which struck me as a little bit too weird... I've been working on a lot of very short term projects which meant being moved around about once a month which I found very frustrating – it gave me a severe sense of dislocation to not actually have an area you could call home..." (M-D-4)

This respondent's feelings are indicative of the sense of instability and transience among all the respondents when questioned about their feelings towards the hot-desk policy. Although it was unusual for employees to hot-desk daily, almost all the respondents had moved desks during the course of the research, some several times – even within the design-studio. This constant upheaval was not enjoyed by any of the respondents and even when it was unlikely that people would have to move desks for quite some time, the **possibility** of having to move at some point in the future still impacted on their sense of security. Importantly for my purposes here, people felt that this was reflected in the degree of personalisation their desks exhibited. As I have already mentioned above, several respondents explained to me how the permanent desks they had occupied in Dept. X's previous office space had been covered with personal effects and how repeated moves had meant they personalised their desks less and less. The general feeling that they no longer personalised to the same degree as they had done before was retold to me in the majority of cases with a tinge of nostalgic sadness as the following interview extracts show:

"I think this desk is probably the most impersonal of all the desks I've had because I used to sit round the corner for ages and ages and that was great cos I had all sorts of pictures and photographs and stuff and then the project came to an end and it was like 'oh you can't sit there anymore'. And then I went to America and when I came back and everything I had was in a box... but I'm loathe to get all this out of a box again, to put it all up when [sigh]... Hot-desking. I can't stand it.... You see I'm loathe to put anything up now cos I'll have to take it all down again, and that's always a bit sad because you know you've been sat there sometimes for the best part

of a year and then had to take everything down… its not even a case of not being bothered, its just, I dunno – when projects are typically four to six weeks long, you don't ever feel settled in one place…" (M-D-2)

This respondent too talks of similar experiences of hot-desking and personalisation:

"For the first three months when I got here, I was moved around so much that I do recall thinking maybe I shouldn't put anything up to tempt fate! And the other thing is that I'm actually sat in someone else's desk – it's reserved for someone else who's on a project – so even though she'll probably never sit at that desk, it's still got the reserved

sign up there – so I don't feel that it's mine particularly, which is probably why I haven't really put much stuff up." (F-D-2)

This sense of being unsettled by hot-desking was echoed right through the data. Words respondents used to capture this feeling ranged from *"putting down roots"* when they had been in a desk for a while (or felt as though they would be there for some time – regardless of the reality of the situation) to feeling like *"floating bodies"* when a project ended and the *"alien experience"* of no longer having a place dedicated personally to them. The respondents' observations that they personalised less when they perceived they would have to hot-desk frequently was matched by my own observations of the environment. Desks with the most transient occupancy were those that displayed the least amount of personal objects, whereas some of the designers desks were almost totally covered in personal paraphernalia.

Thus, rather than an expression of individual territorial control, the extent to which a desk had been personalised (in this particular study) showed the degree of permanence the occupant felt in that place and moreover, the extent to which they felt a sense of 'belonging' – given that personalisation appeared to be a group norm – within the community of designers at least – something writers on group dynamics have long identified as an important element in the cohesiveness of the group (Tuckman 1965) but which is absent from the existing literature concerned with personalisation of organizational space.

142

Conclusion

We have seen from the above discussion of the data generated by this project how the practice of hot-desking discouraged the respondents from personalising their workspace, despite the fact that the management of Dept. X did not actively discourage employees from displaying personal objects and material on and around their work areas. Personalisation was seen by the respondents as important, even if they did not extensively personalise their own space. The data suggests that personalisation is a meaningful conduit for emotional and aesthetic expression – something that respondents felt helped them maintain a sense of balance between their work and non-work selves, as well as contributing to a more psychologically comfortable work environment. Moreover, displays of personal objects were important in the creation of a 'work-self' or identity – based not on a need to establish individual territory or autonomy, but stemming from a desire to identify with a wider organizational group or community. Objects and personal displays expressed the degree to which the occupant felt they belonged to their space and the affiliation they felt with their community. Consequently, differences in the degree of personalisation exhibited can be linked to the regularity with which the occupant felt he or she had to move desks. Those who felt their occupation to be transient generally regretted that they were unable to make their space 'home' by displaying personal items on and around their desks.

Although the findings of this study are limited in scope and not intended to be generalised to other organizational populations, the parallels between the data presented here and other studies and theoretical treatments of object-subject attachment outside the organizational arena is notable. Furthermore, these data resonate with the findings from one of the most recent and wide-ranging studies of the physical work environment carried out by The Industrial Society (Nathan and Doyle 2002).

I therefore conclude by suggesting that hot-desking as a flexible, 'speedy' organizational practice may sit uncomfortably with employees' psychological and social needs at work. Despite representing significant benefits to the organization, the need for speed that the practice of hot-desking embodies seems to be clearly at odds with employees' desire for stability, permanence and belonging at work.

References

Altman, Irwin (1975) *Environment and Social Behaviour: Privacy, personal space, territory and crowding*, Pacific Grove CA: Brooks/Cole.

Ashworth, Jon (1997) 'Virtual office becomes a reality for BA', *The Times*, London p. 371.

Banks, Stephen & Banks, Anna (eds.) (1998) *Fiction and Social Research: By ice or fire,* Walnut Creek CA: Altamira Press.

Belk, Russell (1988) 'Possessions and the Extended Self', *Journal of Consumer Research,* Vol. 15 pp. 139–168.

Berger, Peter & Luckmann, Thomas (1967) *The Social Construction of Reality: A treatise in the sociology of knowledge,* London: Allen Lane.

Callon, M. (1986) 'Some Elements of a Sociology of Translation: Domestication of the Scallops and the Fisherman of St. Brieuc Bay' in J. Law (ed.) *Power, Action and Belief: a new sociology of knowledge?* London: Routledge & Kegan Paul.

Coffey, Amanda (1999) *The Ethnographic Self: Fieldwork and the representation of identity,* London: Sage.

Conroy, Harry (2000) 'The stuff of life: British designers Luke Pearson and Tom Lloyd are dedicated to injecting life into inanimate functional items', *Financial Times: Inside Business,* London 1/7/00 p. 1128.

Csikszentmihalyi, Mihalyi & Rochberg-Halton, Eugene (1981) *The Meaning of Things: Domestic Symbols and the self,* Cambridge: Cambridge University Press.

Czarniawska, Barbara (1999). *Writing Management: Organization theory as literary genre,* Oxford: Oxford University Press.

Daniels, Shirley (1994) 'The Hot Desk Shuffle', *Work Study,* Vol. 43 (7) pp. 7.

Davis, Tim (1984) 'The Influence of the Physical Environment in Offices', *Academy of Management Review,* Vol. 9(2) pp. 271–283.

Denzin, Norman (1994) 'The Art and Politics of Interpretation' in N. Denzin & Y. Lincoln (eds.) *Handbook of Qualitative Research,* London: Sage.

Eadie, Alison (2000) 'A Wheely good wheeze for the office', *Daily Telegraph: City: Business File: Management Matters,* London 13/7/00 p. 541.

Emmison, Michael and Smith, Philip (2000) *Researching the Visual,* London: Sage.

Flexibility Forum www.flexiblity.co.uk/forum accessed 9/4/02.

Geertz, Clifford (1988) *Works and Lives: The anthropologist as author,* Stanford CA: Stanford University Press.

Gillies, Midge (1998) 'Don't get too fond of that desk – it's hot', *The Observer: Workplace,* London 17/5/98 pp. 755.

Goodwin, Bill (2000) 'Hot-desking forms the new ICL eco-system', *Computer Weekly,* 30/11/00 p. 12.

Gottschalk, Simon (1998) 'Postmodern Sensibilities and Ethnographic Possibilities' in S. Banks and A. Banks (eds) *Fiction and Social Research: By ice or fire,* Walnut Creek, CA: Altamira Press, pp. 205–233.

Gummesson, Evert (1999) *Qualitative Methods in Management Research,* London: Sage.

Hammersley, Martin and Atkinson, Paul (1995) *Ethnography: Principles in Practice,* London: Routledge.

Hilper, Kate (2000) 'The sweet smell – and colour – of success', *The Guardian: Office Hours,* London & Manchester 9/10/00.

Hoare, Stephen (1999) 'How to feel at home without the office', *The Times,* London 23/11/99 p. 912.

Kwint, Marius (1999) 'The Physical Past' in M. Kwint, C. Breward, & J. Aynsley (eds.) *Material Memories: Design and evocation,* Oxford: Berg pp. 1–16.

Kwint, Marius, Breward, Christopher & Aynsley, Jeremy (eds.) (1999) *Material Memories: Design and evocation,* Oxford: Berg.

Latour, Bruno (1999) 'On Recalling ANT' in J. Law and J. Hassard (eds.) *Actor Network Theory and After,* Blackwell: Oxford pp. 15–25.

Law, John (1986) 'Notes on the Theory of the Actor-Network: Ordering, Strategy and Heterogeneity', *Systems Practice,* Vol. 5 pp. 379–393.

Linstead, Stephen (1994) 'Objectivity, Reflexivity, and Fiction: Humanity, inhumanity and the science of the social' *Human Relations,* Vol. 47 (11) pp. 1321–1346.

Management Development Review (1997) "Welcome to the office 'hotel'", *Management Development Review,* Vol. 10 (4) pp. 145–147.

Mead, George Herbert (1934) *Mind, Self and Society: From the standpoint of a social behaviorist,* London: University of Chicago Press.

Mitchell, Richard & Charmaz, Kathy (1996) 'Telling Tales and Writing Stories: Postmodern visions and realist images in Ethnographic Writing', *Journal of Contemporary Ethnography,* Vol. 25 (1) pp. 144–166.

Murphy, John (1995) 'Space: The final frontier', *Computer Weekly,* 23/2/95 pp. 30–32.

Nathan, Max & Doyle, Judith (2002) *The State of the Office: The politics and geography of working space,* London: The Industrial Society.

Patton, Michael (1990) *Qualitative Evaluation and Research Methods,* London: Sage.

Pink, Sarah (2001) *Doing Visual Ethnography,* London: Sage.

Remenyi, D., Williams, B., Money, A. & Swartz, E. (1998) *Doing Research in Business and Management: An introduction to process and method,* London: Sage.

Sanger, Jack (1996) *The Compleat Observer: A field research guide to observation,* London: Falmer Press.

Saunders, Bill (2002) 'The Inside Track: Hot-desking', *Guardian On-line,* accessed 9/4/02 http://jobs.guardian.co.uk/officehours/story/0,9897,644306,00.htm.

Scheiberg, Susan (1990) 'Emotions on Display: The personal decoration of workspace', *American Behavioral Scientist,* Vol. 33 (3) pp. 330–338.

Schultz Kleine, Susan, Kleine III, Robert & Allen, Chris (1995) 'How is a possession "me" or "not me"? Characterizing types and an antecedant of material possession attachment', *Journal of Consumer Research,* Vol. 22 (3) pp. 327–344.

Schwartz, Dona (1994) 'Visual Ethnography: Using photography in qualitative research', *Qualitative Sociology,* Vol. 12(2) pp. 119–154.

Steele, Fred (1973) *Physical Settings and Organizational Development,* London: Addison-Wesley.

Sommer, Robert and Steiner, Katherine (1988) 'Office Politics in a State Legislature', *Environment and Behavior,* Vol. 10 (5) pp. 550–575.

Stretton, Mark (2000) 'Bean Counters Call in the Bean bags', *Sunday Times,* London 9/7/00 p. 232.

Sundstrom, Eric (1986) *Workplaces: The psychology of the physical environment in offices and factories,* London: Cambridge University Press.

Wagner, Jon (1979) *Images of Information,* London: Sage.

Walker, Rob & Wiedel, Janine (1985) 'Using photographs in a discipline of words' in R. Burgess *Field Methods in the Study of Education* London: Falmer Press.

Wallendorf, Melanie & Arnould, Eric (1988) '"My favorite things": A cross-cultural inquiry into object attachment, possessiveness, and social linkage', *Journal of Consumer Research,* Vol. 14 pp. 531–547.

Warren, Samantha (2005a) *Consuming Work: An exploration of organizational aestheticization,* Unpublished PhD thesis, University of Portsmouth, UK.

Warren, Samantha (2005b) 'Photography and voice in critical, qualitative, management research', *Accounting, Auditing and Accountability Journal,* Vol. 18 (6) *forthcoming.*

Wells, Meredith (2000) 'Office Clutter or Meaningful Personal Displays: The role of office personalization in employee and organizational well-being', *Journal of Environmental Psychology,* Vol. 20 (3) pp. 239–255.

Appendix 1

Respondents are referred to using a three digit code which identifies their sex, occupation and number in the study eg: M-D-2. The code can be interpreted as follows:

M – Male
F – Female
D – Graphic Designer
P – Project Producer
T – Technical (programmer)
S – Support staff

Chapter 7

Mythologies of Speed and Israel's Hi-Tech Industry

Tammar B. Zilber

Acknowledgments. Research and writing were supported by The Israel Science Foundation (grant No. 1230/05), as well as by The Harvey L. Silbert Center for Israel Studies and The Levi Eshkol Institute for Social, Economic and Political Research in Israel, both of the Social Science Faculty; and by the Recanati Foundation and The Asper Center for Entrepreneurship, both of the Jerusalem School of Business Administration, all at the Hebrew University of Jerusalem. Thanks to Nurit Cohen for her help in collecting the data. Special thanks to Yehuda Goodman for the ongoing discussion of this paper.

> Speed, *noun*. … Old English *sped* (originally in the sense: success); related to *spowan* to succeed, Latin *spes* hope, Old Slavonic *spèti* to be lucky (Collins English Dictionary).

> The dream and the vision … [like] video conference on the go, these things will happen, but they happen in a much slower pace than what we have thought before. … reality starts to dictate its pace, it isn't just our dreams setting up the tempo (Co-founder and current VP in one of Israel's most successful start-ups, talking in a Business Conference, December 2001).

In this chapter, I explore the role of speed as a (Western) cultural theme working its way anew within hi-tech mythology. I aim at deconstructing "speed" as a "knowledge/power" construct in high-tech. "Speed" has been glorified in hi-tech rhetoric, just as much as "hi-tech" has been glorified in the economical and social discourse during the bubble years (De Cock, Fitchett & Farr, 2001; De Cock, Fitchett & Volkmann, 2005; Thrift, 2001; Zilber, 2006). Both were glorified, I argue, because they are perceived as embodiments of our aspirations for the modern ideal of progress and of success in conquering the world.

Hi-Tech Organizations and Speed

The hi-tech industry is a major sector of the Israeli economy in the past decade (Carmel & de Fontenay, 2004; Kipnis, 2004). Until lately it was considered as "the engine" which was pulling the economy forward. According to the Central Bureau of Statistics, in the year 2000 the hi-tech industry employed about 150,000 people (8% of the work force in the business division); Its annual growth rate was 58%. It contributed 21% of the national product and one third of Israeli export ($15 Billion US), and it was responsible to 74% of the national product growth (start-up companies amounted to half of that growth). In terms of hi-tech entrepreneurship, Israel was ranked quite high in comparison to other (and larger) countries (Reynolds, Hay & Camp, 1999; Reynolds, Hay, Bygrave, Camp & Autio, 2000). Once the consequences of the March 2000 NASDAQ harsh fall were slowly being apprehended, the hi-tech industry was portrayed as the weight that drags the economic markets – both in Israel and abroad – into a recession. Either way, hi-tech is central to the Israeli economy – and is still a major player in the world economy at large.

Yet, hi-tech is not only an economic sector, and its significance stems not only from its economic consequences or technological innovations. Hi-tech "mythology" (after Barthes, 1972 [1957]) – images, symbols and myths that constitute it as a cultural phenomenon – has diffused very quickly to other arenas of social life. For example, whereas in 1995 some 437 articles in *Haaretz* Israeli daily newspaper included the term "hi-tech" (about one a day), in the year 2000, 1533 such articles were published (about five a day).[1] Moreover, whereas in 1995 most of the articles that mentioned the term "hi-tech" appeared in the business sections, as we move on in time, this term was spread to all other sections as well, including news, opinion columns, art, fashion, sports and cooking. This remarkable growth in the number of items on hi-tech (3.5 times more over a period of 6 years), and the move of hi-tech terminology from the business section to other parts of the newspaper, mirrors (and affects) the transformation of the hi-tech industry from a merely economic enterprise into a cultural-symbolic phenomenon. As such, deconstructing "speed" in hi-tech enables us to learn not only about hi-tech alone, but about the broader cultural world as well.

The very definition of "hi-tech firms" is debated in the literature (Baruch, 1997; Koberg, Sarason & Rosse, 1996; Medcof, 1999). Yet, reviewing the research literature on high-technology organizations, it seems that there is

---

[1] *Haaretz*'s computerized archive covers the years from mid-1994 to the present and is the most elaborated among Israeli daily newspapers. The growth of Israel's hi-tech industry is dated to the last ten years (Khavul, 2000), thus 1995 serves as a good starting point. It is reasonable to assume that findings from earlier years would have been even more impressing.

general agreement that these organizations are characterized by operating under severe time pressures (e.g. Kunda, 1992; Perlow, 1998, 1999; Perlow, Okhuysen & Repenning, 2002). The fast-paced, high-pressure atmosphere characteristic of high-tech firms was also portrayed in the popular depictions of hi-tech, under titles like: "*Amazon.com: Get Big Fast*" (Spector, 2002); "*21 Dog Years: Doing Time @ Amazon.com*" (Daisey, 2002); "*dot.bomb: My Days and Nights at an Internet Goliath*" (Kuo, 2001); and "*Show-stopper! The breakneck race to create Windows NT and the next generation at Microsoft*" (Zachary, 1994; for an early example, see also Kidder, 1981).

According to the literature, these characteristics stem from the nature of the environment within which hi-tech organizations are operating. The risky, dynamic, uncertain and highly competitive environment creates the need to operate fast in order to capitalize on their innovations (e.g.. Bahrami, 1992; Bahrami & Evans, 1989; Evans, 1991; Galunic & Eisenhardt, 1996; Hansen, Chesbrough, Nohria, & Sull, 2000; Koberg, Uhlenbruck, & Sarason, 1996).

It is my claim here that speed is not only a technical, or functional requirement, stemming from the "objective" characteristic of the hi-tech industry. Rather, I will show that to fully understand "speed" in hi-tech, we need to attend to its symbolic powers. Looking at the symbolic meanings of "speed" in hi-tech, we will be able to better appreciate it as a driving force of this industry.

Methods

Data and analysis. Hi-tech imagery was gathered from various social arenas (multi-sited research) and at different levels: From individual (e.g. hi-tech employees); to organizational (stories told in hi-tech firms); to industry (educational and training programs for hi-tech entrepreneurs and managers; hi-tech conferences) and to the societal (media representations of hi-tech, such as hi-tech want-ads and advertisement, press coverage of hi-tech).

The main data-collection methods included interviewing (Kvale, 1996; Rubin & Rubin, 1995), participant observation (Jorgensen, 1989; Spradley, 1980) and media inspection (Altheide, 1996; Berger, 1998). Data collection spanned from late 2001 to 2003.

I used various methods of textual analysis (Boje, 2001; Lieblich, Tuval-Mashiach & Zilber, 1998; Stillar, 1998) and media analysis (Altheide, 1996; Berger, 1998; Silverblatt, 1995), in accordance with grounded-theory approaches and the cyclic nature of qualitative inquiry (Glaser & Strauss, 1967; Strauss & Corbin, 1990).

Deconstructing Hi-Tech Speed

Speed runs through and is "manufactured" in many arenas of the hi-tech industry – thus affecting, legitimizing and reinforcing various organizational structures, practices and goals. This power of speed is manifested in four main dimensions: (1) Technology; (2) Change of scale; (3) Competition; (4) Evaluation of the year 2000 crisis.

Technology: Dreaming fast

To begin with, hi-tech takes pride in the ever-growing acceleration of transferring information – achieved through wide band, processor/memory/chips/disks/boards/cards and systems speeds, and by compression. This rhetoric of speed is evident in hi-tech advertisements in which one of the most important driving forces of a new product is its better speed compared to its predecessors. Paying a higher price for a product or replacing an older one is thus legitimated mainly on the factor of speed.

Visual images in hi-tech want-ads, for example, are flooded with movement – depicting the human body, cars, animals and hi-tech objects (like cell phones) in motion. One ad depicts an elephant standing on a skateboard, "riding" on a graph which describes the security market between 1999–2002. The caption reads: "Join a market on the rise." Note the image of the elephant – one of the heaviest animals. It too can become fast, like a circus-elephant standing on a ball. The ad alludes to the circus, magic, play – and, at the same time, to prospects of great wealth. Thus, it couples speed with fortune. In other ads, the captions couple speed with wisdom. For example, in an ad for Actelis Networks:[2] "act fast, act smart – act actelis." Sometimes, speed is coupled with progress, like in the following ad for Analog Devices Israel:[3] "Come and build with us an advanced, faster and smarter world."

Interestingly, many of the speed-enabling technological possibilities or features turned out to be too much (too early?) for consumers and markets' needs (serving as a partial explanation of the "burst of the bubble"). Yet, this didn't seem to affect the industry's excitement about them.

Speed functions not only as an objective scale, but also as a cultural and symbolic phenomenon. In an ad by Galileo Technology,[4] the visual image depicts a male figure standing with arms wide open, as if celebrating a victory

---

[2] http://www.actelis.com/ The firm offers a solution for data delivery over the existing copper plant.

[3] http://www.analog.com. Analog devices Israel Ltd., is an R&D center of an USA based semiconductor company that develops, manufactures and markets high performance integrated circuits (ics) used in signal processing applications.

[4] Galileo Technology, which designs and markets complex semiconductor devices, is now part of Marvell Technology Group http://www.marvell.com/.

or worshipping. The caption reads: "1,000,000,000,000 Bits per second." Underneath, the caption claims: "At this pace, everything is possible." What is "everything"? It seems as if speed itself opens new opportunities. When hi-tech firms claim to be "setting the tempo" they do not mean just in technical and narrowly defined terms (inventing and/or manufacturing the infrastructure which enables hi-speed information transfer, etc.). They mean that they are pacing the world itself. Motorola semiconductor Israel,[5] for example, claimed to be "moving the world forward", and Intel Israel[6] professed: "One little improvement can move the world forward, much faster....". This ad showed a turtle that has wheels instead of legs, and the visual effects make it seem to be in fast motion. Note the visual image of the turtle, the slowest animal in Western mythology. Yet, as the fable about the tortoise and the hare tells us,[7] it is not enough being fast, one needs to be committed as well. Of course, imagine what happens if one is *both*!

Change of scale

Speed seemed to resonate and to be manufactured not only in relation to technical specifications, but in the hi-tech rhetoric and in various organizational practices and conceptions as well.

Economic time scales, for example, seemed to be shrinking: Reviewing financial data in the media and in hi-tech conferences, "history" was measured in quarters not years. Eight quarters back were represented as "ancient times". Historically, the hi-tech industry in the West is more than 50 years old, certainly some 30 years in Israel. Yet in the rare occasions that "history" was discussed, people were usually talking about two or three years back (ten years max). "I would like to give an histori-

---

[5] Motorola semiconductor Israel was founded in 1964, and is one of Motorola's world-wide sites. The company provides integrated communications and embedded electronic solutions. It has 5 R&D and one manufacturing sites in Israel, and employs some 4,000 people. http://israel.motorola.com/
[6] Intel Israel was founded in 1974, as Intel's first R&D center outside the USA. Intel supplies computer and communication solutions. Today, Inter Israel has 6 R&D and manufacturing centers in Israel, and employs some 6,000 people. http://www.intel.com/il/index.htm
[7] The Tortoise and the hare (source: http://www.first-school.ws/t/turtlehareen.htm): A Hare one day ridiculed the short feet and slow pace of the Tortoise, who replied, laughing: "Though you be swift as the wind, I will beat you in a race." The Hare, believing this assertion to be simply impossible, assented to the proposal; and they agreed that the Fox should choose the course and fix the goal. On the day appointed for the race the two started together. The Tortoise never for a moment stopped, but went on with a slow but steady pace straight to the end of the course. The Hare, lying down by the wayside, fell fast asleep. At last waking up, and moving as fast as he could, he saw the Tortoise had reached the goal, and was comfortably dozing after his fatigue. "Slow but steady wins the race."

cal review", said the Hi-Tech partner in the Israeli branch of a Big Four[8] accounting firm, "and I mean *real* history, the beginning of 2000, one year backwards, which is – for us – like 30 years back" (Entrepreneurs course, 11.3.2001). In two key-note addresses in the Annual Hi-Tech Conference 2001 sponsored by the Israeli branch of a Big Four accounting firm, reviews of the "state of the industry" were given (one for the US and another for the Israeli market). The PowerPoint presentations included a handful of slides, depicting graphs of start-up fund raising, rounds, VC's and so on – the data usually dated back as far as 1998.

Organizational trajectory within this industry was also transformed: The common depiction of a "successful" hi-tech start-up life-cycle outlined a wondrous jump or a very expeditious development from a small-scale initiative, based on a technological innovation, through a few rounds of capital-raising, and quickly becoming a multinational firm with eight figures markets (or bought by such a firm). Falling short of this pace has been conceived as a "failure". For example, in a hi-tech entrepreneurs course in September–December 2000, a presenter talked about the order of capital raising rounds of hi-tech start-ups. He mentioned four such stages: Seed, 1st, 2nd, 3rd (expansion or mezzanine) and "exit" (IPO or M&A[9]). These were considered to be the preferred ways to make money out of the business (as against running the company for a long time and making profits through sales.) He advised his audience to always raise more money than they think they would need, as "CEO's do not like to be busy with capital raising all the time". He repeated this advice a couple of times, creating the impression that these rounds are quite close to each other, each of them – and the entire cycle – happening very fast. Two meetings were dedicated to a computerized start-up simulation. In the instructions, the goal was defined as: "to manage the start-up for five years. Good luck."

All real cases presented in two entrepreneur courses I attended depicted this wondrous jump. A representative of an Israeli investment bank for start-ups, introduced the story of "Europe's premier" company offering an on-line service. The slide shows two time scales. One, at the bottom, is measured by months, and marks four significant events in the life of the firm. In April 1998, the company raised $850,000 from private sources. In February 1999, it raised $12M at the valuation of $45M from European VCs. Four months later, in June, it raised $30M (at an evaluation of $260M) from a French private holding company. Finally, in October that same year, the firm floated on the London Stock Exchange and NASDAQ, raising $90M (at an

---

[8] One of the four internationally leading accounting firms. In fact, back in 2000–2001, there were still Big Five (in 2002 Arthur Andersen surrendered its license as a result of the Enron scandal).

[9] IPO – Initial Public Offering. M&A – Merger and acquisition.

evaluation of $375M). The success came about, then, within just 18 months. To further highlight the speed of success (it is, after all, a success story), a yellow "star" hovers over the conventional time table, with a caption that reads: "Just 18 months from start-up to almost $400M valuation." The yellow "star" is similar to the representation of explosion, common in the graphic language of comics. That is, even the shortened time scale, collapses into a big (The Big) bang.

The presentation of such success stories defines "success" in hi-tech. Nothing short of a wondrous and fantastic organizational development would do. Organic and natural development was out. Only supernatural growth was acceptable. Not only the conception of success was changed, but along with it the very understanding of "mature" development, time horizon and "experience".

Hi-tech presentations. Speed is evident in how the industry is depicted, and in the very form of its presentation. In entrepreneurs' courses, would-be entrepreneurs were instructed on how to connect with and present themselves to venture capitalists (VCs) in order to raise money for their start-ups. The message was: be fast, do it short – send a business plan, but be sure that they will only read the executive summary. Present your business in 15 minutes or less. Be prepared to present your idea/company in a 3 minutes "elevator pitch", in "One sentence, one [PowerPoint] bullet" (A VC partner talking at an entrepreneurs' course). The need to be speedy is nicely represented in the following quotation, where the speaker connects speed with height:

> Do remember one thing in regard to your presentation. The idea is to run from A to Z, very fast. We in Garage [.com] used to say: fly at 30,000 feet height .... Don't go too low. Come down low – and you will crash. (A Vc partner, talking at an entrepreneur course, 11.3.2001)

Indeed, at all public events I attended and recorded, people made constant remarks about speed. Almost all presenters apologized for being in a hurry and hence not having the time to elaborate. Many of them talked much about all the things they would have liked to have addressed, if not limited by time.

VC's. Speed was celebrated from the VCs' side as well. For example, one of Israel's most known and (temporarily) very successful investment bank for hi-tech start-ups, prided itself for the speedy processing of applications – eight weeks maximum for investments of hundreds of thousands of US dollars. In fact, their entire business plan and innovation was based upon this speed processing. Their logo showed a baby turning into a man. They promised to help start-up companies develop "with the speed of the Internet".

Speed transformed the *typical employee and managers* profile as well, calling off (and challenging) not only geographical boundaries, but also social ones. The successful entrepreneur was rhetorically and visually constructed as creative, unconventional, relatively inexperienced, and – *young*. No wonder, then, that hi-tech want-ads featured only young-people's images. Moreover, young hi-tech employees were presented as role models, their consumption choices as rational choices to be followed by all. A campaign for a Ford focus car centered around the images of hi-tech young employees. Some of the captions were: "You can identify them by the gadgets on the table, the options in their pocket, and also by the cars parked outside"; "They can teach you the new hot thing on the Internet, which stocks to buy, and also in which car to invest"; "Those who spend their days inventing the new hot thing, can probably identify success"; "They demand an unconventional work environment, above the average salary, and a real nonstandard car"; And, in an ad showing a young Israeli woman with a man and a woman of Asian origin, the caption read: "They were impressed by your speedy decisions, your business thinking, and the way with which you take the curves…".

An aura of *childish playfulness* characterized many campaigns – including quotations from children books (Alice in Wonderland), balloons, marbles, and children games and popular pastime, as if saying that work in high tech is like play. With speed, the young manage to transform work into play, and still succeed on the grown-ups' field. With speed, the young grow up fast enough to stay young and take the place of the old.

Known Western perceptions of *"career" and future life plans* were transformed by a fantasy of becoming rich enough to quit work at the age one's parents were barely starting to get anxious about their mid-life crisis. Hence, a pension plan advertisement featured a man sitting at his desk, but instead of looking at his computer, his legs were on top of the desk, and he was dressed up for a fishing trip and holding a fishhook in his hand. The caption read: "Imagine that one day you will quit work, and do what you really love." According to the small print, one of the unique features of that pension plan was the accumulation of pensions privileges in a short period of ten years. No wonder, then, that the man in the ad was surprisingly young.

The rhetoric of speed is part of a new rhetoric of scale that characterized the hi-tech-bubble-period, and the "new economy" at large. This rhetoric marks a drastic change of scales. Technological gadgets had to be smaller and smaller. Start-ups valuations grew higher and higher. Management and employees turned younger. These changes marked and grew out of a total change of scales and measures. In this context, speed became a must – technology should work faster, organizational life cycles turned faster.

This change of scales in general, and the rhetoric of speed in particular, might be related to a loss of a central notion of time, that of the time yet to come. The "future" as a time zone further away hardly exists in the material

I gathered. Rather, the future is represented as appearing now. Hi-tech firms claimed to be "inventing" the future. For example, IXI Mobile, a privately held firm that develops wireless data services and devices,[10] claimed "The future is in our hands", and Elishra[11] announced: "When the hi-tech world works on tomorrow's projects, in Elishra we think about the day after tomorrow. Tomorrow is over." With no time horizon further ahead, other time perceptions changed as well. The present becomes the never-ending workday. The celebration of young age and disrespect for experience works in the same direction, of turning known and traditional time scales upside down.

Competition: Speeding up (to the top)

"Speed" is not only a feature of objects and practices, it is a dynamic motivational force working especially as a comparative notion. In order to be fast, you should be faster than someone else, who is necessarily slower than you are. Hence, the rhetoric of speed is actually a rhetoric of competition.[12] Indeed, many of the want-ads that related to speed, coupled it with winning a competition. The ad for a company named "Be Connected" features three round images: a speedometer with the title "be fast"; a sperm forcing its way into an ovum, with the title "be first", and the company logo (green circle with the words "be connected" in it). Meaning, only by being fast – like we in "Be Connected" are – will you be able to succeed like the sperms that compete for the ovum in the reproduction process. Another ad, by Actelis Networks,[13] quotes Albert Einstein's saying that "knowledge will take you to the last mile, imagination will take you there faster". The ad features a graphic image of movement, and the caption reads: "Actelis. The first to cross the last mile." In an ad for SuperCom,[14] we see the audience at a sports match. The people in the center hold a banner, which reads: "When progress and technology are the name of the game, SuperCom will get you a front

---

[10] IXI Mobile was founded in August 2000 in Tel Aviv, Israel. It is now headquartered in Redwood City, California with a research and development center outside of Tel Aviv, Israel. IXI employs 65 people, the majority of them in R&D. IXI is privately held. The company specializes in custom-made cellular devices. http://www.iximobile.com/

[11] Elishra, part of Tadiran Telecom (http://www.tadirantele.com), develops military communications equipment.

[12] I would like to thank Nurit Cohen for this insight.

[13] See note 2 above.

[14] http://www.supercomgroup.com. Founded in 1988, publicly traded since 1999. A technology integrator and a solution provider of high-end smart card production systems and secured governmental document publishing solutions.

row ticket." InfraCom,[15] which developed infrared communication, offered "success at your fingertips", and its logo read: "light years ahead".

The rhetoric of competition was also evident in the way two start-ups CEOs presented their companies in a start-up show at the Israel's hi-tech industry 2002 annual meeting:

> XXX is quite a veteran company. It was founded in 1990 ... [we operate in] a total market, potential market of one billion dollars per year. Our technology is ahead of our competitors by 18 to 24 months. We are racing ahead to increase this gap as much as we can.

> The company started to sell its product about 6 months ago, it's going very fast, and slowly becoming a leader in its field.

Celebrating speed is actually celebrating winning, in a zero-sum game. Hence, the rhetoric of hi-tech speed in the past decade re-infuses "speed" with its original lexical meanings – that is, of prosperity, success, hope and good luck.

The bursting of the bubble: From dreams to a realistic tempo?

With the speed of light, the rhetoric of hi-tech turned around, from celebrating the industry to lamenting it. This change was clearly evident in hi-tech inner circles. Speed has a central place in this rhetoric of repentance, which testifies to its central role in the rhetoric of hi-tech before the "bursting of the bubble":

> [Our last] conference was held two years ago, in 1999. Just two years ago, [yet] in the previous century. We heard talks about the Internet, as a huge wave that will sweep us all toward a bright and amazing future. We heard analyses that foresaw the collapse of the Old Economy. We heard commentaries in which the hidden overpowered the bare, in which wishes overpowered business common sense. We heard optimistic forecasts on incomes, evaluations and huge profits in various markets. Dozens of entrepreneurs walked about here, but most of their start-ups went the way of all flesh. We had "Angels", we had "First Tuesday".[16] We climbed up from the garage to

---

[15] http://www.infra-com.com. a technology company focusing on the development and commercialization of Optical Wireless Broadband solutions.

[16] First Tuesday International was a London-based business networking subsidiary, that brought entrepreneurs and investors together at networking parties held on the first Tuesday of each month. It was established in 1999 and went global within a couple of months, acquired by YAZAM.COM, an Israeli investment bank for start-ups on July 2000 for an estimated 50M$ in a shares deal. On April 2001 the company was purchased by its network of First Tuesday sites, comprising a majority of the city licensees, and by a group of private investors. Many see it as an example of the New Economy hype: a London-based matchmaking club for Internet entrepreneurs turned into a big international business, connected with big multinational names.

the management floor. In the Oval Office we spoke about reforms, about the boiling stock exchange.... We were dreaming. [Now] optimism turned into sobriety. The New Economy returned in shame to the boardrooms. Haste returned to the devil. (The coordinator, opening remarks, hi-tech conference, 2.12.2001)

As part of after-the-bubble remorse, the rhetoric of speed was brought to ridicule:[17]

Two years ago, if an investor blinked his eyes, he would have lost the investment.... In the time of the bubble, seed-stage venture capital firms had the pretense to "bring companies from A to Z at the speed of light". (Hi-tech partner, Israeli branch of a Big Four accounting firm, hi-tech conference, 2.12.2001)

We had instant start-ups. I mean, take some start-up powder, add hot water, mix, and oops, it came out good, Mirabilis![18] It doesn't work this way. One needs to go back to basics, to study business, marketing, talk with customers all the time. It's hard work. (Hi-tech partner, Israeli branch of a Big Four accounting firm, entrepreneurs course, 11.3.2001)

On the face of it, it seems as if the hi-tech industry has gone through a reality-check, and came back to the real world (see the second quotation at the beginning of this chapter). Yet, even in this after-the-bubble rhetoric, speed is still there, just a bit more hidden, but in fact framing the very estimation of the length of the current crisis:

In my opinion, the recession in which we are in today is not deeper than recessions in other industries and economies in the last century. On the contrary, I think that the current capability of people, economies and central banks to handle the recession and the drop in world economies, this capability improved. .... In my opinion, this recession is going to be *shorter* than [other recessions] in the previous century.... We will get out of this recession *faster* than we did in the case of other recessions. .... In my opinion, there is

---

[17] And with it, the celebration of youthfulness: "It [the bubble years] was like a family, where the kids took over, and not just any kids, but confused kids, adolescents. Like, the parents look at the kid and really don't know how such a thing grew up, and what to do with it." (An organizational consultant, working in "an old fashioned" hi-tech firm, characterizing and criticizing the bubble years, at an Organization Behavior seminar at the Hebrew University, April 2002).

[18] Mirabilis was founded in July 1996 by four young Israeli avid computer users. Only four months later they came up with their product – ICQ. On June 1998 America Online acquired all Mirabilis' assets for 287 M $, one of the largest hi-tech cash deals in Israel's history. As of 2005, ICQ had more than 190 million registered users worldwide and offered instant messaging and enhanced communications features.

no economic war going on, there is no nightmare. There is no dream either. All in all, there is a return to reality. .... Running a company, running any business.... It is like running long distance. It's a marathon.... and you know how to win a marathon, of course. You start with a sprint, and then increase [the tempo] a little more, a little more, a little more. (Co-founder and current VP in one of Israel's most successful start-ups, now an international and profitable firm. Conference, 2.12.2001)

Slowing Down to Think: Speed, Organizations, and the Modern Moment

As I showed above speed is a major driving force both in terms of technological specification of the industry and as a symbolic and ethical powerful resource. Speed is manifested in changing career trajectories and concepts of the self (and self esteem) and in changing more traditional time scales. Moreover, speed plays a major role in changing the very notion of what is a business success.

As I showed, speed is a diffused notion that moves on from the technical and economical into the symbolic and vise versa. We should think then about this relationship as working on all levels of the industry: Its practices, structures, values and economical and technological standards. We should also try to deconstruct speed historically: The imagery of speed is so powerful because the hi-tech imagery of speed in Israel is embedded within Israeli and Zionist ideals, and also suggest renewed ways for following them.

This dialectical relationship between the past and the present, and between collective memory and the historical moment is essential for the success of the symbolic in the social and economical realms. New images must echo to some extent socio-cultural themes, or otherwise they will not be understood, and they will not have their motivational and driving force. At the same time, they have to offer something new, or they will not be interesting and hence will not "catch on". On the symbolic level, speed became so central in hi-tech, and hi-tech so central in the economic and socio-cultural realm (for a while), for the same reasons – both speed and hi-tech hold a promise to be ideal embodiments of the modern moment in general and of the Israeli and Zionist aspirations in particular (Zilber, 2006). Speed itself – the ever rapid tempo of change – is celebrated in the modern experience (Levine, 1999). Moreover, speed resonates so well with the modern western notions of progress achieved through improved technology and understood as a deep marker of success and of mankind's victories over "nature" (Whimster & Lash, 1987). It is rooted historically in the Judaeo-Christian tradition of Man conquering earth, surpassing limitations, and of controlling the world and the animal kingdom by the decree of God.

References

Altheide, D.L. (1996) *Qualitative media analysis.* Thousand Oaks, CA: Sage.

Bahrami, H. (1992) The Emerging Flexible Organization: Perspectives from Silicon Valley. *California Management Review,* 34(4), 33–52.

Bahrami, H. & Evans, S. (1989) Emerging organizational regimes in high technology firms: The bi-modal form. *Human Resource Management,* 28(1), 25–50.

Barthes, R. (1972 [1957]) *Mythologies* (A. Lavers, Trans.). New York: Farrar, Straus and Giroux.

Baruch, Y. (1997) High technology organization: What it is, what it isn't. *International Journal of Technology Management,* 13(2), 179–195.

Berger, A.A. (1998) *Media analysis techniques.* Thousand Oaks, CA: Sage.

Boje, D.M. (2001) *Narrative methods for organizational and communication research.* London: Sage.

Carmel, E. and De Fontenay, C. (2004) Israel's Silicon Wadi: The Forces Behind Cluster Formation. In: Building High-Tech Clusters, T. Bresnahan and A. Gambardella (eds.), Cambridge, UK, Cambridge University Press, pp. 40–77.

Daisey, M. (2002) *21 dog years: Doing time @ Amazon.com.* New York: Free Press.

De Cock, C., Fitchett, J.A. & Farr, M. (2001) Myths of a near future: Advertising the new economy. *ephemera: critical dialogues on organization,* 1(3), 201–228.

De Cock, C., Fitchett, J.A. & Volkmann, C. (2005) Constructing the new economy: A discursive perspective.

Evans, J.S. (1991) Strategic flexibility for high technology maneuvers: A conceptual-framework. *Journal of Management Studies,* 28(1), 69–89.

Galunic, D.C. & Eisenhardt, K.M. (1996) The evolution of intracorporate domains: Divisional charter losses in high-technology, multidivisional corporations. *Organization Science,* 7(3), 255–282.

Glaser, B.G. & Strauss, A. (1967) *The discovery of grounded theory: Strategies for qualitative research.* New York: Aldine.

Hansen, M.T., Chesbrough, H.W., Nohria, N. & Sull, D.N. (2000) Networked incubators: Hothouses of the new economy. *Harvard Business Review,* 78(5), 74–84.

Jorgensen, D.L. (1989) *Participant observation: A methodology for human studies.* Newbury Park, CA: Sage.

Khavul, S. (2000) *Money and knowledge: Sources of seed capital and the performance of Israeli high-technology start-ups.* Unpublished Ph.D., London Business School.

Kidder, T. (1981) *The soul of a new machine.* New York: Little Brown & Company.

Kipnis, B.A. (2004) Tel Aviv, Israel – A World City in Evolution: Urban Development at a Deadend of the Global Economy. In: M Pak (ed) *Cities in Transition.* Ljubljana: Department of Geography, University of Ljubljana, pp. 183–194.

Koberg, C.S., Sarason, Y. & Rosse, J. (1996) A taxonomic approach to studying high-technology firms: Deciphering the tower of Babel. *The Journal of High Technology Management Research,* 7(1), 15–36.

Koberg, C.S., Uhlenbruck, N. & Sarason, Y. (1996) Facilitators of organizational innovation: The role of life-cycle stage. *Journal of Business Venturing,* 11 (2): 133–149.

Kou, D. (2001) *dot.bomb: My days and nights at an Internet Goliath*. New York: Little Brown & Company.

Kunda, G. (1992) *Engineering culture: control and commitment in a high-tech corporation*. Philadelphia: Temple University Press.

Kvale, S. (1996) *InterViews: An introduction to qualitative research interviewing*. Thousand Oaks, CA: Sage.

Levine, D.P. (1999) Creativity and Change: On the Psychodynamics of Modernity. *American Behavioral Scientist*, 43: 225–244.

Lieblich, A., Tuval-Mashiach, R. & Zilber, T. (1998) *Narrative research: Reading, analysis and interpretation*. Newbury Park, CA: Sage.

Medcof, J.W. (1999) Identifying 'super-technology' industries. *Research-Technology Management*, 42(4), 31–36.

Perlow, L.A. (1998) Boundary control: The social ordering of work and family time in a high-tech corporation. *Administrative Science Quarterly*, 43(2), 328–357.

Perlow, L.A. (1999) The time famine: Toward a sociology of work time. *Administrative Science Quarterly*, 44(1), 57–81.

Perlow, L.A., Okhuysen, G.A. & Repenning, N.P. (2002) The speed trap: Exploring the relationship between decision making and temporal context. *Academy of Management Journal*, 45 (5): 931–955.

Reynolds, P.D., Hay, M., Bygrave, W.D., Camp, S.M. & Autio, E. (2000) *Global entrepreneurship monitor*. Kauffman center for entrepreneurial leadership at the Ewing Marion Kauffman Foundation.

Reynolds, P.D., Hay, M. & Camp, S.M. (1999) *Global entrepreneurship monitor*. Kauffman center for entrepreneurial leadership at the Ewing Marion Kauffman Foundation.

Silverblatt, A. (1995) *Media literacy: Keys to interpreting media messages*. Westport, Connecticut: Praeger.

Spector, R. (2000) *Amazon.com: Get big fast*. New York: Harper Business.

Spradley, J.P. (1980) *Participant observation*. New York: Holt, Rinehart and Winston.

Stillar, G.F. (1998) *Analyzing everyday texts: Discourse, rhetoric, and social perspectives*. Thousand Oaks, CA: Sage.

Strauss, A. & Corbin, J. (1990) *Basics of qualitative research: Grounded theory procedures and techniques*. Newbury Park, CA: Sage.

Thrift, N. (2001) 'It's the romance, not the finance, that makes the business worth pursuing': Disclosing a new market culture. *Economy and Society*, 30(4), 412–432.

Whimster, S. & Lash, S. (1987) *Max Weber, Rationality, and Modernity*. London: Allen & Unwin.

Zachary, G.P. (1994) *Show-stopper! The breakneck race to create Windows NT and the next generation at Microsoft*. New York: Free Press.

Zilber, T.B. (2006) The Work of the Symbolic in Institutional Processes: Translation of Rational Myths in Israeli Hi-Tech. *Academy of Management Journal*, 49(2), 279–301.

SECTION III

The Speed of
Organizational Imagery

Chapter 8

Pushing Speed? The Marketing of Fast and Convenience Food

Joanna Brewis and Gavin Jack

Our sous-chefs: acknowledgements

This piece originally appeared in *Consumption, Markets and Culture* (2005, vol.8: 46–67). We are grateful to the publishers, Taylor and Francis, http://www.tandf.co.uk, for their kind permission to reproduce it here. We are also indebted to Stephen Brown, Richard Christy, Donncha Kavanagh, Martin Parker, Samantha Warren and Edward Wray-Bliss who all provided invaluable assistance in the form of references and suggestions. And grateful thanks are due to Jan McHugh who initially alerted us to the Slow Food movement and thus inspired this chapter in the first instance. Finally, two anonymous *Consumption, Markets and Culture* reviewers and the editors and reviewers of this text have helped us considerably in developing and sharpening our arguments.

Starter: fast food nation, fast food globe

> A world on the move is still a world that eats – almost non-stop it seems …
> (Kennison, 2001: 125)

Recent evidence suggests that:
- There are 26,500 McDonald's restaurants across the world, in some 119 countries.
- Four new McDonald's open per day, and roughly 2000 each year.
- An estimated one out of every eight US workers has at some point been employed by McDonald's.
- There are more than 1000 McDonald's restaurants in the UK, serving over 2.5 million people on a daily basis.
- Some 5 million Big Macs and 2.3 million cheeseburgers were sold in Greece, a country with a population of just 10.5 million, in 2000.

– Every day 0.5% of the population of the world visits a McDonald's. (Bellos *et al.*, 2001; Schlosser, 2002: 3, 4; *McDonald's*, n.d.)

It seems that Fredric Jameson's late 1980s prediction that "we'll soon be able to watch *Dallas* or eat a Big Mac in any part of the inhabited world" (cited in Hebdige, 1989: 51) may be well on its way to coming true. McDonald's, in other words, is the global brand par excellence, having superseded Coca-Cola in this respect. The familiar golden arches of its logo, a better known symbol than the Christian cross, shine out at us from tens of thousands of branches, from billboards, televisions, cinema screens and sports stadia (the firm was an 'official partner' of football's 2002 World Cup), from countless examples of merchandise, from tightly clutched brown paper bags as harried workers scuttle down our cities' streets and from rubbish in bins, gutters, train stations, playgrounds and car parks. Indeed, if we needed any more persuading of the extent to which McDonald's has become an almost unremarkable part of our cultural 'furniture', 96% of US schoolchildren were apparently able to identify corporation mascot Ronald McDonald in a recent survey. Only Santa Claus came higher in terms of recognition levels (Schlosser, 2002: 4).

Much has been written about the deleterious environmental (eg, rainforest depletion), political (eg, lobbying to ensure the passage of controversial but industry-friendly legislation), social (eg, poor employment conditions), cultural (eg, its colonization of schools and hospitals) and health (eg, obesity) effects of McDonald's business activities. This chapter, however, takes its inspiration from the fact that the best known product in the world consists of a hamburger (/cheeseburger/ Filet o' Fish/ Big Mac/ Quarter Pounder/ Egg McMuffin/ Happy Meal ...) served politely, to rigorous standards of production, hygienically, cheaply, *but above all quickly*, pretty well wherever we might find ourselves in geographical terms. In other words, McDonald's is first and foremost *fast* food, the dominant player in an ever-expanding sector in the global economy. Consider, for example, the fact that Americans spend more on fast food than on PCs, software, cars and college education and, even more dramatically, that their expenditure in this sector outstrips their spending on films, books, newspapers, videos and music – *combined* (Schlosser, 2002, 3). Similarly, in the UK, analysis of data from the Dietary and Nutritional Survey of British Adults suggests that more than a third of British men prefer a diet consisting mainly of fast food and beer (Pryer *et al.*, 2001). Moreover, the British Retail Price Index (RPI) included takeaway burgers and kebabs in its representative 'basket' of 650 goods and services (used as a measure of inflation) for the first time in February 2003, to reflect increasing spending in these areas (*National Statistics Online*, 2003).

Furthermore, it seems that we increasingly require the food we prepare ourselves to be quick and expeditious: Gleick (1999: 148, 150), for instance, claims that so-called convenience meals now take up more room in the average American supermarket than fresh fruit and vegetables. Equally noteworthy are soaring UK sales of chilled ready meals – rising by 67% between 1993 and 1997 – and the fact that 1 in 4 British women rely heavily on convenience food, as well as the recent addition of dried potted snacks to the RPI 'basket' along with certain takeaway meals as described above (Reed *et al.*, 2000, 235; Pryer *et al.*, 2001; *National Statistics Online*, 2003). It appears in fact that traditional "domestic eating" is beginning to "assume the status of a weekend and special-occasion hobby" (Taylor and Lyon, 1995: 64), whereas fast and/ or convenience food consumption increasingly represents the workaday nutritional choice, in the West at least. In short, time seems increasingly to be of the essence when it comes to Western food habits.

This chapter sets out to explore some of the putative links between fast/ convenience food marketing and Western constructions of time, to which the marked rise in the uptake of 'speedy' methods for acquiring and preparing food would seem to speak. Our starting point is a cursory scan of British television advertisements for such products. This reveals, for us at least, a set of apparent paradoxes around the ways in which they are articulated: the ads seem to celebrate both speed – time being constructed in terms of 'the same', continuity, a sense in which we can do everything we already do, only faster – and nostalgia – an emphasis on slowing down, where time is represented in terms of 'the different', discontinuity, a return to 'the good old days' when food was tastier, healthier, more varied and so on. On one level, such a paradoxical use of temporal tropes like 'speed' and 'nostalgia' might be read as nothing more than an outcome of the brand differentiation and positioning strategies of competing producers. We would argue, however, that these paradoxes can be more productively read in terms of their wider relations to the systemic and cultural vicissitudes of contemporary global capitalism, based on a range of empirical and conceptual evidence. In this regard, we contend that their relations are not so much paradoxical as dialectical and that, as such, these ads for fast and convenience foods instantiate an essential and continuing ideological structure of Modernity.

Our argument is intended to be something of a think piece, a broad-brush polemic, on the relationship between fast/ convenience food and time, situated in wider data-based and theoretical arguments about marketing and Modernity. We would not wish to argue that what *we* see in these advertisements is what the advertisers *intend us to see*, or indeed what *other consumers would see*: ours is only one of a potential series of interpretations. Instead of some form of 'authoritative' or 'expert' translation, then, what we aim to provide is a speculative and deliberately provocative reading of these texts as popular cultural artefacts which may (if our interpretation resonates at all) say something interesting about what marketers do with time, and what that implies about the Western relationship to time in a broader sense.[1]

In this we are following a trajectory outlined by Lears (1994) in his socio-historical analysis of American advertising. He asserts that advertisements are "perhaps the most dynamic and sensuous representations of cultural values in the world" (Lears, 1994: 2), whilst also explicitly acknowledging as idiosyncratic his own interpretation of how the advertising texts he deciphers connect to wider social developments. Lears also detects apparently contradictory attitudes – around two of our key themes, past and present, for example – in these texts. However, our argument differs from his in that our suggestions about the "broader cultural significance of advertising" (Lears, 1994: 3) are both narrower and broader; narrower because the argument here focuses specifically on one key social value – time – and broader in our claim that the seemingly paradoxical combination of the tropes of speed and nostalgia can be identified as enduring in marketing activities *up to and including* the present day. Lears' analysis, on the other hand, is at its most detailed when it focuses on advertisements from the period between the late nineteenth century and the onset of World War II.

Main course: speeding up and slowing down

No time to stand and stare

Starting with the advertisements, a common way of framing an understanding of time in relation to fast and convenience foods (in our eyes anyway) is in terms of speed. We see, for example, McDonald's making a deliberate play on their fast service in comparing Wimbledon 2001 men's singles champion Goran Ivanisevic's serve (134 miles per hour) and the assembling of a meal in one of their restaurants (135 miles per hour). Kentucky Fried Chicken also based a series of ads on people in a hurry – including a pair of rally drivers and a woman in labour – nonetheless having enough time to drop in and pick up a Zinger Burger. Similarly Chicago Town Pizza emphasize that their products can be eaten on the run – one advert actually shows a man being offered a pizza whilst out jogging – and a Dolmio Ready Meals advertisement suggests that their food can be prepared in the length of time it would take your upstairs neighbour to descend from their apartment to

---

[1] Nonetheless, and although we do not place any empirically grounded store by our reading of the advertisements, it is perhaps worth pointing out that the fast food industry relies much more heavily on television advertising than it does on other media (Yoon and Kim, 2001) and that the British consumer is also notable for their high consumption of convenience food especially as compared to their counterparts in mainland Europe (*Breakfast*, 2003). Even our quasi-journalistic analysis of British television advertisements may therefore be instructive with regard to the marketing uses of time, and their wider implications, in this context.

knock on your door with an unwanted invitation for the evening, thus giving you a ready excuse to decline. For us, the emphasis on time as speed in these advertising texts suggests that *fast* food of whatever type should and does appeal to us Westerners for a variety of reasons, both functional and symbolic. Indeed the economic, cultural and social contingencies of 'time poverty' appear to be writ large across the Western milieu – and Gleick (1999: 11) certainly has it that fast and convenience food companies understand, profit from and simultaneously encourage a pre-existing preoccupation with haste. Such an understanding of time poverty might lead us to interpret the increasing popularity of fast and convenience food in relation to systemic changes in Western labour markets, and the concomitant position of labour in the process of capital accumulation.

In terms of the functional appeal of these food products, the available data do imply that time *shortage* and *speed* of provision are pressing imperatives for working adults in particular. First, and as regards the consumption of fast food, it seems that this rises as available time decreases. For example, families in which both parents work spend more money on food prepared away from home than other families and much of this goes on fast food – 35.5% in 1999 in the US, up from 14.3% in 1967 (Jekanowski et al., 2001: 58). Customers also seem to want their fast food to be just that. As Davis and Heineke (1998: 72) suggest, "The perception of the waiting time [in a fast food restaurant] is particularly important when customers feel time-pressured" such that the customer in a rush will be especially sensitive to perceived waiting times. Groth and Gilliland's (2001) data point to much the same conclusion. And the fast food chains themselves are nothing if not sensitive to the importance of (perceived) speedy service – consider, for example, Gleick's (1999: 244–245) description of the text that occasionally appears through one's car window while waiting at a drive-thru McDonald's. This contains instructions to the consumer as to how to assist the restaurant in optimizing pace of service, such as having the correct change ready.

Perhaps even more salient is the same chain's ongoing efforts to increase service speed. In March 1998 the McDonald's Made For You menu was launched in the US, with the promise that customers could buy a take-away meal which would be cooked on the spot (so as to address competitive pressure from other outlets, like Wendy's International, which offered fresher and more varied food), but would still only take 90 seconds from order to exit. The system appears, however, to have failed – recent statistics from mystery shoppers suggest that service standards are being met only 46% of the time and 30% of customers have to wait more than four minutes (ie, at least 2.6 times longer than McDonald's say is the norm) to receive their food. Calls to a US freephone customer line also confirm that slow service is a major source of dissatisfaction (Gibson, 2002). Indeed in eight of the nine financial quarters prior to March 2003 the company showed what

Alexander (2003) describes as "disappointing results". Speed, then, has become a renewed McDonald's priority, and consideration is being given to returning to boxing burgers instead of wrapping them in paper as well as re-introducing assembly-line style sandwich making and warming bins (Alexander, 2003). Perhaps McDonald's is just no longer fast enough, if it ever was.

When we consider the relationship between *convenience* food and time poverty, on the other hand, it is interesting to note the claim by some researchers that hours worked, especially by women, and use of such meals and snacks are *not* positively correlated: also, those who define themselves as very 'time poor' eat a lot of fast food away from home but are much less reliant on frozen dinners etcetera (Darian and Cohen, 1995; Candel, 2001). As with McDonald's, subsequent analysis suggests that this is because so-called convenience foods are in fact *not convenient enough* – perhaps because portions are too small, and so salads or sandwiches also need to be made as a supplement, or because it is difficult to prepare more than one such meal at a time for a family due to limited microwave space. Fast food is defined as quicker and easier because little forward planning, preparation or clearing up are required, and those seeking speed and efficiency therefore seem to prefer eating takeaways or in fast food restaurants to using ready meals. Nonetheless, convenience food is still more expeditious than meals made from scratch, even if it compares unfavourably to fast food in this regard – and we should not ignore competing data which suggest that its purchase *does* in fact increase with hours worked (eg, Park and Capps, cited in Jae *et al.*, 2000: 253).

On balance, then, there would seem to be a broadly direct correlation between working hours and the consumption of fast/ convenience foods, something which reflects the fact that many of us in the West apparently suffer from time poverty. Indeed it is not much more than a truism to state that those employed in all manner of occupations often need to work long hours, perhaps with few breaks, to work antisocial hours, or even to take second or third jobs to make ends meet. Consider the fact that one in nine full time employees in the UK currently works more than 60 hours a week, although the recommended maximum is 48, and that 80% of employers have staff working over and above their standard hours (almost half of whom get no extra pay). Nightwork and other 'unsociable' shift patterns are also increasingly common, especially in retail, so as to service the emerging 24/7 society: for example, 1 in 4 British adults work at some point between 6 pm and 6 am and 34% of parents work weekends (Summerskill, 2000: 6; *The Editor*, 2000: 4). We could therefore argue that the fact that fast and convenience foods are quick and easy to buy, prepare and eat (as well as reducing washing up time) speaks to their utility in the fast-paced, tightly packed lifestyles of today – that we simply don't have enough time to buy, prepare and eat meals in the conventional way (Reed *et al.*, 2000: 235).[2] As Lyon and Colquhoun put it,

> It is something of an understatement to speak of the UK, and many similar societies, as being obsessed with the mastery of time ... the need to co-ordinate activities in time, and accomplish tasks with ever greater speed, has permeated virtually all aspects of everyday life. Many goods and services are sold on the basis of speed, efficiency or explicitly in terms of how much time they can save us. The specific characteristic of speed becomes the master variable on which we distinguish between brands and judge the progress made by manufacturers or providers. (Lyon and Colquhoun, 1999: 191)

Importantly, they offer fast food, microwaveable ready meals, pizza delivery and so on as key examples of their argument.

The intensification of the labour process and the extension of the working day may consequently be seen to provide reasons for the increasing attractiveness of expeditious forms of nutrition. Such systemic change has, for many, arguably reconfigured the socio-spatial relations associated with acquiring, making and consuming food. However, to point to a relationship between time poverty and consumer behaviour in terms of simple causalities (we have less time due to changes in working arrangements in the West and this dictates our relation to food) is to provide a reductionist and reified understanding of the role of time in consumption. To go beyond such an impoverished view, we now extend our focus on the connections between fast/ convenience food usage and time poverty to consider the wider social, historical and cultural contexts within which our notions of time have developed. In this regard we suggest that the relationship between time poverty and the consumption of fast and convenience food is not just a function of structural changes in many Western labour markets, but also an outcome of the ways in which our understandings of time have been discursively conditioned. In short, it might be claimed that the contemporary preoccupation with speed in the Western working world derives from the way in which time as an analytic category has emerged as part of Western consumer capitalism. From this perspective, we may gain some insight into the ideological nature of marketers' use of temporal tropes. That is to say, it could reveal something about how the deployment of time in this regard works in the interests of the owners of capital, instantiated here in the activities of those responsible for branding and advertising fast and convenience food.

---

[2] There is perhaps an interesting connection to be made between fast food and food avoidance (*fast*ing). If time-consuming 'traditional' meals are no longer routinely feasible in our fast-moving world, then food is theoretically relegated from the position of sustenance for life to that of a distraction from or interruption of workaday life. Do we therefore seek to sideline it by using fast food, or indeed neglect it altogether by fasting?

In unravelling this argument, we firstly acknowledge the socially constructed nature of time. Kavanagh *et al.* (2002: 17) point out, following Castoriadis, that

> all societal institutions, including that of time, are intensely and inherently 'imaginary'. And different societies, bearing different institutional forms, construct their temporality differently. All temporality is 'phantastic' and just because we in the West can convince ourselves that others all now rationally share our rational version of time, that does not mean that our time is any less rhetorical than anyone else's.

Notions of time, then, are 'imaginary' in the sense that they are a product of human minds and inscribed with particular meaning and form at particular historical moments and in particular cultural locations. As Moore (cited in Hassard, 1991: 113) tells us, "the temporal order is a social order". In this regard, and bearing in mind that we should not place *too* much faith in arguments about definitive differences between national cultures, it is worth at least mentioning Edward Hall's (1976) research into cultural attitudes to time. Hall's semi-ethnographic work argues that cultures can be roughly divided in terms of viewing time in 'monochronic' (M-time) and 'polychronic' (P-time) terms. In M-time cultures, which he suggests predominate in the industrialized West,

> time is [seen to be] linear and segmented like a road or a ribbon extending forward into the future and backward into the past. It is also [perceived as] tangible; they speak of it being saved, spent, wasted, lost, made up, accelerated, slowed down, crawling and running out. (Hall, 1976: 19)

We might therefore say that a particular conception of time – one that is Euclidean in form – has come to be significant in Western cultural systems. Importantly, though, this cultural understanding of time must be read against the historical background of the development of industrial capitalism in the West, and especially in the UK and the US. In this regard, the linear conception of time, and its possibilities of measurement, quantification and therefore control, are fundamental to capitalist relations of production, where the management of labour time and the working day lie at the heart of the mechanics for extracting surplus value (see Marx, 1976 [1867], chapter 10 of *Capital*, in this respect). Castoriadis, likewise, suggests that "the explicit institution of time in capitalism, as identitary time or the time of marking, is that of a measurable, homogeneous, uniform and wholly arithmetizable flux" (cited in Kavanagh *et al.*, 2002: 17). Similarly, although Hassard suggests that the Western sense of time has its roots in the onset of Christianity and the concept of life as a path progressing from "sin on earth, through redemption, to eternal salvation in heaven" (Hassard, 1996: 582), he goes on to assert that this metaphor of time-as-a-line took on a different

170

character under industrial capitalism. Here its linearity began to be associated with value, and thus it also became understood as both measurable and scarce. Work under capitalism is therefore typically organized according to timetables and the majority of workers are remunerated according to time spent at work.[3]

Moreover, as we witness the increasing encroachment of capitalist systems of exchange across the world, under the aegis of globalization, there is evidence that such Western conceptions of time are travelling and becoming assimilated by other cultures. Gleick (1999: 10), for instance, argues that certain enclaves in the Far East such as Tokyo, Shanghai and Hong Kong are equally obsessed with M-time. This is a theme that might also be identified as part of Ritzer's (1996) McDonaldization thesis, his impassioned critique of the spread of a particular form of technocratic rationality across the globe. For Rifkin (1989), similarly, we pay a significant price for our insistence on the precise (yet artificially imposed) quantification of time and the importance of punctuality – namely, the loss of a more organic and rhythmic sense of time as the natural context of life. Many of us could therefore be seen as cultural slaves to M-time – we seem to perceive time as a threat, as something in chronically short supply which we need to manage and dispose of with great care, having learnt "to organize our temporal expectations in accordance with particular social and cultural rules" (Hassard, 1991: 109). Importantly, it is this cultural construction of time as a quantifiable phenomenon which makes time poverty as a social and linguistic, as much as material, entity possible. And in ideological terms, the spread of this profoundly Western (European and American) understanding of time can be interpreted as a key cultural structure in the neo-imperialist impulses of contemporary global capitalism.

A related dimension in this argument is the highly symbolic nature of time poverty as a marker of having 'arrived', in the West in particular. Following this line of interpretation, it is possible to read time as part of a continuing but increasingly global history of class struggle in which time poverty can be seen as an important mediator of class relations. Accordingly, the display of time shortage positions us and others socially. For example, Bauman's (1998; also see Brewis and Linstead, 2000, 244–245) analysis of the 'first' and 'second' worlds suggests that, as capitalism globalizes, divisions (which are not always or even predominantly geographical) are developing between

---

[3] However, and further to our point above about over-relying on analyses such as Hall's, Hassard (1991, 1996) also reminds us that generalizations about prevailing constructions of time are not always helpful – for example, in his suggestion that sociology has a tendency to "gloss over the fact that the industrial world is not simply composed of machine-paced work systems, but includes a wealth of processes based on self-paced production" (Hassard, 1996: 584).

those bound by *time* and those bound by *space*. In other words, the "winners" in the new global economy are high fliers both literally and metaphorically – they are enabled to move rapidly around the planet, to follow the ever-changing dynamics of capital investment, by electronic communications and the revolution in air transportation. These are the high income groups, the professionals, the first world knowledge workers on whom emerging forms of economic activity depend for their expertise. They are also 'time poor'. For example, Gleick (1999: 91) cites Hewlett-Packard's 1998 claim that there are more than 58 million Americans and British who are "'mobile professionals', ... with a need to scan and fax contracts, newspaper articles, and market reports 'spontaneously' while they are someplace defined as between other places: driving between sales calls, or on an airplane, or waiting for an airplane".

A corollary of this analysis is that we may *aspire* to be 'time poor' – or at least to be viewed as such. As Gleick remarks, it is as if

> The more time you have on your hands, the less important you must be. So sleep in the office. Never own up to an available lunch slot ... Overwork equals importance. An overfull schedule is a sign of talisman and rank ... A peculiarly modern righteousness comes with that fifty-hour – no, sixty-hour – no, seventy-hour work week. (Gleick, 1999: 155, 159)

Reeves agrees:

> to be seen to have time to spare is a sign of low status: arranging lunch, it is never done to be available too soon ... Similarly, being late is moving from a sign of rudeness to a sign of status. (Reeves, 1999: 17)

Time therefore appears to be a negative status symbol – the less we have, the more prestige we accrue. Although Veblen's (1961 [1902]) arguments about consumption identify conspicuous *leisure* as a means for displaying social status in the early stages of Western capitalist development (as in the assumption that those at leisure can afford to be), he goes on to propose that, as capitalism takes hold, commodity consumption begins to outstrip the consumption of leisure as evidence of a high-class lifestyle. Veblen suggests that conspicuous consumption has yet to completely supersede conspicuous leisure in this regard: however, more than a century later, we could suggest that this is no longer the case. The aspirational characteristics of time poverty may as a consequence also explain, at least in part, the growing popularity of fast/ convenience foods – as Mennell (cited in Toivonen, 1997: 331) suggests, food has always been used as a means of 'social climbing'. Moreover, it is worth recalling Gleick's (1999: chapter 20) insightful argument about the difficulties of measuring the working week, or indeed the time we spend actually working when we are 'at work', as well as the evidence which suggests that we actually spend no less time at leisure despite the above-mentioned claims of a "work explosion" (Gleick, 1999: 159). With this in mind, and although many of us may not in any measurable sense be time poor, we may well perceive ourselves to be, *or at least wish to be defined*, as busy, busy people.

The speed associated with fast and convenience foods – fitting one's nutritional needs into one's 'frantic' lifestyle ever more efficiently, an emphasis on doing the same but 'better' – is therefore, we suggest, attractive to Western adults for several reasons, economic, social and cultural. It is also a moot point as to whether speed is part of such foods' function/ use value or an aspect of their form/ sign value (Bourdieu, 1984), or indeed whether the two can be easily or meaningfully separated. But in any case, whether we privilege a systemic understanding of changes in the labour market as the basis for concomitant changes in food consumption, or a more culturally inspired (where culture means ideology) understanding of time as a quantifiable commodity mediating increasingly global class relations, time is nonetheless conceived as part of the persistence of capitalist relations of production and consumption. Speed, as a temporal marketing message, speaks of and profits from a continuation of our extant cultural and economic trajectory.

Stop the world, I want to get off

On the other hand, and to return to our quick and dirty, researcher-as-couch-potato reading of British television advertisements for fast/ convenience food, we interpreted many other campaigns as referring only in passing to the 'speedy' attributes of the commodity in question. In fact some advertisements seem to shy away from the speed trope altogether, drawing on a multiplicity of other bases for differentiation. These campaigns sell their products – or so it seems to us – as not just fast but also:

- delicious/ high quality: eg, Pizza Ristorante frozen pizza, the advertising for which plays on all the tropes of the 'genuine' Italian restaurant experience, or Freshbake Ready Meals' claim that these products are as good as, if not better than, 'Grandma used to make';
- diverse: take the Village Bistro range of six varieties of microwave meals, "all" of which we will apparently "want to try";
- good for body and soul: like New Findus Wok vegetables, which are "so fresh you can taste the crunch", or the many McDonald's adverts featuring top sports players such as Ivanisevic and British footballers Alan Shearer and Teddy Sheringham;
- filling: eg, McDonald's Big Breakfast Bun and its depiction of people literally running out of 'fuel' because they haven't eaten 'properly' first thing;
- having other familiar associations: including childhood – such as Burger King's free ice-cream promotion, where the protagonist announced the

give-away from an ice-cream van as it travelled through the streets of an anonymous British Anytown – and celebrity – the aforementioned use of sports stars in particular;
- ideal for sharing: eg, Domino's Pizza of Two Halves, which features two sets of different toppings;
- representing value for money: like the McDonald's McChoice Menu ads which proudly proclaim the low, low price of 99 pence for any item – or various promotional campaigns, such as Pot Noodle's Not Poodle with its £10 000 prize …

… and so on and so on.

As we have already suggested, these multiple articulations of fast and convenience food products seem to us to speak of a rather different understanding of time than a preoccupation with speed – that is to say, nostalgia for the past, for a halcyon era when life apparently moved *much more slowly*, when things were *different* (/ better) and we had time to make 'proper', healthy, varied and nutritious food, with copious amounts of fresh ingredients, using complicated methods and traditional technologies and to share it with family and friends. Again, this is scarcely an undocumented phenomenon in the contemporary climate – and Ritzer and Rifkin's aforementioned concerns about fast-paced lifestyles seem to us to reflect exactly this kind of nostalgia. Perhaps the most overt instance in culinary terms is the Slow Food movement, founded in Italy in 1986 after McDonald's opened its first branch in Rome. Its key aim is to "protect the right to pleasure, the respect of the rhythms of life and a harmonious relationship with nature", given that "We are enslaved by speed and have all succumbed to the same insidious virus: *Fast Life*, which disrupts our habits, pervades the privacy of our homes and forces us to eat *Fast Foods*." Slow Food now has 77,000 members worldwide, in 48 countries. It stages culinary events and debates, has its own publishing company specializing in food, wine and tourism and supports initiatives like the Ark of Taste, the aim of which is to list and thereby protect products, dishes and animals which are threatened by our contemporary way of life. It also believes that foodstuffs and recipes are deeply redolent of their place of origin, and thus urges attention to this aspect of material culture, works to preserve traditional methods of agriculture and values outlets like cake shops and cafés as worthy of protection in historical, artistic and environmental terms (*Slow Food*, n.d.).

Slow Food might be read as a 're-imagination' of the time and timing of food. Indeed, and in contrast to the emphasis on continuity in the last section, it could be argued that the movement advocates a radical disjuncture with and discontinuation of our current economic and cultural modes, one that stands in opposition to the mediation of food provision by capitalist relations of production. Slow Food stands for a relaxed pace instead of speed, a harmonious rather than exploitative relationship to nature, an emphasis on the past rather than the present. We suggest moreover that, contained within such examples, there are a number of cues to help explain what we see as the repetitious use of nostalgia as a basis for creating fast and convenience food brand identities; something which Brown (1999, 2001a, 2001b) describes as *retromarketing*. As he tells us, it seems as though "the past is this season's present and old the new 'new'" (Brown, 1999: 363). Indeed Brown points to the present proliferation of nostalgic symbolism not just in promotion but across the marketing mix in product design, packaging, retail outlets and distribution channels (eg, online auction sites). We now pursue the extent to which the use of nostalgia as part of the wider phenomenon of retromarketing can be interpreted as a marker of discontinuity in the relationship between food marketing, consumption and Modernity.

We begin by considering how the nostalgic construction of time is perhaps played upon in marketing to enhance the perceived quality of products and, in turn and more significantly, their *trustworthiness*. Lyon *et al.* (1997: iv) posit that food manufacturers have picked up on a general cultural tendency to look to the past to the extent that terms such as "premium, luxury, heritage, traditional, countrystyle and farmhouse ... vale, glen, valley and garden" are now commonly used to signify the high standard of their offerings. This point is extended by Lien (1997) in her ethnographic study of the work of product managers in three ready-made food manufacturers in Norway.

She asserts that the use of nostalgic themes can be seen to form part of a product's wider claim to some kind of 'authenticity'. In one of her studies of a poultry processing company, she demonstrates that the manufacture of authenticity as part of the marketing effort for turkey-based convenience foods represents the materialization of the product manager's concern about a generic (/ nostalgic) consumer suspicion regarding the quality of the raw materials used in processed food. In her analysis, Lien explains that such claims to authenticity indicate "an enhanced awareness of the inauthentic" (Lien, 1997: 248) amongst consumers; that is, some doubt that the raw material may have been processed in an 'unwanted' way during manufacture. To Lien, then, the product manager for this range was responding to an implicit and culturally encoded dichotomy between raw material that is industrially processed (and therefore 'dubious') and that which is not (and therefore 'uncontaminated'). The assumption she identifies in the managers' work is that the use of tropes of 'authenticity' (such as those connected to nostalgia) might enhance the trustworthiness of the brand.

But this concern with 'authenticity' also forms part of a wider story told about the 'contaminating' nature of modern times, at the heart of which lies the idea of our apparent present-day discontinuities/ disaffection with Modernity. Lyon and Colquhoun (1999: 192), for example, argue that the use of the "past as a leisure resource[,] ... a consciously therapeutic dimension to our lives" represents one response to the demands and challenges of our seemingly fast-moving lifestyles. They identify a key contradiction as lying within the fact that many contemporary systems and structures limit our 'control' over time, exacerbating our sense that it is always running out, while also promoting the illusion that we are masters of our own lives in this regard. A specific instance is the exponential growth in technological innovation, which means – they suggest – that our relationship to such changes has also altered. No longer subscribers to the progressivist 'white heat' ideology of the 1950s and 1960s, instead we are now as likely to bemoan what we have lost in the pace of technological development (such as the virtual destruction of British manufacturing) as we are to celebrate our gains. In other words, our attitudes to change have themselves changed – radically and fundamentally (Lyon *et al.*, 2000). Gleick (1999: 11) agrees, citing Zeldin's claim that "Technology has been a rapid heartbeat, compressing housework, travel, entertainment, squeezing more and more into the allotted span ... Nobody expected that it would create the feeling that life moves too fast."

On the basis of this paradox, Lyon *et al.* argue that we seek to maximize our psychological experience of time in terms of quantity *and* quality, to alleviate the fragmentation and uncertainty of contemporary experience in the West, by looking to the past. They borrow especially from Toffler's discussion of alienation as a response to the "future shock" induced by "too much change in too short a time" (Toffler, cited in Lyon *et al.*, 2000: 19) in this regard. Similarly, Holt and Schor (2000: viii) aver that, as our lives speed up, we tend to "look back to an earlier era when there *was* time enough, even if living standards were less opulent. Many long for a simpler, more authentic, less materialist past."

However, we prefer to argue that any notion of nostalgia as some kind of quest for authenticity needs to be interpreted against the *historical trajectory* of Modernity as an economic and cultural project. That is to say, we agree with Brown that the claim that our retro-fever speaks to a fin-de-siècle sense of societal turmoil, that it is a collective attempt to cope with the impression that life is *now* changing much too quickly, is problematic. Brown backs this up with an array of evidence that earlier epochs in Modernity were also heavily retro in their sensibilities, both with regard to marketing and wider social trends. In fact he suggests, following Lowenthal, that "the progressive forward-looking, things-can-only-get-better mindset is [perhaps] the exception rather than the rule of western culture ... the *lingua franca* of modernity" (Brown, 1999: 370). This claim is also redolent of Jameson's (1991) definition of postmodernism as the cultural logic of late capitalism. Whilst the economic structures of late capitalism remain largely unchanged in the West, they have, he argues, spawned a new cultural logic characterized by superficiality, a sense of the impersonal and a loss of historicity, resulting in a nostalgic *cannibalization* of past styles. There is no systemic or structural discontinuity between Modernity and Postmodernity – we still live in thoroughly Modern times – but perhaps we fail to apprehend this because of the speed at which we have come to live and see ourselves living in the vacuum of the contemporary.

Marketing's use of the 'return to the good old days' theme is (for us at least) therefore part of a *longstanding* narrative around Modernity to which the makers of our ads seem to be responding; namely that a search for authenticity – the 'good life that has been lost' – represents an attempt to counteract the purported alienation of Modern life and its apparatuses of production and consumption. As Meethan (2001: 91 – emphasis added) points out with regard to the marketing of tourist destinations, we have here a "reiteration of the *long and well-worn* theme concerning the corrosive nature of modernity on traditional life", something which is obviously characteristic of the Slow Food philosophy, the work of Ritzer and Rifkin and many other commentaries on Modern economy and society. Perhaps then the nostalgic representation of fast and convenience food is nothing but a cultural logic whose ideological function continues to serve the economic structures of consumer capital: that is to say, there is no profound discontinuity in our times, and the sense that we twenty-first century Westerners have 'lost' something is little more than an enduring ideological chimera.

Also it is far from clear as to whether nostalgia, as an ideological reaction to this pervasive cultural construction of loss, is a good or a bad thing in any case. Much seems to depend on our attitudes to change and a concomitant assumption that times are indeed different. Lyon *et al.* (2000: 20) do not problematize the nostalgic response, suggesting instead that most of us utilize the past only episodically and then as a coping mechanism. Holt and Schor (2000: viii), whilst recognizing that living standards may historically have been lower, construct 'the past' as both distinguishable from 'the present' and describe it in positive terms ("more authentic", "less materialist" and so on). But Laudan (2001, 36) is rather more critical. She points out that there is a good deal that is *elitist* in such constructions, especially as far as food is concerned. For Laudan it has become "a mark of sophistication" to eschew processed food (Slow Food is a good example, and one that she uses) and to seek out the 'authentic', the 'fresh', the 'pure'.[4]

---

[4] Relatedly, Holt's empirical application of Bourdieu's discussion of the "social patterning of consumption" (Holt, 2000: 213) to a group of American respondents suggests that those he identifies as possessing high levels of cultural capital – and thus who can also be considered to belong to the cultural 'elite' in this context – tend to dismiss anything mass produced, "popular" or "routinized". Instead they engage in a quest for "decommodified authenticity" in their consumption of "traditional" and "unique" household objects, clothes, films, holidays and music (Holt, 2000: 238–241).

This she refers to as Culinary Luddism. Parker (2002) offers much the same sort of argument in his critique of Ritzer. Parker suggests that Ritzer shares the aforementioned 'sense of loss' with neo-Marxist and Frankfurt School critics of Modernist mass (/ capitalist) culture, a profound longing "for an older, quieter, slower world" (Parker, 2002: 32; *cf* Meethan, 2001), but also contends that Ritzer is much more conservative than these other writers. For example, Parker mentions Ritzer's complaint that McDonald's restaurants are "sterile" and "superficial", selling "mediocre" food which is not of the "highest quality", as well as the suggestion that TV dinners and microwave meals are inferior to those prepared from fresh ingredients. He also points to Ritzer's side-swipe at McDonald's customers, the claim that they are sadly mistaken if they think the food is good value or that they are using their time efficiently by consuming it (Parker, 2002: 32). In short, for Parker, as for Laudan, culinary nostalgia is often disdainful of those who consume fast and convenience foods. Such charges of elitism shed additional light on the ideological nature of claims and judgements about social and economic change.

Furthermore, Laudan points out that our apparent nostalgia for the food of yesteryear is in any case misplaced, suggesting that what we prize about the past would have seemed inexcusably backward to those living in it. She argues that our ancestors were much less than keen on the fresh and the natural – on the basis that fresh foods quickly go off, seasonal variations do not allow for constant year-round production of all foodstuffs, raw food is difficult to digest and so on. She notes that these men and women therefore "bred, ground, soaked, leached, curdled, fermented, and cooked naturally occurring plants and animals until they were literally beaten into submission". Further, Laudan points out that culinary nostalgia omits to take account of the fact that many of our ancestors, especially the peasants of whose food we frequently speak so fondly, had very short life expectancies and were bedevilled by diseases, often as a result of their diets (Laudan, 2001: 40–41). Moreover, modern methods of processing and the mass production of food have released thousands of people worldwide from the drudgery of field labour and food preparation (pp. 41–42). In short, she remarks with a degree of acerbity that "the sunlit past of the Culinary Luddites never existed" (p. 42). For Laudan, then, the longed-for 'past' exists ideologically to co-construct a vision of the present that is profoundly negative, essentially different and in need of repair.

Moreover, and despite not agreeing with Laudan on the potentially problematic nature of the trends described above, Lyon and Colquhoun concur that our culinary memories are at best selective – that "We require the best that yesterday had to offer, we do not require those aspects of it that were dull, tedious, uncomfortable or inconvenient" (Lyon and Colquhoun, 1999: 194). We don't, for example, wish to relive Second World War austerity meals or post-war rationing. Moreover, just as we now habitually buy 'pre-aged' products such as faded jeans and distressed leather jackets (Gleick, 1999: 102), these days we simply don't have (*or don't believe that we have*) the time to recreate bubble and squeak or steak and kidney pie from their constituent ingredients. Food nostalgia therefore represents a pastiche, an ersatz and stereotypical portrait of history which eschews both straightforward historical representation and any satirical impulse (Jameson, 1988: 16): it depicts "nobody's past", as Williamson (cited in Lyon *et al.*, 1997: iii) puts it. Brown, likewise, echoes Laudan, Lyon, Gleick and others in his suggestion that the "sepia-hued retroscape" which marketing often seeks to evoke didn't actually exist anywhere "outside of Hollywood studio back lots", because it consists of an "amalgam of new-and-improved with as good-as-always" (Brown, 1999: 368, 2001a: 84, 2001b: 306).

In the same vein, Lears identifies a now-and-then pastiche in several of the advertising texts he discusses, some of which as we already know date back to the nineteenth century. However, he argues that this "pseudotraditionalism" became especially pronounced in marketing messages during the Depression, apparently as a form of restorative balm against economic crisis and the resultant sense of psychic insecurity (Lears, 1994: 383). Lears marks the ways in which advertisers of the time linked all manner of modern, factory-manufactured goods with "an imagined world of preindustrial domestic harmony" (p. 124). An apposite example is the Hurff's Soup campaign of 1936, where a tagline proclaiming the high expectations that country folk have from their soup accompanied a picture of a large family awaiting the arrival of a steaming tureen at their farmhouse dinner table. As Lears puts it, ads like this "scramble" past and present: in conjuring up oxymoronic images of "home-cooked canned goods" and "mass-produced craftmanship" (p. 385), they suggest that the relevant products preserve "all the charms of yesterday amid the comforts of tomorrow" (p. 386).

Whether interpreted positively or negatively, it is exactly this *faux*-yet-enduring nostalgia that we identify running alongside appeals to speed in the advertisements that we have discussed here, as well as in wider Western cultural trends. These ads are, after all, campaigns for *fast* or *convenience* foods – processed, mass customized, laden with preservatives and additives – which could never have existed in the history to which the relevant texts appear to hark back, overtly or not. For us, as for Lears, there is an attempt here to sell foodstuffs which offer the best of all possible worlds – in terms of our desire for speed *but also* for quality, taste, variety, enjoyment, nutritional value, community, value for money and so on. These texts seem to suggest that we want *even our junk food* to be both "expeditious and dense ... [to effect] the best possible ratio between economy and efficacy" (Barthes, 1972: 63, here discussing steak), to exhibit both function *and* form. Perhaps speed alone is insufficient to secure our hearts, minds and bellies: in order to achieve competitive advantage, these manufacturers need to provide more. Perhaps it has become a 'qualifier', where previously it was an 'order-winner' (Hill 2000). Or, to put it another way, we require our food to be fast, but not *Fast*, in the pejorative Slow Food sense. As McDonald's themselves admit, and as is also very visible in their aforementioned difficulties with the Made for You system, "our customers [are] now veterans in the quick-service market and their expectations [have] gone through the roof" (cited in Taylor and Lyon, 1995: 65). Many of the fast/ convenience food adverts we have discussed, from our perspective in any case, seemingly labour to represent the various nostalgic (/ different/ 'real') pleasures to be had from the experience of eating the products concerned, *while at the same time* harping on the theme of speed (/ the same-only-faster-and-better) *or* leaving the fact that they are quick and convenient largely to speak for itself. There is here an implicit appeal to the 'discerning' consumer, the one who wants speed and convenience but is at the same time unwilling to relinquish taste and 'authenticity'.

Coffee and dessert: some concluding cogitations

In conclusion, our discussion appears to be suggestive of a double-edged relationship to speed in the contemporary Western cultural context. However, it also seems to us that this relationship is not as paradoxical as it might at first appear. If we are preoccupied with 'the best of all possible worlds', then maybe we want all the privileges of the past as well as the glittering prizes of continued technoscientific progress. Our use of Lears' (1994) analysis certainly points to such a conclusion. Moreover, and to borrow from Stephen Brown again, his suggestion of the importance of 'new-and-improved' and 'as-good-as-always' in the marketing endeavours he discusses implies that the poles of 'same' and 'different' are in any case reversible when we consider these varying constructions of time. That is to say, if 'good' food is framed as necessarily 'fast*er*' these days, then it is also and simultaneously *different* – whereas if it is marked as 'traditional' or 'authentic' then it is the *same as it has always been*. Speed and nostalgia therefore appear to fold in on each other in this regard, a point at which the stability of the paradox collapses.

This seeming contradiction between a continuous and a discontinuous version of time in the marketing of fast and convenience foods is then no paradox at all. Indeed we would argue that it speaks of a key dynamic in capital's accumulative processes of production, distribution and consumption – the dialectical nature of the relationship between capital and time (Godfrey *et al.*, 2004). This dialectic takes form in the productive tensions of capital's continuous search for new markets and sources of productive capacity (as it cannot survive on constancy) and the discontinuities not only at the systemic level of the economy, but also at the level of the desiring consumer's constant search for something 'different'. Here Marx's paradoxical phrasing of the 'constant revolutionizing' of the means of production (and thereby distribution and consumption) becomes especially prescient in addressing marketing appeals for fast and convenience food. It encourages us to read such appeals ideologically as forms of signification mediated by wider systemic changes in the relationship between capital and time, and as instantiations of capital's dialectical material base. In this respect, marketing as a cultural phenomenon continues to serve the ambivalences of capital's trajectory. These ads for fast and convenience foods instantiate an essential and continuing ideological structure of Modernity, dressed up in the ever-changing clothing of brand identities. Therefore, and although discontinuity might be a manufactured piece of culture, its ideological function has key material effects and it should not be easily consigned to the dustheap of meaningless ephemera. The contradiction it represents would seem to be meaningful for understanding the continuation and expansion of markets and marketing.

In the final analysis, we would suggest that fast/ convenience food can, speculatively at least, be culturally understood as *accelerated* food, using the distinction drawn by Kavanagh *et al.* (2002: 2) between speed and acceleration:

> Things *are* moving fast*er*, but we are not getting more speed ... The difference is that speed indicates movement or change, while acceleration involves an intensification along an existing trajectory ... speed is about transformation while acceleration is about translation. In this sense, speed is radical while acceleration is conservative.

Perhaps there is also little that is new about our desire for fast/ convenience food. Laudan (2001: 38–39) certainly argues that societies throughout history have relied on food which can be eaten quickly, often away from the homebase – and gives many illustrative examples of her point. Her earlier cited claims also point to a longstanding emphasis on making food preparation as expeditious as possible by means of drying, smoking, fermenting and so on. Fast/ convenience food as we know it today could therefore be seen to represent the latest stage in an acceleration, an increasing *codification*, of meal-making and meal consumption. As Kavanagh *et al.* (2002: 4) claim, maybe we moderns are "running ... to stand still": we are putatively Janus-faced in the sense that we want to do pretty much what we have always done but to do it "ever faster", faster, *faster*.

References

Alexander, D. (2003) 'McDonald's focus flips back to fast', *News for McDonald's®
Franchise Owners*, 16th March. Online. Available at http://www.licenseenews.
com/news/news159.html (accessed 2nd October 2003).

Barthes, R. (1972) *Mythologies*, London: Jonathan Cape.

Bauman, Z. (1998) *Globalization: The Human Consequences*, Cambridge: Polity
Press.

Bellos, A., Borger, J., Harding, L. and Howard, M. (2001) 'Planet Mac', *The
Guardian* (G2 section), 6th April: 2–5.

Bourdieu, P. (1984) *Distinction: A Social Critique of the Judgement of Taste*,
Cambridge, Massachusetts: Harvard University Press.

Breakfast (2003) BBC Radio Five Live, 21st February.

Brewis, J. and Linstead, S. (2000) *Sex, Work and Sex Work: Eroticizing Organization*,
London: Routledge.

Brown, S. (1999) 'Retro-marketing: yesterday's tomorrows, today!', *Marketing
Intelligence and Planning*, 17: 363–376.

Brown, S. (2001a) 'Torment your customers (they'll love it)', *Harvard Business
Review*, October: 83–88.

Brown, S. (2001b) 'The retromarketing revolution: *l'imagination au pouvoir*', *International Journal of Management Reviews* 3 (December): 303–320.

Candel, M.J.J.M. (2001) 'Consumers' convenience orientation towards meal preparation: conceptualization and measurement', *Appetite*, 36: 15–28.

Darian, J.C. and Cohen, J. (1995) 'Segmenting by consumer time shortage', *Journal
of Consumer Marketing*, 12 (1): 32–44.

Davis, M.M. and Heineke, J. (1998) 'How disconfirmation, perception and actual
waiting times impact customer satisfaction', *International Journal of Service
Industry Management*, 9 (1): 64–73.

The Editor (2000) 'We're all worked out', supplement with *The Guardian*, 24th
November: 4.

Gibson, R. (2002) 'McDonald's sees need to speed up US improvements', *News for
McDonald's® Franchise Owners*, 3rd September. Online. Available at http://www.
licenseenews.com/news/news66.html. (accessed 2nd October 2003).

Gleick, J. (1999) *Faster: The Acceleration of Just About Everything*, New York:
Pantheon.

Godfrey, R., Jack, G. and Jones, C. (2004) 'Sucking, bleeding, breaking: on the
continuities of vampirism, capital and time', *Culture and Organization*, 10 (1):
25–36.

Groth, M. and Gilliland, S.W. (2001) 'The role of procedural justice in the delivery of services: a study of customers' reactions to waiting', *Journal of Quality
Management*, 6: 77–97.

Hall, E.T. (1976) *Beyond Culture*, New York: Doubleday.

Hassard, J. (1991) 'Aspects of time in organization', *Human Relations*, 44 (2):
105–125.

Hassard, J. (1996) 'Images of time in work and organization', In S.R. Clegg, C.
Hardy and W.R. Nord (eds) *Handbook of Organization Studies*, London: Sage,
pp. 581–598.

Hebdige, D. (1989) 'After the masses', *Marxism Today*, January: 48–53.

Hill, T. (2000) *Manufacturing Strategy: Text and Cases*, Basingstoke: Palgrave.

Holt, D.B. (2000) 'Does cultural capital structure American consumption?', in J.B. Schor and D. Holt (eds) *The Consumer Society Reader,* New York: The New Press, pp. 212–252.

Holt, D.B. and Schor, J.B. (2000) 'Introduction: do Americans consume too much?' in J.B. Schor and D. Holt (eds) *The Consumer Society Reader,* New York: The New Press, pp. vii–xxiii.

Jae, M.K., Ryu, J.S. and Abdel-Ghany, M. (2000) 'Family characteristics and convenience food expenditure in urban Korea', *Journal of Consumer Studies and Home Economics,* 24 (4): 252–256.

Jameson, F. (1988) 'Postmodernism and consumer society', in E.A Kaplan (ed.) *Postmodernism and its Discontents,* London: Verso, pp. 13–29.

Jameson, F. (1991) *Postmodernism, or the Cultural Logic of Late Capitalism,* Durham, North Carolina: Duke University Press.

Jekanowski, M.D., Binkley, J.K. and Eales, J. (2001) 'Convenience, accessibility and the demand for fast food', *Journal of Agricultural and Resource Economics,* 26(1): 58–74.

Kavanagh, D., Lightfoot, G. and Lilley, S. (2002) 'Running to stand still: the consumption of speed by acceleration', paper presented to the *20th Standing Conference on Organizational Symbolism,* International Business School, Budapest, Hungary, July.

Kennison, R. (2001) 'World on a platter? Consuming geographies and the place of food in Society', *Body and Society,* 7 (1): 121–125.

Laudan, R. (2001) 'A plea for culinary modernism: why we should love new, fast, processed food', *Gastronomica,* February: 36–44.

Lears, J. (1994) *Fables of Abundance: A Cultural History of Advertising in America,* New York: Basic Books.

Lien, M.E. (1997) *Marketing and Modernity,* Oxford: Berg.

Lyon, P. and Colquhoun, A. (1999) 'Selectively living in the past: nostalgia and lifestyle', *Journal of Consumer Studies and Home Economics,* 23 (3): 191–196.

Lyon, P., Colquhoun, A. and Reid, A. (1997) 'Consuming the past: time, context and food', *Nutrition and Food Science,* January/ February: i–xii.

Lyon, P., Colquhoun, A. Kinney, D. and Murphy, P. (2000) 'Time travel: escape from the late 20th century', *Jaargang,* 18 (1): 13–24.

Marx, K. (1976 [1867]) *Capital,* London: Penguin.

McDonald's (n.d.). Online. Available at http://www.mcdonalds.com (accessed 3rd October 2003).

Meethan, K. (2001) *Tourism in Global Society: Place, Culture, Consumption,* Basingstoke: Palgrave.

National Statistics Online (2003) 'Calculating inflation: takeaways go into the RPI basket', 17th March. Online. Available at http://www.statistics.gov.uk (accessed 28th March 2003).

Parker, M. (2002) *Against Management: Organization in the Age of Managerialism,* Cambridge: Polity Press.

Pryer, J.A., Nichols, R., Elliott, P., Thakrar, B., Brunner, E. and Marmot, M. (2001) 'Dietary patterns among a national random sample of British adults', *Journal of Epidemiology and Community Health,* 55 (1): 29–37.

Reed, Z., McIlveen, H. and Strugnell, C. (2000) 'The retailing environment in Ireland and its effect on the chilled ready meal market', *Journal of Consumer Studies and Home Economics,* 24 (4): 234–241.

Reeves, R. (1999) 'The mad rush to save time', *The Observer,* 3rd October: 17.

Rifkin, J. (1989) *Time Wars: The Primary Conflict in Human History,* New York: Simon and Schuster.

Ritzer, G. (1996) *The McDonaldization of Society: An Investigation into the Changing Character of Contemporary Social Life,* Thousand Oaks, California: Pine Forge Press.

Schlosser, E. (2002) *Fast Food Nation: What the All-American Meal is Doing to the World,* London: Penguin.

Slow Food (n.d.). Online. Available at http://www.slowfood.com (accessed 2nd October 2003).

Summerskill, B. (2000) 'One in four Britons now works nights', *The Observer,* 10th September: 6.

Taylor, S. and Lyon, P. (1995) 'Paradigm lost: the rise and fall of McDonaldization', *International Journal of Contemporary Hospitality Management,* 7 (2/3): 64–68.

Toivonen, T. (1997) 'Food and social class', *Journal of Consumer Studies and Home Economics,* 4 (21): 329–347.

Veblen, T. (1961 [1902]) *The Theory of the Leisure Class: An Economic Study of Institutions,* New York: Modern Library.

Yoon, S.-J. and Kim, J.-H. (2001) 'The effects of perceived consumer characteristics on the choice and use of internet ads', *Journal of Brand Management,* 8 (4–5): 346–364.

Chapter 9

"Outdistance the Competition": The Bicycle Messenger as a Corporate Icon

Nina Kivinen

Introduction

Some say that we live in a new society, a networked society (Castells 1996), a postmodern world, a risk society (Beck 1992), a consumer society (Baudrillard 1970/1998); the boundaries between 'economy' and 'culture' have become blurred, or perhaps the two always have been inseparable (as argued in du Gay & Pryke 2002). Most of us can agree that things and people have changed shape, meaning and behaviour, and we have seen new phenomena appear as information and communication technologies have become part of the everyday life for a number of people in many parts of the world. One can also argue that in today's society a different kind of visualisation is appearing. The sheer number of images that we see, interpret and attribute meanings to during an ordinary day is staggering, but so is also the number of images we ignore or do not even notice. Not only is everything we see an image, but we also see explicit images in newspapers and books, in advertisements and billboards, on television and on the internet, and now also in our mobile phones. Consequently, the study of visual practices has received more attention both through the study of images circulating in society as well as through images, typically photographs, produced by researchers themselves.

Visual representations have usually been of interest within fields such as marketing, and more explicitly consumer marketing (see e.g. Schroeder 2002a), cultural studies, art history and art studies. Studying visual data in social sciences in general is a more recent phenomenon. My view on what visual data could encompass follows a definition laid out by Emmison & Smith who write that visual data can potentially be any "object, person, place, event or happening which is observable to the human eye" (Emmison & Smith 2000, 4).

This chapter will focus on the analysis of one single image, the single image that could be found on the homepage of a large energy sector company in the autumn of 2001. What goes on on the internet on a corporate website? One might argue that the webpages are marketing material directed at current and future customers and are therefore only of interest for marketing research. But if the webpages also are directed to the members of the organization, are not the pages then involved in the process through which the organization constructs its identity; a process that is also closely linked to the process of construction of brand identity? I am not interested in the effects or outcomes of the homepage. Instead I am intrigued by what it is that comes into being on the page, the form and practices of culture, if you will, in and through which culture is produced, enacted and consumed (Lister & Wills 2001). My interest lies in understanding the visual performance of concepts, things and people, such as in this case, organizational identity or organizational imagery.

The questions this chapter will ask are: how does this picture construct the identity of the company? How is the intangible visualised? And how is speed constructed in this image, if at all? Are these spatial and temporal constructs necessities in order to maintain the view of an ever more rapid circulation of signs in contemporary society? The literature on aesthetics, art and art history are used as a background reading and I take as my starting point my reading of organization and management for interpreting the world of visual representations around me. The issues raised here draw upon my wish to critically examine 'globalisation' and the role of information technology in organizing and in the economy in general.

Internet, Images, Identities and Signs

The World Wide Web has provided a new medium for the circulation of information, texts and images. I suggest that the implications of these technologies are often exaggerated. We are intrigued by transitions and we seem to have a need to believe that we are experiencing new and fundamentally different phenomena; a view that is central in the modern project. Modern writers tend to view the development of Western societies as a linear and rational process in which globalisation, for example, would be only a natural stage in a continuum. The discourse makes development and evolution seem like necessities that need to be achieved at any cost. A post-modern twist again would have us breaking with history, seeing today's existence as a-historic, an in-between-state, breaking with that which was and refusing to predict what is to be. I argue that, indeed, the process of *becoming* is more interesting than the state of *being*. But this process is still in some ways connected to something which has been. So the internet is based on new technology that did not exist before, but the structure, layout and design of

186

the internet draw upon much older conventions as argued by Sean Cubitt (Cubitt 1998). Similarly Schroeder and Borgerson (Schroeder and Borgerson 2002) argue that information technology has more similarities than differences with, for example, renaissance art.

The internet effectively circulates signs in contemporary society and as argued by Jean Baudrillard in his critique of Marx, everything is a sign and exchange is the basis of utility (Baudrillard 1981/2000). Similarly Lash & Urry (1994) stress in their book *Economies of Signs and Space* the contemporary importance of the sign or the symbolic content of commodities over their material content. According to Lash & Urry, the production of signs has taken two forms: a cognitive form – through a flow of information, digital codes and other abstract symbols, and an aesthetic form – the expressive side of economic life. Contrary to du Gay & Pryke (2002) they argue for keeping the two separate, based on a notion that the two have distinct forms of knowledge and reflexivity. Lash & Urry's argument is based on the view that a cognitive reading by necessity is semiotic and therefore structures are central, whereas the aesthetic form refers to an anthropological reading, thus culture. An attempt to make these two readings simultaneously would implicitly posit structure over culture. du Gay & Pryke write that dichotomies such as economy – culture should be questioned and attempts should be made at treating phenomena without this separation.

The internet has provided firms, organizations, and people with new ways by which to construct and re-construct their identities. One obvious implication is the possibility to construct and maintain multiple identities in chat rooms, for example. This is, however, not a discussion I will bring in here. I am more interested in the constructions of organizational identity and brand identity that the World Wide Web has made possible. I am particularly referring to the homepages of organizations. For identity construction the web offers a medium which is flexible as it can easily be changed and remade daily. The web is accessible to both members and non-members of an organization; this will have implications on how the pages are designed. Another implication of the web is that the use and circulation of images and other visual material is easy. There is a huge flow of images on the web; a homepage containing only texts might be considered boring and non-creative.

The growing interest in visualisation is linked to the field of organizational aesthetics, which emerged in the late 1980s (Gagliardi 1990; Strati 1999; Linstead & Höpfl 2000). Combining art and management, or art and business, has become a popular topic in European management research, in Scandinavia particularly following the work of Pierre Guillet de Monthoux (see e.g. Guillet de Monthoux 1993, 1998). The breaking of boundaries between the artist, a romantic, misunderstood and tragic figure who never sells a painting in his lifetime, and the business man, a shrewd profit seeker who never has the time to enjoy life and the arts, has provided some interesting research on areas where these two aspects of life for a long time have lived side by side such as in theatre, opera and music production. Needless to say the dichotomy that separated business from art in the first place was more of a 19ᵗʰ century construct. For me this body of literature on aesthetics and management has been a door opener to the realisation that I have previously ignored what I *see* as a source of data to be interpreted and analysed, as opposed to what I *read*.

My Way of Seeing

Visual representations of beliefs, values and meanings have always played an important part. But somehow it seems that the world of images was moved to a world of culture and art, and in the process we perhaps lost some of our abilities for reading images. Social sciences have come to focus on the spoken or written word as a valid source of data to be analysed and understood. But nonetheless one cannot claim that the study of the visual in social sciences is only a contemporary phenomenon. Seeing the world around us, and analysing what we see has always been important in social sciences. According to Ball & Smith (1992), Georg Simmel raised the issue in 1908 by writing that the eye has a sociological function. For example, by seeing and interpreting facial expressions we recognise the intentions of others.

In ethnographic work photography has been used since the invention of the camera, and earlier sketches were drawn for providing 'accurate' descriptions of what had been seen and described in field notes. Photographs of 'strange people' could for instance be used for measuring their physical characteristics and thereby determine their 'race'. But generally photographs were used more for descriptive purposes than as the focus of analysis in their own right (Ball & Smith 1992). Photographs provided proof; the ethnographer had really visited the place in question and seen the objects and people described in writing. Pictures and images were therefore capturing the 'real world'. This approach to using photography is used by many contemporary visual anthropologists and visual sociologists.

Other researchers choose to study the photographs and images created by the society and culture studied. According to Emmison & Smith (2000) studying existing images is a more European phenomenon, which they attribute to the influence of structuralism and semiotics which open up the images to interpretation. Within visual sociology critical work has been emphasised by for instance Chaplin (1994), who encourages more studies that would explore the potential of the visual as sociological knowledge and critical text. Similarly Pink (2001) argues for reflexivity in visual studies for understanding how visual and ethnographic materials are both produced and interpreted.

My analysis emerges from my understanding of semiotics, following

Ferdinand de Saussure, C.S. Pierce and Roland Barthes, while maintaining a post-structuralist reading of the production of meanings. Rose (2001) writes that semiology (or semiotics) can be used as a critical visual methodology as it "offers a range of tools for looking at images carefully; it is centrally concerned with the ways in which social differences are created; and at least some of its practitioners advocate reflexivity in its deployment" (Rose 2001, 73). van Leeuwen (2001), among others, makes a distinction between semiotics and iconography, where the first deals with the image itself, whereas the latter also studies the context in which the picture is produced and circulated, and how and why cultural meanings and their visual expressions come about historically. van Leeuwen argues that semiotics, referring explicitly to the visual semiotics of Roland Barthes, treats cultural meanings as given, shared by everyone with some insight into contemporary culture. In my view visual semiotics is not necessarily limited to such a view and I do recognise the need for a historically sensitive reading on images.

A few more words are needed on the work of Roland Barthes (see e.g. Barthes 1961/1982a, 1964/1982b, 1981) on photography and images. In his essay *Rhetoric of the Image* (1964/1982b), Barthes deconstructs an advertisement for Panzani pasta, which he separates into three different messages: a linguistic message (referring to the text in the advertisement), a coded iconic message (connoted to a larger system of signs), and the non-coded iconic message (the denoted image referring to the objects depicted in the image). Denotation therefore refers to that which is depicted in an image, whereas connotation refers to the ideas and values that are expressed through what is represented. A Barthian analysis would thus often start from trying to describe the image without making references to symbolic meanings outside the image itself. This could be compared to Pierce's way of discussing icons where signs of this type directly resemble something else and can therefore be recognised (Berger 1997). But clearly both Barthes and Pierce recognise these as signs, i.e. the images do not relate to other objects through any natural relation.

Berger approaches the analysis of images in terms of five elements: 1) the *artist*, who creates images, 2) the *audience*, which receives the images, 3) the *work of art*, which is the image itself, 4) the *society* in which the images are found, and finally, 5) the *medium*, which affects the images (Berger 1997, 46). All these elements work together in constructing multiple meanings and interpretations of every single image. Similarly when describing possible approaches to studying the visual within cultural studies, Lister and Wills (2001) break down their analysis into analysing the context of viewing (Where is the image? What is its location in the physical and social world?), and the context of production (How did the image get there?), before turning to the image itself. Lister and Wells separate looking – form and meaning (i.e. analysing the image) and looking – recognition and identity (considering the viewer of the image). A common feature of most approaches to studying the visual is that images are today seen as circulating in society and they affect the meanings and interpretations of other images. But do we know how to read images? We often claim that we are not fooled by advertisements, but how much time to we really spend on studying the number of images that we see every day and every waking second?

Visualising Identity

I will now move more explicitly to the area of my study, where I am analysing a manufacturer of equipment used in the energy sector and five of its large customers. In this chapter I have chosen one of these companies and the single image on their webpage as my only source of data, in order to study the meanings that an image can represent. Why this image? My arguments for using this particular image are that this company has intrigued me since the start of the project. This image was also the only image on the opening page of the website of the company in the autumn of 2001. The location of this particular image is such that I see it as a representation of the (corporate) image of the company as it has been chosen by the organization and given a prominent position. From a marketing perspective imagery and identity have been studied for some time (see for example Stern & Schroeder 1994 and Schroeder 2002a), but I would argue that imagery is not only a concern for marketing but also for other processes and social practices in organizations and in society in general.

Looking at this picture I recognise that there are a number of choices I need to make concerning how to proceed with my analysis. I can begin by analysing the context in which this image can be seen and the context in which it is produced (Lister & Wells 2001), or I can take my starting point in the picture itself. As this image out of a number of images was the one that felt intriguing in the first place, I decide to set out looking at that image in question. Relating to Berger's (1997) five dimensions, I choose in this chapter to ignore the artist and the audience and thus, I will not discuss the photographer who took the picture, the web designers who outlined the webpages, nor the possible intentions or un-intentions of the company I am studying. Nor will I dwell upon the possible effects the webpages might have or to whom they are directed, the audience in this case is simply me. I do, however, take into account the society within which this image is produced and circulated. My study has brought me to visit a number of offices of energy sector companies worldwide[1] and I have conducted some

---

[1] In 2000–2001 I conducted interviews in Finland, Spain, Bangladesh, the Philippines, Thailand, Hong Kong and the US for my PhD-project. In 1999 I did interviews for another project within the same industry in Guinea, Egypt, the Seychelles and Tanzania.

40 interviews with people who work in the industry within this and other studies. My training in management and organization, and social sciences in general, are the main features of my positioned reading of images; this is my 'way of seeing'.

So what do I see in this image? To me it is first and foremost a photograph of a man on a bicycle. He appears to be young, perhaps in his early 20s and he is dressed in a bright yellow jacket and black bike shorts. He wears gloves, a helmet and a rucksack, all in black. The bicycle is a mountain bike, or that is what we call them in Finland. They should perhaps be called street bikes as they have become a common sight in the streets. His bike is bright blue, but the colour of the bike does not really match the clothing of the biker. The helmet is somehow strange. It seems to be of solid manufacture but I cannot really make out its contours. It would appear that there is something on the biker's head that does not belong there. The picture is too blurred to really make out the details. In the background one can barely see buildings that look like office buildings and perhaps a car or two. I would therefore place the bike on a street in a larger city, perhaps in the US. But again the picture is too blurred to say for sure, which brings me to the more technical details of the image.

The picture is blurred in two ways. First of all the biker is not clear; he is not in sharp focus. In addition, the background is blurred in a different way, as if the object in front of the picture is moving in relation to a fixed background. The photograph shows movement. The composition of the image is traditional with the object practically in the centre of the picture. The biker appears to be moving from right to left. The dominant colour of the photograph is blue. Not only is the picture not clear, it is also divided by white lines into 20 squares, three of which are semi-transparent and coloured in a light green. Goldman & Papson (1996) write in their interesting monograph on the sociology of advertising that a grainy picture often signifies 'reality'. A clear picture would lead you to think that the picture has been taken in studio surroundings whereas the grainy picture makes you see it as a representation of an actual incident. The grainier the picture, the more real it seems. On the other hand a black-and-white photograph could also have made a reference to documentary images as used in newspapers and other media. This is a reference to earlier film techniques. Up till the 1970s colours were associated with studio pictures, thus referring to for instance musicals and other fantasies, whereas black-and-white was used outdoors and signified documentaries. The picture has been digitally manipulated at least by placing the coloured squares on the original photograph. This to me is a reference to IT and high tech.

The man on the bike is probably a bike messenger, delivering mail and packages for corporate customers in urban surroundings. In order to be good at his job he needs to be fit, have strong legs and good reflexes, as assumingly he will be travelling at a speed considerably higher than that of your ordinary biker. According to an article in the largest Swedish daily newspaper, Dagens Nyheter, where a reporter trailed a bike messenger in Stockholm for a day (Liljestrand 2002), the average bike messenger is 22–23 years old and male. He does not stay in the business for long, approx. six months, and on average he would be paid a provision of 30% for every delivered package. So the faster he is, the more deliveries he can make during the course of a day. The article actually mentions a "flexible attitude towards traffic laws" (Liljestrand 2002, 7) as an advantage, were you to seek employment as a bike messenger. The other qualities mentioned are good physique, good knowledge of the city, capacity to do multiple tasks simultaneously, and a good memory. On an ordinary day a bike messenger in Stockholm would deliver around 25–30 packages and cover a distance of 80 to 100 km.

What is the role of this young and fit man? Is he an employee of the company, a manager or 'is' he the company? I read him as representing the company in question. If the image had pictured a group of people I would probably have viewed them as individuals within the organization. But this man being alone in the picture I read as being the company. An image of a single person often conveys the image of individuality and power. This is, however, not a portrait where these values would be more evident. No, the movement shown in the image makes me draw other conclusions. The bike messenger is moving whereas the buildings behind him stand still. His vehicle is not the fastest possible in absolute terms. If he had wanted he could have chosen to drive a sports car or high speed train or why not even a moon rocket. Out of many possibilities he has chosen the bicycle, an invention that is over a century old, as this is probably the fastest means of transport in his specific context. In relative terms he is the fastest. He will arrive ahead of anyone else. He is able to cut corners and pass through bottlenecks. He clearly has an advantage over the others. But his only advantage is his speed.

He has not constructed a new vehicle; instead he takes an old solution and uses it to solve a modern problem. He is creative, but he is well aware of history and he has not forgotten his past. The first bicycle, called the *draisienne*, was built by Baron Karl de Drais de Sauerbrun and it was first exhibited in Paris on April 6, 1818. This first bicycle, a two-wheeled, rider-propelled machine was made of wood and the rider would move the bicycle by pushing his feet against the ground. Pedals were added to the design a few years later.[2] So his means of transport is not a new invention. The bike messenger has used on old solution to a new problem; this is innovative thought. What about his surroundings? The bike will be the fastest trans-

---

[2] http://www.britannica.com/eb/article?eu=81256&tocid=8248&query=bicycle accessed June 14, 2002.

portation, but only in a larger, western city, which has grown so fast that the system of public transport is lagging behind. He could probably not be operating in a metropolis in a third world country. Not only would the streets be crowded with people, animals and other vehicles, but the pollution would also make it difficult to breath. I make this crude generalisation based on my experience of Manila and Dacca. But would he have a solution for this specific context as well? I am not entirely convinced, but it is possible as this image does construct the space in which the biker is effective. The modern bike, the mountain bike, is also a reference for having chosen a means of transport designed for rough terrain in the 'wild' and now it is used in the rough world of urban traffic and global economy. So solutions designed for a specific context in the end can be fast enough in other surroundings as well. Within the city limits he can be everywhere and reach everywhere. In the city, his space and place, he rules, he is in control.

Fast Subjects

"[S]o the stories go", Nigel Thrift writes, "firms now live in a permanent stage of emergency, always bordering on the edge of chaos" (Thrift 2002, 201). Firms need to be flexible, adaptive, creative and fast. "Firms will therefore become faster, more agile [...]. They will be able to live life in a blur of change." (ibid.) Thrift, a critical geographer, argues in his article *Performing cultures in the new economy* that discourses on business have created new kinds of 'fast' subject positions. Managers of today are living in a constant stage of emergency. According to Thrift this entails a creation of new spaces of intensity through which the creative manager, or creative management, is constructed.

Thrift writes that we need to render visible the space which is to be governed; space has to be represented and marked out. In his article he describes three procedures which both show and value the new things which are necessary to create the 'fast' subjects. He calls them: sight – new spaces of visualisation, cite – new spaces of embodiment, and site – new spaces of circulation. Thrift emphasises that this is a production of new spaces, spaces that are more active, more performative than those of old (drawing partly on the work of Butler 1990 but also on the work within science and technology studies, e.g. Callon 1998; Law 1994 and Latour 1999), and that information technology is instrumental in this production, both as a cultural artefact, a medium and as agency. I will here in short describe what Thrift argues concerning sight. In this article Thrift explores the world of business magazines and their visualisation of managers and control. Magazines such as *Fortune* traditionally presented a masculine and serious picture of making business where control was represented by a dark suit and a leather armchair. The business magazine of the new economy, *Fast Company*, portrayed a different manager. The mangers were often shown in action, dressed more casually. The language of the images in the magazines showed constant and unremitting change, high technology and adaptation as the way of life.

This language can perhaps also be seen in the image I am analysing. The energy sector is more than a century old, but nonetheless the image can be read as showing youth and creativity, terms more closely linked to businesses in the new economy. The image is still gendered, but not as strongly as it could have been. The rhetoric of the new economy is emphasising the equal opportunities of both men and women, whilst the imaging still maintains a masculine gender.

Turning back to the image. What is this bike messenger carrying? What is his message and for whom is he working? As knowledge and information are key words in contemporary society it is easy to make that reading of the picture. The biker is a key component in a larger network as he makes a reference to someone having information and someone else needing it, without the messenger the network will break down or at least be much slower. This can also be seen as a reference to the IT-sector, but it could also be seen as the embodiment of the invisible commodity that the company presumably is selling, energy. The visualisation of immaterial products and services make some things visible while hiding others (Schroeder 2002b). Or he can be seen as a trader of energy. Someone has excess energy whereas someone else is in need of it. The bike messenger then provides a faster way of transporting whatever needs to be transported from A to B, while clearly not being the only possible means of transport. There are other more conventional ways of going about, for instance your regular postal service. But he is able to provide something which they do not. And again we come back to speed.

Who are his customers? Presumably anyone can use the services of a bike messenger as long as they are active in the same space, the same city. The cost of using their services should be accessible to just about any business and why not any person. So who needs these services? Whatever is transported cannot be large in size and it cannot be transferred digitally. But somehow, presumably, it is often something which is needed in the IT-business in particular. The company is therefore approachable and open to new ideas but it is limited in its action to a specific context, a specific space.

Virtual/Real Identities and the Internet

The relevance of imaging in general and webpages in particular, for me is significant in cultural production of society, but I choose to relate to the most obvious discussions, namely (corporate or organizational) identity construction and branding, as the production and consumption of images in contemporary society is closely linked to branding (see e.g. Schroeder

2002a). Whether brand identity can be separated from organizational identity I leave open at this time, and choose to discuss the processes by which identity is performed on the internet. Brand meaning is not created by the market alone, but also through culture, aesthetics and history (Schroeder 2002c). The intention of the analysis of a single image was to show some possible interpretations, or entries to further interpretation of a company, a reading, and by no means an exhaustive reading, of the image of the company.

The new media has provided new ways of constructing the subject, and as Poster argues (1990, 1995) there are new conditions for subject formation, which amounts to the dispersal and decentring of the subject. But is there a difference between the 'virtual' and the 'real' and is it necessary to maintain a dichotomy of online – offline? Hine writes that there are two distinct ways of viewing the internet: firstly, the internet represents a place, cyberspace, where culture is formed and reformed, and secondly, the internet is a cultural artefact, suggesting it could have been otherwise, "what it is and what it does are the products of culturally produced understandings that can vary" (Hine 2000, 9). The latter argument again follows the work of sociologists like John Law and Bruno Latour. Hine argues that rather than transcending time or space, as argued by e.g. Castells (1996), the internet can be shown to have multiple temporal and spatial orderings, which break down the boundary between online/offline. Still following Hine, she argues that spatiality is defined more through connection than distance and she sees the internet as both a performative space and a performed space, thus trying to combine both approaches to studying the internet.

So in the End...

The internet is an interesting phenomenon to consider in contemporary social practices. The image and identity of the company studied in this chapter are found on the web, and at the same time the image and identity are constructed through the internet. The image makes references to continuous constructions of time and space (or timing and spacing as Bruno Latour (1997) called these processes), a time/space that is favourable to the bike messenger. He can deliver information or energy faster than anybody else and he can adapt to new circumstances using both old and new technology.

"... *we continued to outdistance the competition*", Kenneth L. Lay, chairman and Jeffrey K. Skilling, president and chief executive officer of Enron, one of the largest energy sector companies in the world, wrote in the annual report of 2000[3], a message explicitly directed to their shareholders. This

---

[3] Enron Annual Report 2000, 2.

message is also included in the single image chosen for the Enron website. The image of Enron differed from how the industry previously had been seen: an engineering-driven, traditional, and perhaps slow-moving industry. But Enron created a new image, the image of a young and fit man who races through the crowded street and cuts corners in order to arrive ahead of everybody else.

On December 2, 2001, the spectacular story of Enron came to an end as the firm filed for Chapter 11 bankruptcy protection. Several executives were indicted for fraud, conspiracy, insider trading and money laundering, leaving thousands of employees without work and retirement savings. In the end, cutting corners proved to be a strategy worth avoiding.

References

Ball, Michael S. & Gregory W. H. Smith (1992) *Analyzing Visual Data.* Qualitative research methods series no 24. Beverly Hills, California: Sage Publications.

Barthes, Roland (1981) *Camera Lucida. Reflections on Photography.* Translated by Richard Howard. New York: Hill and Wang. (Original: "La chambre claire", Editions du Seuil 1980.)

Barthes, Roland (1982a) *The Photographic Message,* in *Image-Music-Text,* essays selected and translated by Stephen Heath. Huntington: Fontana Paperbacks. (Original: "Le message photographique", *Communications* 1, 1961.)

Barthes, Roland (1982b) *Rhetoric of the Image,* in *Image-Music-Text,* essays selected and translated by Stephen Heath. Huntington: Fontana Paperbacks. (Original: "Rhétorique de l'image", *Communications* 4, 1964.)

Baudrillard, Jean (1981/2000) "The Ideological Genesis of Needs", in Juliet B. Schor and Douglas B. Holt (eds.) (2000) *The Consumer Society Reader.* New York: The New Press. pp. 57–80.

Baudrillard, Jean (1970/1998) *The Consumer Society: Myths and Structures.* Theory, Culture & Society. London & Thousand Oaks, California: Sage publications.

Beck, Ulrich (1992) *Risk Society. Towards a New Modernity.* London: Sage Publications.

Berger, Arthur Asa (1997) *Seeing is Believing. An Introduction to Visual Communication.* Mountain View, California: Mayfield Publishing Company.

Butler, Judith (1990) *Gender Trouble.* New York: Routledge.

Callon, Michel (ed.) (1998) *Laws of the Markets.* Oxford: Blackwell.

Castells, Manuel (1996) *The Rise of the Network Society.* Cambridge, Massachusetts: Blackwell.

Chaplin, Elizabeth (1994) *Sociology and Visual Representations.* London: Routledge.

Cubitt, Sean (1998) *Digital Aesthetics.* London: Sage Publications.

Emmison, Michael & Philip Smith (2000) *Researching the Visual.* London: Sage Publications.

Gagliardi, Pasquale (ed.) (1990) *Symbols and Artifacts: Views of the Corporate Landscape.* Berlin: de Gruyter.

du Gay, Paul & Michael Pryke (eds.) (2002) *Cultural Economy – cultural analysis and commercial life*. London: Sage Publications.

Goldman, Robert & Stephen Papson (1996) *Sign Wars. The Cluttered Landscape of Advertising*. New York: The Guilford Press.

Guillet de Monthoux, Pierre (1993) *Det sublimas konstnärliga ledning. Estetik, konst och företag*. Stockholm: Nerenius och Santérus förlag.

Guillet de Monthoux, Pierre (1998) *Konstföretaget: mellan spektakelkultur och kulturspektakel*. Stockholm: Korpen.

Hine, Christine (2000) *Virtual Ethnography*. London: Sage Publications.

Lash, Scott & John Urry (1994) *Economies of Signs and Spaces*. London: Sage Publications.

Latour, Bruno (1997) "Trains of thought. Piaget, formalism and the fifth dimension", *Common Knowledge*, vol. 6, no. 3, pp. 170–191.

Latour, Bruno (1999) *We Have Never Been Modern*. Cambridge, Massachusetts: Harvard University Press.

Law, John (1994) *Organizing Modernity*. Oxford: Blackwell.

van Leeuwen, Theo (2001) "Semiotics and iconography", in Theo van Leeuwen & Carey Jewitt (eds.) (2001) *Handbook of Visual Analysis*. London: Sage Publications. pp. 92–118.

Liljestrand, Jens (2002) "Starka ben" [Strong legs], På stan april 19–25, *Dagens Nyheter*, (April 19, 2002) pp. 4–7.

Linstead, Stephen & Heather Höpfl (eds.) (2000) *The Aesthetics of Organization*. London: Sage Publications.

Lister, Martin & Liz Wells (2001) "Seeing beyond belief: Cultural Studies as an approach to analysing the visual", in Theo van Leeuwen & Carey Jewitt (eds.) (2001) *Handbook of Visual Analysis*. London: Sage Publications. pp. 61–91.

Pink, Sarah (2001) *Doing Visual Ethnography. Images, Media and Representation in Research*. London, Thousand Oaks, California: Sage Publications.

Poster, Mark (1990) *The Mode of Information. Poststructuralism and Social Context*. Cambridge: Polity Press.

Poster, Mark (1995) *The Second Media Age*. Cambridge: Polity Press.

Rose, Gillian (2001) *Visual Methodologies*. London: Sage Publications.

Schroeder, Jonathan E. (2002a) *Visual Consumption*. Routledge interpretive marketing research. London: Routledge.

Schroeder, Jonathan E. (2002b) "Building Brands: Architectural Expression in the Electronic Age", in Linda M. Scott & Rajeev Batra (eds.) *Persuasive Imagery: A Consumer Response Perspective*. Mahwah, New Jersey, London: Lawrence Erlbaum.

Schroeder, Jonathan E. (2002c) "The Artist and the Brand". Paper presented at the European Academy of Management Annual Conference in May 2002.

Schroeder, Jonathan E. & Janet L. Borgerson (2002) "Innovations in Information Technology: Insights from Italian Renaissance Art", *Consumption, Markets and Culture*. Vol. 5 (2), pp. 153–169.

Stern, Barbara B. & Jonathan E. Schroeder (1994) "Interpretative Methodology from Art and Literary Criticism: A Humanistic Approach to Advertising Imagery", *European Journal of Marketing*. Vol. 28 No. 8/9, pp. 114–132.

Strati, Antonio (1999) *Organization and Aesthetics*. London: Sage Publications.

Thrift, Nigel (2002) "Performing cultures in the new economy", in Paul du Gay & Michael Pryke (eds.) (2002) *Cultural Economy – cultural analysis and commercial life*. London: Sage Publications. pp. 201–233.

Chapter 10

The Carousel Event

Steffen Böhm

Child on the carousel. The platform bearing the docile animals moves close to the ground. It is at the height which, in dreams, is best for flying. Music starts, and the child moves away from his mother with a jerk. At first he is afraid to leave her. But then he notices how brave he himself is. He is ensconced, like the just ruler, over a world that belongs to him. Tangential trees and natives line his way. Then, in an Orient, his mother reappears. Next, emerging from the jungle, comes a treetop, exactly as the child saw it thousands of years ago – just now on the carousel. His beast is devoted: like a mute Arion he rides his silent fish, or a wooden Zeus-buss carries him off like an immaculate Europa. The eternal return of all things has long become child's wisdom, and life a primeval frenzy of domination, with the booming orchestrion as the crown jewels at the center. As the music slows, space begins to stammer and the trees to come to their senses. The carousel becomes uncertain ground. And his mother appears, the much-hammered stake about which the landing child winds the rope of his gaze. (Walter Benjamin, 1928, *One-Way Street*)

A child on a carousel. This imagery, taken from Walter Benjamin's book of aphorisms, *One-Way Street*, describes an event of speed. It is a typical example of Benjamin's poetic writing that invites us into a mysterious world of dreams, images and allegories. What do they mean; what does Benjamin want to tell us? Instead of attempting to decipher the symbolic construction of his writing, an understanding of Benjamin's texts is only possible, I would argue, by immersing oneself into precisely the event of speed he describes. As he tells us in his essay 'The Task of the Translator' (1999a: 70ff), an exact translation of language is impossible; a translation is always already a 'destruction' of the 'original' text. Thus, the task of writing cannot be to interpret the true meaning of a work, but to immerse oneself into an author's textual apparatus in order to repeat, that is translate, the event that has been produced by exactly this apparatus. It is like stepping onto the platform of a carousel; one is suddenly part of a different machine. The experience of speed; one is taken away onto a journey. The machine spins around its axis. The world stands still, yet it simultaneously flits by. It is this moment of the simultaneity of speed and stillness that describes the event of translation. What I would like to do in this chapter is to attempt to repeat Benjamin's carousel event, a repetition, as I said, that can only be a translation. The specific translation that is attempted here is to explore the significance of the carousel event for the study of organisation – organisation being understood in a broad sense as the study of the social organisation of contemporary capitalist modernity. What I will argue is that Benjamin's carousel is a two-fold event: First, it points to the 'goings-on' of capital. I will engage with Marx's writings to show how capitalist social organisation eternally returns to itself and thus creates what Benjamin calls the dream-like phantasmagoria of modernity. This phantasmagoria is an event of speed as repetition. Second, in an affirmative reading, I will argue that the carousel event presents possibilities for a political event of decision: in the moment of the simultaneity of speed and stillness history presents itself as an image, which enables carousel passengers to see time differently. The carousel event is thus a dialectical moment that points to both the eternal return of the ever-same and the transcendence of the same by the different.

* * * *

In January 1928 the German publisher Rowohlt published two books by Walter Benjamin, *Ursprung des deutschen Trauerspiels* (*The Origin of German Tragic Drama*) and *Einbahnstraße* (*One-Way Street*), which were written at roughly the same time – in the period between 1923 and 1926. The first, the so-called *Trauerspiel* book, was a highly original engagement with German baroque literature that tried to establish allegory as the main organisational principle of the baroque. Brodersen has called this book a "quite provocatively 'unacademic' work, at least in the customary under-standing of the term …. From the work's epigraph to specific aspects of his manner of procedure, to the form in which the material was presented, the book was a complete parody of what German professors understood to be a systematic, methodologically reasoned work" (1996: 149). In a letter to his friend Gerhard Scholem, Benjamin wrote about the *Trauerspiel* book: "what surprises me most of all … is that what I have written consists, as it were, almost entirely of quotations. It is the craziest mosaic technique you can imagine" (1994: 256). It is no wonder, then, that this 'crazy mosaic' of quotations did not serve its intended purpose as an *habilitation* thesis, which was required to become a professor at a German university. After receiving a doctorate for his thesis *The Concept of Art Criticism in German Romanticism* in 1919, Benjamin tried to start a career as a university lec-turer in Bern, Heidelberg, Gießen and Frankfurt am Main. Although he had considerable support from friends, he failed – for various reasons – in all of these institutions to gain a foothold in the German university system and put his life on a stable economic basis. The *Trauerspiel* text, which he submit-ted to the University of Frankfurt in 1925, was his last attempt to become a 'respectable' member of the academic profession. However, he withdrew

200

his application for an *habilitation* after it became clear that his text had not received any appreciation in several departments of the university.

Benjamin had written part of the *Trauerspiel* book on the Italian island of Capri, where he stayed for several months in 1924. During this visit he met and fell in love with Asja Lacis, a Latvian Bolshevik who "was part of a politically active avant-garde dedicated to developing the cultural practice of the Soviet Communist Party". She worked "with Brecht's theatre in the 1920s and on Erwin Piscator's agitprop spectaculars. She wanted to generate a revolutionary pedagogy, specifically through theatre work with proletarian children" (Leslie, 2000: 3). What must have partly attracted Benjamin to Lacis was her intellectual background in politico-economic materialism and her insights into Soviet communism, the most progressive political, cultural, economic and social event of the first two decades of the twentieth century. Taking a keen interest in new book publications, Benjamin had also just got hold of Lukács' *History and Class Consciousness*, which was published in 1923. This and other Marxian reading material must have been a key talking point for Lacis and Benjamin during their stay in Italy.

Something had happened to Benjamin in Capri. Instead of fully concentrating on his *Trauerspiel* book, which was supposed to guarantee him an academic career and a stable economic base, he was flirting with new ideas, with new theoretical and political vistas. In his letters to Scholem he expressed his feeling that "they were indications of a change that awakened in me the will not to mask the actual and political elements of my ideas in the Old Franconian way I did before, but also to develop them by experimenting and taking extreme measures. This of course means that the literary exegesis of German literature will now take a back seat" (1994: 258). So, while he was still engaged with his study of German baroque literature, his mind was already travelling ahead of him. He was making plans for new writing projects. It seems as if his flirtation with 'Bolshevist theory' – in the practice of Lacis and Lukács – had encouraged him to rethink the politics of his writings, which up to then, although unusual in their style, had remained somewhat abstract and, perhaps, meta-theoretical and thus disconnected from the actual materialist realities of his time. The profoundness of this rethinking is expressed in a letter to Scholem, written on 29 May 1926 in Paris, in which he signals his attempt to "leave the purely theoretical sphere. This will be humanly possible", he went on to say, "in only two ways, in religious or political observance" (1994: 300). Benjamin thus formulated the problem of the dialectical relationship between theory and practice, which, it seems, he felt he needed to rethink during that time. The formulation of this problem was undoubtedly influenced by his study of Lukács' *History and Class Consciousness*, which was firmly based on a materialist conception of the theory/practice dialectic. His flirtation with new Marxist theories and practices opened up new ways for him to think about the political purposes and implications of his intellectual work. In a letter to Scholem he writes: "anyone of our generation who feels and understands the historical moment in which he [sic] exists in this world, not as mere words, but as a battle, cannot renounce the study and the practice of the mechanism through which things (and conditions) and the masses interact" (1994: 300). By the time he wrote these words in May 1926, he had clearly begun to appreciate the importance of a materialist thinking, which he first experimented with in *One-Way Street*, a book that Benjamin dedicated to Asja Lacis with the following words: "This street is named | Asja Lacis Street | after her who | as an engineer | cut it through the author" (1996: 444).

The simultaneous publication of the *Trauerspiel* book and *One-Way Street* marked an event that pointed to the end of what Benjamin called his German literature production cycle and the start of a new production cycle that would let him engage with modern reality in a more materialist and political fashion. While the *Trauerspiel* book, despite its somewhat 'unacademic style', was clearly targeted at the academic reader who has a firm knowledge of philosophical concepts, *One-Way Street* was a collection of aphorisms, mental images and even dreams of modern city life. The break of Benjamin's writing style is also represented by the different typography and book-covers chosen for the two books. The *Trauerspiel* book was uniform and reserved in its design; it used a Gothic typeface. It clearly tried to appeal to an establishment of German academic intellectualism (Brodersen, 1996: 146). *One-Way Street*, in contrast, had a very modern feel to it. A Roman typeface was used and the cover, designed by Sascha Stone, "gave an immediate, forceful impression of modernity, openness, *speed*, quick-wittedness and simultaneity; in short, the impression of a book that was abreast of the times in every respect" (*ibid.*, emphasis added). However, *One-Way Street* was not simply intended as a book that would be able to keep up with the fashion of the day. Instead, Benjamin warned Hugo von Hofmannsthal, editor of *Neue Deutsche Blätter* and publisher of several of Benjamin's essays, "that you not see everything striking about the book's internal and external design as a compromise with the 'tenor of the age'. Precisely in terms of its eccentric aspects, the book is, if not a trophy, nonetheless a document of an internal struggle" (1994: 325). This struggle – that which led him to broaden his horizon towards new materialist theories and radical political practices – was represented by the aphoristic nature of *One-Way Street*. Instead of a coherent argument, Benjamin offered a series of what he called 'profane motifs' that, as he said, "march past in this project, hellishly intensified" (1994: 322).

These 'profane motifs' are images of modern city life: carousels, panoramas, breakfast rooms, cellars, clocks, embassies, flags, books, diaries, antiques, toys, stamps, betting offices, beer halls, planetariums, and many other things and technologies that characterise a modern urban environment. What

Benjamin wanted to achieve with these aphoristic images was "to attain the most extreme concreteness for an era, as it occasionally manifested itself in children's games, a building, or a real-life situation" (1994: 348). *One-Way Street* engaged with the materialities of the 'profane' world; it aimed to "grasp topicality as the reverse of the eternal in history and to make an impression of this, the side of the medallion hidden from view" (1994: 325). Instead of taking the materiality of here and now for granted and seeing history as a given return of the eternal, Benjamin wanted to explore the possibilities of being "'concrete' in the context of the philosophy of history" (1994: 333). That is, he tried to see the history inscribed into the 'profane' things of modern city life.

Capri was an event that cut through Benjamin's work and life. It opened him up to materialist theories and practices and encouraged him to confront the political implications of his thought in a more direct way. In May 1925, a month or two before he withdrew his application for an *habilitation* at the University of Frankfurt, Benjamin announced to Scholem that he would hasten his "involvement with Marxist politics and join the party" (1994: 268). By that time he had already studied some parts of Lukács' *History and Class Consciousness*, a book that, in his words, had astonished him (1994: 248). It was Lukács' writing that made him reconsider the relationship between theory and practice: "the problem with 'theory and practice' seems to me in effect to be that, given the disparity that must be preserved between

Book cover of
The Origin of German Tragic Drama,
1928

Book cover of
One-Way Street, 1928

these two realms, any definitive insight into theory is precisely dependent on practice" (*ibid.*). Capri was an event that made Benjamin reconsider his engagement with the theory/practice bind. His study of Lukács' and his relationship with Lacis confronted him with the concrete political urgencies of his lifetime. It seems as if he made a decision in Capri; and the first result of this decision was *One-Way Street*.

* * * *

Part of what Benjamin tries to do in *One-Way Street* is to show how in modern cities human relations become increasingly reified or thing-like. This language mirrors Lukács who, in *History and Class Consciousness*, uses the concept of reification to analyse the process of commodification, which he describes as the "central, structural problem of capitalist society" (1971: 83). Following Marx, Lukács defines the basis for the commodity-structure as the relation between people that "takes on the character of a thing and thus acquires a 'phantom objectivity', an autonomy that seems so strictly rational and all-embracing as to conceal every trace of its fundamental nature: the relation between people" (*ibid.*).

Benjamin adopts this diagnosis to characterise what he regards as the coldness of the modern metropolis that constantly threatens to freeze the human subject to death (1996: 453–454). In his view, the urban subject becomes a material thing: "Bus conductors, officials, workmen, salesmen – they all feel themselves to be the representatives of a refractory material world whose menace they take pains to demonstrate through their own surliness" (1996: 454). What is at the heart of modern social relations is not, according to him, the warmth of a community but the coldness of money, which "stands ruinously at the center of every vital interest" (1996: 451–452).

For Benjamin, money crushes the vitality of life as it alters the way human beings interact with each other: "the freedom of conversation is being lost. If, earlier, it was a matter of course in conversation to take interest in one's interlocutor, now this is replaced by inquiry into the cost of his shoes or of his umbrella. Irresistibly intruding on any convivial exchange is the theme of the conditions of life, of money" (1996: 453). In Benjamin's view, money is the theme that determines the language and communication in the modern metropolis. Money territorialises, as Deleuze and Guattari (1987) put it, all language and vital interests. Money reifies life and makes it available for capital's reproduction machinery.

Benjamin cannot help but see the modern metropolis as a theatre stage: "It is as if one were trapped in a theater and had to follow the events on the stage whether one wanted to or not – had to make them again and again, willingly or unwillingly, the subject of one's thought and speech" (1996: 453). In Marx, too, the commodity presents itself on a kind of stage. Marx uses the image of a wooden table to describe the transformation of an ordinary thing into something with a life of its own. As soon as the table "emerges as a commodity, it changes into a thing which transcends sensuousness. It not only stands with its feet on the ground, but, in relation to all other commodities, it stands on its head, and evolves out of its wooden brain grotesque ideas, far more wonderful than if it were to begin dancing of its own free will" (Marx, 1976: 163). The point of Marx's dancing table is to show how an ordinary thing, the table, acquires an extra-sensuousness once it has been turned into a commodity. This extra-sensuousness defines the attractiveness of the commodity; it has to look beautiful on stage in order to excite its viewers.

Benjamin's walk along the one-way streets of the modern city shows how ordinary things and beings are transformed into extra-sensuous commodities. For him, the commodity animates the urban theatre in a new way; it accelerates the rhythms of life: "One need recall only the experience of velocities by virtue of which mankind is now preparing to embark on incalculable journeys into the interior of time, to encounter there rhythms from which the sick shall draw strength ... The 'Lunaparks' are a prefiguration of sanatoria" (1996: 487). Instead of sending the sick to sanatoria, capital provides them with Lunaparks, carousels and other fun machines. In Benjamin's view, the commodity injects life into sick landscapes of modernity; it is a machinery of speed that accelerates social relations beyond the point of recognition.

* * * *

Owing to the extensive use of machinery and to division of labour, the work of the proletarians has lost all individual character, and, consequently, all charm for the workman. He becomes an appendage of the machine, and it is only the most simple, most monotonous, and most easily acquired knack that is required of him. Hence, the cost of production of a workman is restricted almost entirely to the means of subsistence that he requires for his maintenance and for the propagation of his race. But the price of a commodity, and therefore also of labour, is equal to its cost of production. In proportion, therefore, as the repulsiveness of the work increases, the wage decreases. Nay more, in proportion as the use of machinery and division of labour increases, in the same proportion the burden of toil also increases, whether by prolongation of the working hours, by increase of the work exacted in a given time, or by increased speed of the machinery, etc. (Karl Marx and Friedrich Engels, 1848, *The Communist Manifesto*)

* * * *

A dozen automata bent over the garments, sewing, machining, pressing, at top speed. Speed! Speed! That was the keynote. No time even to wipe your nose, the coats must be kept flying about the workshop, on the move all the while. Speed! Speed! The quickest worker set the pace. (Simon Blumenfeld, 1935, *Jew Boy*)

* * * *

It was now that the tempo of the shift moved from hard and fast work to a controlled frenzy of washing-up. Conversation came to an end. We were, I suppose, cheaper than industrial dishwashing machines but we imitated them quite well. First we put all the cutlery into great wire trays and lowered them into a large sink of piping-hot detergent and water, then with a big old wooden brush with mangled bristles we reached in and scrubbed them all in a general sort of way. Now we shook and joggled the steaming heavy trays, swooshing them up and down, before lifting them into an even hotter sink of clean water with more swooshing and joggling. There was no time to leave them to dry, so they had to be wiped down fast and put back on to the cutlery trolley, all facing the same way. After that came mountains of plastic plates and the plastic trays used by the youngest children: trays like airline dishes with indentations for different kinds of foods. All these were also dunked and scrubbed and stacked at high speed.... Why so fast and frantic? Because there were now only thirty-five paid minutes left to get it done. After that, it would be in our own time and Wilma was rightly determined that we would all be out of there every day by 2.10 at the latest – and we always were. In theory our shift ended at 2.30, but that was only if we took the full half-hour unpaid for lunch, a waste of time for everyone. As it was we took under five minutes' unpaid for lunch and worked flat out instead. We usually managed to get the work done in our paid three hours, plus five or sometimes ten minutes' unpaid. But it could only be done in that time by working at this maniacal rate. (Polly Toynbee, 2003, *Hard Work: Life in Low-Pay Britain*)

* * * *

As Marx (1976) shows throughout *Capital*, capital is not a thing that sits in somebody's pocket, but a process. "The material manifestation of this process exists as a transformation from money into commodities back into money plus profit" (Harvey, 1982: 20). Capital is a process of the expansion of value; it needs to be constantly on the move in order to expand and reproduce itself. Capital is able to expand its value by employing labour as a commodity in the production process. For Marx, the capitalist production process, which is controlled and dominated by capital, and which employs the labour commodity in return for wages, defines the definite class relations and antagonisms between capital and labour. Capital only regards labour as valuable in the form of what Marx calls labour-power. That is, the capitalist only sees the labourer as a commodity that can be made use of in the labour process in order to produce other commodities. However, as Marx (1976: 274–280) explains, the capitalist purchases labour's labour-power for a certain amount of time not simply to produce commodities. The whole purpose of employing labour power is for the capitalist to produce surplus value, that is, produce greater value that it itself has. And what is important in this context is that it is only labour that is able to produce surplus value for capital by putting its labour-power to work. Labour and capital are thus locked into an antagonistic class relationship, which is always already dominated by capital, as it is the capitalist who owns labour-power and the value that is produced in excess of the labourer's own reproduction.

Since the labour process is the sole origin of surplus value, capital's incentive is to maximise the usage and exploitation of labour-power. Marx (1976) distinguishes between two main ways to produce surplus value; absolute and relative surplus value. His celebrated chapter in *Capital* on the working day (1976: 340–411) shows in detail that the capitalist seeks to gain *absolute* surplus value and valorise itself by extending the hours a labourer works a day. In this chapter Marx analyses the struggle between collective labour and the capitalist class over the extent of the working day. As "capital is dead labour which, vampire-like, lives only by sucking living labour, and lives the more, the more labour it sucks" (1976: 342), the capitalist class constantly seeks to make the working day as long as possible, as the rate of absolute surplus value is directly dependent on the amount of time capital can employ labour-power. In contrast, labourers claim that they need to reproduce themselves and satisfy their physical, social and intellectual needs (1976: 341). For Marx (1976: 344), it is this struggle that defines the antagonistic class relationship between labour and capital, which manifests itself in the way both capitalists and labourers seek collectivity and institutional representation in order to fight this battle more effectively.

According to Marx, capital "was celebrating its orgies" (1976: 390) in the first half of the 19th century. Workers, "'young persons and children were worked all night, all day or both *ad libitum*'" (*ibid.*). There were few regulations as to how many hours a labourer should be allowed to work per day, and the few laws that had been introduced were not enforced. But resistance and the collectivisation of labour gained in momentum and between 1833 and the late 1860s several parliamentary acts were passed to regulate the working day among other labour matters (see Marx, 1976: 389ff).

The shortening of the working day was clearly due to the success of the early labour resistance movements. However, it was partly made possible by capital's advances in increasing *relative* surplus value that were the result of the introduction of large-scale production machinery and the more efficient organisation of the production process (see Marx, 1976: 429ff). Marx's concept of relative surplus value points to the exploitation of labour by way of the constant revolutionising of the technological and organisational conditions of the production process. The productivity of labour can be increased when the proportion of the working day necessary for the reproduction of the value of labour-power falls (1976: 432). That is, if a labourer's work is embedded in a more advanced technological and organisational production arrangement, the capitalist can increase surplus value without extending the working day.

For Marx, the shortening of the working day "makes it possible for the worker to set more labour-power in motion within a given time. As soon as that shortening becomes compulsory, machinery becomes in the hands of capital the objective means, systematically employed, for squeezing out more labour in a given time. This occurs in two ways: the speed of the machines is increased, and the same worker receives a greater quantity of machinery to supervise or operate" (1976: 536). Increasing the speed of the labour process is thus the prime means to enhance the productivity of labour-power and hence advance relative surplus value for the capitalist. The introduction of large-scale machinery and more efficient organisational principles, such as Taylor's Scientific Management, can be seen as the direct response to pressures to shorten the working day and increase the productivity of labour-power by way of speeding up the production process (Taylor, 1911/1972).

One of the contributions of Braverman's work (1974) is to show how this Taylorist process of speeding up production has deskilled workers and made them mere extensions of machines. As Harvey (1982: 31) argues, however, the concept of 'deskilling' is rather inelegant, as productivity-driven reorganisations of the workplace seemed to have resulted in a *re*skilling of the labourer. Taylorist reorganisations and the introduction of large scale machinery, such as Ford's assembly line, have established new hierarchies in the workplace. On one hand, the bulk of workers now define themselves in relation to a particular skill that is harvested by the production process turning the labourer into 'living automatons' (Dugald Stewart, cited by Marx, 1976: 481) that follow the rhythms of the industrial machines. The new skill of the workers is to see themselves as fragments that operate in a larger machinic assembly; Taylorism and other reorganisations of the labour process reconfigure the worker's body. On the other hand, 'mental' skills are now needed, which are exercised by a "special kind of wage-labourer" – the manager – who commands "the labour process in the name of capital" (Marx, 1976: 450). A new breed of wage-labourer is introduced, one that is disconnected from the shopfloor and reskilled as a servant of capital. The task of managers is to oversee the workplace and organise the production process in an ever more efficient way.

Since surplus values produced through advanced technological and organisational production methods are always relative and ephemeral – precisely because competition would soon catch up with these advances rendering the relative advantage in surplus value production non-existent – capital demands that its managers continuously revolutionise production processes. We are thus talking about a second dimension of speed in relation to the production of relative surplus value. Not only does the drive for relative surplus value speed up the labour process and thus the exploitation of wage-labourers, the ephemerality of any relative surplus value requires the frenetic search for new technological and organisational production methods that once again would enable capital to gain a relative competitive advantage.

* * * *

When, as children, we were made a present of those great encyclopaedic works – World and Mankind or The Earth or the latest volume of the New Universe – wasn't it into the multicoloured 'Carboniferous Landscape' or 'European Animal Kingdom of the Ice Age' that we plunged first of all, and weren't we, as though at first sight, drawn by an indeterminate affinity between the ichthyosaurs and bisons, the mammoths and the woodlands? Yet this same strange rapport and primordial relatedness is revealed in the landscape of an arcade. Organic world and inorganic world, abject poverty and insolent luxury enter into the most contradictory communication; the commodity intermingles and interbreeds as promiscuously as images in the most tangled of dreams. Primordial landscape of consumption. (Walter Benjamin, ca. 1937, *Arcades Project*)

* * * *

Marx is sometimes criticised for concentrating his analysis of the political economy of capitalism on the production process, and, to be more precise, on the labour process. The argument is that Marx's theories are not particularly strong when it comes to explaining the multiple aspects of consumption that seem to dominate large areas of modern capitalist society today. Indeed, the first volume of *Capital* is largely concerned with a detailed analysis of the labour process. However, when one studies the second volume of *Capital* as well as his *Grundrisse* notes, it becomes clear that Marx is as concerned about aspects of consumption and circulation of commodities as he is interested in their production.

In *Grundrisse*, Marx insists again and again that capital is a process rather than a thing that is simply produced in a factory. A product that is produced through the labour process is virtually value-less if it is not circulated, as a commodity, in the market and eventually sold. That is, the surplus value produced in the labour process cannot be realised without the commodity being circulated and sold. For Marx, "circulation therefore belongs within the concept of capital" (1973: 638). In fact, circulation must be seen as an integral part of production, which is to say that any stasis or fixation of the commodity is undesirable: "As long as it remains in the production process it is not capable of circulating; and it is virtually devalued. As long as it remains in circulation, it is not capable of producing, not capable of positing surplus value, not capable of engaging in the process of capital. As long as it cannot be brought to market, it is fixated as product. As long as it has to remain on the market, it is fixated as commodity. As long as it cannot be exchanged for conditions of production, it is fixated as money" (Marx, 1973: 621). This means that fixated capital is tied-down capital; it loses value and thus has to be kept in circulation. Hence capital needs to be in a constant process of circulation.

For Marx, there is a constant dialectical movement between stages of production and circulation, which he describes as follows: (1) creation of surplus value within the production process, which results in the product; (2) bringing the product to market; transformation of the product into a commodity; (3) (a) entry of the commodity into ordinary circulation, which results in the transformation into money; (b) money circulation and retransformation of money into the conditions of production – this means that capital circulates first as a commodity, then as money, and vice versa; (4) renewal of the production process, which appears as reproduction of the original capital, and production process of surplus capital (1973: 619). This makes clear again that the labour process alone cannot explain the vicissitudes of capital. What makes capital capital is its continuous circulation in order to realise surplus value and to initiate a new circle of the production process: capital is a carousel; capital is circulating capital.

One should, however, not simply conflate production and circulation into a single process. Marx is quite clear that production and circulation need to be seen as distinct: "the renewal of the production process can only take place ... when the part of the circulation process which is distinct from the production process has been completed" (1973: 627). So, the transformation of money into capital that can be used to renew the production process – see stage (3b) above – can only take place once commodity and money have completed their circulation. So circulation time – which is distinct from production time, as discussed above – is a very important measure for the capitalist: "the more rapid the circulation, the shorter the circulation time, the more often can the same capital repeat the production process" (*ibid.*). What Marx therefore shows is "that circulation time becomes a determinant moment for labour time, for the creation of value. The independence of labour time is thereby negated, and the production process is itself posited as determined by exchange, so that immediate production is socially linked to it and dependent on this link – not only as a material moment, but also as an economic moment, a determinant, characteristic form" (1973: 628).

It is thus in the capitalist's interest to speed up the circulation of capital because it is directly linked to the production of surplus value. It is an obvious economic logic: the longer a commodity sits on the shelves of a supermarket, the longer it takes to realise the surplus value produced in the labour process, and the longer it takes to turn the commodity into money and again into capital that can be reinvested into the production process. One says, 'time is money'. Perhaps one should specify this and say that for the capitalist a reduction of circulation time has a direct impact on the expansion of value. So, there is considerable pressure to decrease circulation time. The ideal scenario for the capitalist is for circulation time to equal zero, "i.e. the transition of capital from one phase to the next at the speed of thought" (Marx, 1973: 631). Over the past ten years one has seen tremendous efforts to turn this ideal into reality. For example, just-in-time (JIT) and point-of-sale (POS) systems have sought to reduce the time products sit unused in warehouses and supermarkets. Equally, the logic behind e-commerce systems is to cut large distribution stages (the so-called 'middle man') out of the value chain. The computer manufacturer Dell, for example, only sells its products over the Internet or the telephone; they only start to produce a computer once it has been ordered by a customer. With such a system circulation time of the commodity is drastically reduced and capital is not tied up in commodities that have not been sold yet: commodities are (almost) circulated at 'the speed of thought'.

* * * *

Interested parties explain the culture industry in technological terms. It is alleged that because millions participate in it, certain reproduction processes are necessary that inevitably require identical needs in innumerable places to be satisfied with identical goods. The technical contrast between the few production centers and the large number of widely dispersed consumption points is said to demand organization and planning by management ... No mention is made of the fact that the basis on which technology acquires power over society is the power of those whose economic hold over society is greatest. A technological rationale is the rationale of domination itself. Automobiles, bombs, and movies keep the whole thing together ... It has made the technology of the culture industry no more than the achievement of standardization and mass production, sacrificing whatever involved a distinction between the logic of the work and that of the social system. This is the result not of a law of movement in technology as such but of its function in today's economy. (Theodor W. Adorno and Max Horkheimer, *Dialectic of Enlightenment*, 1944)

* * * *

Capital is a carousel; it is continuously in circular motion in order to reproduce and valorise itself. However, this carousel is in constant danger of breaking down precisely because there are a number of limits built into the system of reproduction of capital (see Marx, 1973: 415ff). There is not enough space here to discuss these limits in detail. Let us just mention one of these multiple limits: Because the capitalist continuously seeks to maximise surplus value, production of commodities is expanded without the market necessarily being able to swallow all; there is simply not enough demand. The result is a sharp increase in circulation time, the disastrous consequences of which we have discussed above. This is a classic case of overproduction, which, according to Marx (*ibid.*), is a constant danger for the capitalist system. As we have seen, capital constantly seeks to increase the velocity of circulation, and it has found several technological and organisational innovations to speed up the carousel of capital reproduction. However, an important other way to decrease circulation time is to expand demand, that is, the potential market. This is to say that one cure for overproduction is to look for new consumers of a commodity. This is thus the second aspect of the circulation of capital: by conquering ever more markets, that is, by continuously expanding its circulation, it is able to increase the velocity of its reproduction. The speed of the carousel of capital is produced through the expansion of the system itself.

As Marx says in the *Grundrisse*: "The circulation of capital is at the same time its becoming, its growth, its vital process. If anything needed to be compared with the circulation of blood, it was not the formal circulation of money, but the content-filled circulation of capital" (1973: 517). The vampire-image of capital, which Marx uses in the first volume of *Capital* (see above), comes to mind again (see also Godfrey *et al.*, 2004). Marx portrays capital as a living organism that sucks blood out of the social in order to valorise and stay alive itself. But perhaps the vampire is not the best imagery here: rather than sucking the blood out of the social, the organism of capital expands itself rhizomatically and connects its blood vessels with those of other organisms. As Negri puts it: "The social conditions of production are formed, organized and dominated by the organization of circulation, by the impulse capital gives to it. Therefore circulation is, above all, the expansion of the potency of capital; and for the same reason it entails the appropriation of all the social conditions and their placement in valorization" (1991: 112). The expansive circulation of capital is its response to its inherent limits and crises. In order for the carousel to continue to spin around its axis, new life-spheres need to be incorporated into the machinery of capital. Rather than sucking life out of the social, it links its blood vessels to ever more social territories in order to expand its circulation.

In the second volume of *Capital*, Marx (1992: 427ff) identifies the object of the continuous expansion of the circulation of capital: total social capital. This means that capital's expansion of its circularity aims at nothing less than social organisation as such: "the socialization of capital is a process which determines, through circulation, an irresistible compulsion towards expansion, appropriation and homogenization – under the sign of a social totality" (Negri, 1991: 113). In the name of conquering ever newer markets – only the world market is the limit – Marx sees capital as increasingly producing society; in fact, capital becomes the blood of life itself. In Negri's reading of Marx: "capital constitutes society, capital is entirely social capital. Circulation produces the socialization of capital" (1991: 114). In Negri's view, this necessarily means that it is increasingly difficult to distinguish between labour and capital: "capital is the totality of labor and life" (1991: 122). That is, as capital aims to be the social – to circulate into ever new spheres of life – the boundaries between labour/life and capital become increasingly blurred. As the carousel speeds up, our vision becomes increasingly blurred. Where is the sky; where is the ground; where are left and right? Speed blurs our senses.

As Negri and others argue, the historical development of capital is one that is characterised by an increasing socialisation of the labour process. This means that more and more areas of social life are captured by the circulation of capital. In *Empire*, Hardt and Negri (2000) refer to this as the communicative aspects of capital. For them, the concept of communication points to all areas of transport, media, language and information exchanges that characterise the expansive circulation of capital. What is important to realise in this regard is that it is not technology that is driving this process – as Harvey (1982: 100) notes, Marx should not be seen as a technological determinist. Rather, capital is an inherently expansive force; capital is a machine itself, as Deleuze and Guattari (1987) maintain. This means that it is not technology that makes capital into a communicative machine; instead, capital makes use of technology in order to serve its machinic desires. So, when Leslie notes that technology is seen by capitalists and "machine-obsessed modernists as a magical apparatus of social refurbishment whose scientific properties can remedy all predicaments through technical rationality" (2000: 39), she misses the point that it is capital itself which should be seen as such a 'magical apparatus'. Technology is merely an extension of the machinic aspects of capital itself.

The point that the capital machine is seen as a technics of 'social refurbishment' is important here. It would be a mistake to simply say, for example, that Ford's assembly line was a manufacturing system that was used to gain a competitive advantage and produce a higher surplus value. Instead, it was a whole apparatus to produce not only cars but also subjects and social milieus. Ford paid his workers above-average wages for their labour-power precisely because this enabled him to create extra demand for his commodities. Equally, he built social housing for his workers because he could thus enable a better reproduction of labour-power (see also Burawoy, 1982). Ford was a genius when it comes to the expansive speed of the circulation of capital. The event of Ford's Model T car was of course the extension of another event that aided the rapid expansion of the circulation of capital in the 19th century: the railway. In America, for example, the train enabled the conquering of new markets in the mid-West and the Pacific regions; it enabled the emergence of a national economy and the immense acceleration of the division of labour on a vast geographical scale. Railways were signs of progress in the 19th century: one could suddenly move at high speed from one place to the other; a spatial movement that "became so wedded to the concept of historical movement that these could no longer be distinguished" (Buck-Morss, 1989: 91). Through the railway capital had not only conquered new markets and increased its speed of circulation, it also territorialised time and history: the expansion of the circulation of the capital carousel and historical progress became one and the same thing.

But nowadays the train and car are relatively old technologies. Today circulation seems to become more 'virtual': "Now speed moves into a different register: from the movement of people and material objects in space to the movement of images and signals at absolute speed" (Lash, 1999: 289). Today it is not only the train, assembly line and car that 'keep the whole thing together', to evoke Adorno and Horkheimer's words (1979: 121), but TV, the Internet and other information and communication technologies distributing (moving) images, news stories, information and knowledge. Let us recall again Benjamin's words: "One need recall only the experience of velocities by virtue of which mankind is now preparing to

Paula McArdle, 'Carousel'

214

embark on incalculable journeys into the interior of time, to encounter there rhythms from which the sick shall draw strength" (1996: 487). The Internet, for example, is such a journey, not only into the interior of time but also the subject and life itself. The Internet enables the circulation of capital on a new scale – not only geographically but also in terms of the interiors of subjectivity it is able to reach. Life/labour and capital become increasingly indistinguishable.

* * * *

Benjamin's *One-Way Street* was his first major attempt to reflect about the modern cityscape, which, during his time of writing in the 1920s, became increasingly characterised by signs of capital's expansive circulation: advertising, world exhibitions, fashions, film stars, and department stores, to name just a few. Although *One-Way Street* was clearly influenced by the experience of his hometown Berlin, Benjamin said in a letter that "the book owes a lot to Paris, being my first attempt to come to terms with this city. I am continuing this effort in a second book called *Paris Arcades*" (1994: 325). At the end of the 1920s Benjamin therefore started a new writing project, which was a direct continuation of his book *One-Way Street*. He predicted this new project to "take a few weeks" (1994: 322). What has came to be known as the *Arcades Project* (1999b) turned out to be his life-project, which occupied him until his death in 1940 when he committed suicide while fleeing from the Nazis. The project thus remained unfinished.

Benjamin was fascinated by the Parisian arcade because it presented him with the 'world in miniature' (1999b: 31), a world that was characterised by the triumphal rise of the bourgeois class, technological industrialism and the commodity. In the *Arcades Project*, which, similarly to *One-Way Street*, is a collection of quotes and aphorisms, he cites the *Illustrated Guide to Paris* which introduces the arcades as "a recent invention of industrial luxury, [that] are glass-roofed, marble-paneled corridors extending through whole blocks of buildings, whose owners have joined together for such enterprises. Lining both sides of these corridors, which get their light from above, are the most elegant shops, so that the arcade is a city, a world in miniature" (1999b: 31). The Parisian arcades first appeared in the early 1850s and when Benjamin was walking through them – or their remains – in the 1920s and 1930s, it must have been like a journey into the historical archives of capitalism, an encounter with the childhood years of modernity. The purpose of the *Arcades Project* was precisely to encounter the historical 'origins' of capitalist modernity, and for Benjamin it was clearly Paris that stood at the centre of what he (1973) called the passage into 'the era of high capitalism' (see also Böhm, 2006). It was a project that was, as Buck-Morss notes, "constructed with the 'utmost concreteness' out of the historical material itself, the outdated remains of those nineteenth-century buildings, technologies, and commodities that were the precursors of his own era" (1989: 3).

For Benjamin, the 'hero' of Parisian modernity is the *flâneur*, an upper middle class, bourgeois man who walks in places where there are big crowds and 'things' to see – for example, in the arcades. Benjamin sees the *flâneur* as a subject whose experience is characterised by the 'shocks' of the modern city: commodities, advertising images, anonymous crowds. For Benjamin, the *flâneur* has a deep empathy with these objects, these 'things': "The *flâneur* is someone abandoned in the crowd. In this he shares the situation of the commodity" (1973: 55). As if the commodity had a soul, it tries to 'nestle' in the body-house of the *flâneur*: "Like a roving soul in search for a body" the commodity "enters another person" whenever it wishes (*ibid.*). Benjamin writes that this luring sensuousness of the commodity 'intoxicates' the *flâneur*; the narcotic commodity lures him into a 'dream world', in which the most mundane things on sale can be enjoyed.

Benjamin chose the term 'dream world' to describe Parisian modernity precisely because he saw the arcades producing a kind of 'sleeping collectivity', a collective dream consciousness: "The nineteenth century, a space-time '*Zeitraum*' (a dream-time '*Zeit-traum*') in which the individual consciousness more and more secures itself in reflecting, while the collective consciousness sinks into ever deeper sleep ... We must follow in its wake so as to expound the nineteenth century – in fashion and advertising, in buildings and politics – as the outcome of its dream visions" (1999b: 389). For Benjamin, capitalist modernity is the 'dream-time' of the carousel, the merry-go-round: one sits on a toy horse (exchanging views with fellow riders) that speeds around its own axis (Missac, 1995: 108). The movement of this carousel is one that 'eternally returns' to itself; it announces change with every second, but it just returns to us the ever-same. The carousel gives its passengers the impression of being on a speedy train of progress, a train that relentlessly searches for the new, but it just 'eternally returns' to the same station. The name of this station is 'capital'; it is the 'obligatory passage point' for all passengers (Böhm, 2006). For Benjamin, capital constantly announces 'the new'. However, this 'newness' is always already reterritorialised within the specific value system of capital. The carousel of capital gives the impression of speed and change, but for Benjamin this is only a phantasmagoric illusion. Although, capital continuously searches for 'the new' and aims to circulate itself in ever new territories, in the end "there is nothing really new" (1999b: 112) precisely because capital always returns to itself.

Benjamin's usage of the term 'phantasmagoria', which appears in the *Arcades Project* on a number of occasions, can be traced to Marx's discussion of 'commodity fetishism' introduced in the first volume of *Capital*. There Marx writes – and it is worth quoting him at length: "The mysterious character of the commodity-form consists therefore simply in the fact that the commodity reflects the social characteristics of men's [sic] own labour as objective characteristics of the products of labour themselves, as the socio-natural properties of these things. Hence it also reflects the social relation of the producers to the sum total of labour as a social relation between objects, a relation which exists apart from and outside the producers. Through this substitution, the products of labour become commodities, sensuous things which are at the same time supra-sensible or social... It is nothing but the definite social relation between men themselves which assumes here, for them, the fantastic form of a relation between things. In order, therefore, to find an analogy we must take flight into the misty realm of religion. There the products of the human brain appear as autonomous figures endowed with a life of their own, which enter into relations both with each other and with the human race. So it is in the world of commodities with the products of men's hands. I call this the fetishism which attaches itself to the products of labour as soon as they are produced as commodities, and is therefore inseparable from the production of commodities" (Marx, 1976: 165).

The 'commodity fetish' is thus a fantastic illusion, a phantasmagoria. Marx 'takes flight into the misty realm of religion' to explain the workings of the commodity because, like religion, the commodity is not simply a 'thing'. Instead it is the process of the systematic yet illusionary substitution of relations between subjects by relations between objects. This substitution process has real effects on the make up of individuals – it changes their libidinal apparatus. Marx chose the term 'fetishism' with care, as its anthropological origins allude to the study of how tribes' religious beliefs – often centred on some holy artefacts – structure their libidinal economy. Similarly, he sees the commodity structuring our modern lives; its workings create and maintain a specific 'system of needs' – commodity fetishism produces a specific libidinal economy that makes up the modern subject (Pietz, 1993).

In this sense, the commodity has very real effects; it's not simply a subjective illusion. Yet, according to Marx, 'commodity fetishism' must be seen as a systematic misrecognition, which does not imply that it is a 'false' knowledge. That is, the subject with its knowledge is part of the carousel of capital; it does not watch the 'goings-on' of the carousel from an external position. Benjamin's phantasmagoria and Marx's commodity fetishism describe a situation in which capital itself becomes the religious ordering of the social. As Benjamin writes in his short essay 'Capitalism as Religion' (1996: 288–291), "in capitalism, things have a meaning only in their relationship to the cult" (1996: 288). Similarly to Marx, for Benjamin this cult is a permanent feature; "there are no 'weekdays'. There is no day that is not a feast day...; each day commands the utter fealty of each worshipper" (*ibid.*). Benjamin thus describes capital as a parasite (1996: 289), which, in his words, 'destructs' being and reconstructs it along new lines.

* * * *

> The mimetic element in language can, like a flame, manifest itself only through a kind of bearer. This bearer is the semiotic element. Thus, the nexus of meaning of words or sentences is the bearer through which, like a flash, similarity appears. For its production by man – like its perception by him – is in many cases, and particularly the most important, tied to its flashing up. It flits past. It is not improbable that the rapidity of writing and reading heightens the fusion of the semiotic and the mimetic in the sphere of language. "To read what was never written." Such reading is the most ancient: reading prior to all languages, from entrails, the stars, or dances (Walter Benjamin, 'On the Mimetic Faculty', 1933).

* * * *

The question of how to transcend the religious phantasmagoria of capital has interested writers ever since the bourgeoisie became the dominant social class. Is there anything outside the capital-carousel that seems to turn everything social into its passenger? As Marx makes clear throughout *Capital*, despite its natural appearance, capital is hardly a machine that is running smoothly and perfectly. The capital-carousel is not a *perpetuum mobile* in the sense that it just goes on and on without any breaks and faults. Crises are an inherent characteristic of capital. They can materialise at any stage of the capital-process: when capital is turned into a product in the labour process, when the product is brought to market and turned into a commodity, when the commodity is sold and turned into money, when money is circulated, when money is turned again into capital, etc. This also implies that, although capital increasingly becomes labour and life itself, one should not assume that the class antagonisms between capital and labour disappear. That is, even if capital's expansive circulation now covers most areas of 'the social' and life, as Hardt and Negri (2000) argue, this does not mean that we have reached 'the end of history' (Fukuyama, 1992) implying that all social conflict and struggles have come to a conclusion.

In *One-Way Street*, Benjamin is quite articulate about the type of struggle that he sees to define capitalism: "The notion of the class war can be misleading. It does not refer to a trial of strength to decide the question 'Who shall win, who be defeated?' or to a struggle whose outcome is good for the victor and bad for the vanquished. To think in this way is to romanticize and obscure the facts. For whether the bourgeoisie wins or loses the fight, it remains doomed by the inner contradictions that in the course of development will become deadly. The only question is whether its downfall will come through itself or through the proletariat" (1996: 469–470). These words by Benjamin stand in stark contrast to the type of depoliticised reading that is again and again put forward by some of his readers. Caygill, for example, maintains that Benjamin agreed with Lukács' "diagnosis of the reduction of experience by the commodity form under capitalism, but not with the view that it could be superseded by a class-conscious subject" (1998: 130). Rather than suggesting, as Caygill seems to do, that Benjamin was not interested in questions of class struggle, I would maintain that works such as *One-Way Street* and the *Arcades Project* present images of a class struggle that is culturally, socially and economically dispersed.

It is precisely this dispersion that points to the circulation of capital, which has been the subject of this chapter. As Negri maintains, "circulation entails the reproduction of capital, of the working class and of their struggle on a larger scale" (1991: 106). That is, the expansive circulation of capital does not lead to the eradication or disappearance of class struggles, but their dispersion into all areas of the social and life itself. This is one of the central arguments of Hardt and Negri's *Empire*, and one could suggest that Benjamin – after he had made his 'decision' on Capri – went a long way to present aspects of this argument.

In Hardt and Negri (2000), the proletariat is translated into the 'multitude' – a dispersed proletariat that potentially involves every human being on earth. The multitude is a multiplicity of proletarian struggles that cannot be located in only one place – for example, the workplace. Instead, the multitude is a body of struggles that take place everywhere; the multitude is a 'non-place' (Augé, 1995). The multitude constitutes itself precisely because of capital's increasing speed of circulation and its attempt to encompass all aspects of life. Capital, or what Hardt and Negri call 'Empire', tries, on one hand, to be all-encompassing and continuously increase its powers of reproduction and accumulation, but, on the other hand, this also implies the expansion and acceleration of its antagonisms and class struggles. That is, as Empire reaches for the domination of life, life itself becomes impregnated by capitalist class struggles. The speed of the capital-carousel entails the speed of struggles at the same time.

Benjamin presents the speed of the capital-carousel and its inherent struggles by using an aphoristic style of writing. *One-Way Street* and the *Arcades Project* are essentially montages of quotations and fragmentary commentaries that do not form a coherent narrative. Precisely because of their anti-narrative structure, the textual fragments of these works are in constant circulation. Their location is not fixed; they are essentially textual 'non-places'. Now, on one hand, this mimics capital's powers of circulation. That is, by using a fragmentary style of presentation, he shows us how capital infiltrates different aspects of modern city-life in all sorts of different ways. So, on one level Benjamin's quotations and aphorisms seem to be simply part of the wider reproductive mechanisms of the capital carousel.

On the other hand, however, his montages are not simply reproductions. Instead, his quotations seek to interrupt the 'goings-on' of the carousel: "Quotations in my work are like wayside robbers who leap out, armed, and relieve the idle stroller of his conviction" (1996: 481). That is, while Benjamin's textual montages are part of the capital carousel – they cannot simply stand outside of it – they also aim to transcend the reproductive logic of that very carousel.

The difference between capital's carousel and Benjamin's montage is that they have different approaches to time. As we discussed above, despite capital's expansive circulation that seeks to tear down all barriers of time and space, it territorialises time by establishing a logic of homogeneous progress. Benjamin refers to this as the carousel's 'eternal return': capital constantly returns to itself and, by doing so, it spatialises time into a chronological, progressive order. In contrast, a montage challenges those images of history that are continuously emplaced by forces of capital. It dissects the homogenous body of history by inserting alien images of past, present and future. A montage, in other words, is not interested in the 'eternal return' of history, but in seeing those historical images that have been forgotten or marginalised. Benjamin hopes that the fragments of historical images presented in *One-Way Street* and the *Arcades Project* will illuminate the reader and enable certain re-cognitions and new experiences of time. He refers to these illuminations as 'flashes of knowledge' (1999b: 462). Such a flash must be understood as an event, an *Augenblick*, which discontinues and destructs the continuity of the 'eternal image' of history and enables new histories to emerge.

For Benjamin, an *Augenblick*, which can be translated literally as 'the blink of an eye', is a special, short-lived, ephemeral moment; it is an event (see also Böhm, 2006). Benjamin sees this event as a figuration of *kairos* (Kairos being the youngest son of Zeus in Greek mythology and seen as the embodiment of opportunity). Hence, *kairos*, as a concept, signifies a time when conditions are right for the accomplishment of a crucial action – it is a decisive event. This is the event of the carousel; the event that aims to transcend the 'eternal return' of the carousel of capital. This event can be characterised by two *simultaneous* movements: The first movement is that of the halting of the carousel's continuous circulation by turning its endless speed into a momentary stillness: "Marx says, that revolutions are the locomotives of world history. But perhaps it is completely different. Perhaps revolutions are when mankind, which is travelling in this train, reaches for the emergency brake" (Benjamin, 1974: 1232, my translation). Hence, the world is brought to a standstill – the hustle of the 'normal goings-on' of modernity is stopped by way of a speculative thought-image: "Thinking involves not only the flow of thoughts, but their arrest as well. Where thinking suddenly stops in a configuration pregnant with tensions, it gives that configuration a shock" (1999a: 254). A montage is such a thought-image; it speculates about a different time by halting the carousel of capital.

The second movement of this event is that of remembering, which for Benjamin does not mean to recognise 'the way it really was'. Instead, it means to see images of the past as belonging to the present. Benjamin's task for us is to set up constellations of different images of time that do not belong to the same sequence. This is essentially the dialectical event of the carousel, which the Benjamin-reader Missac sees as follows: "the dialectic does not let itself be absorbed by the merry-go-around and the illusion of eternity is provides. Rather, before one finds the mother who waits at the edge of the platform, as though above history, the dialectic must know how to confer significance and effectiveness on the present" (1995: 108). Benjamin's dialectical carousel event is the place where past, present and future come together; where "each 'now' is the now of a particular recognisability" (1999b: 463). Thus, history needs to be recognised; it needs to be worked on and read, as it were. History is a contingent and contested phenomenon that is constructed through the speculative power of thought. For Benjamin, dialectics is when one puts fragments of historical experience and dominant contemporary images of time together in such a way that a powerful constellation is formed, from which a 'flash of knowledge' springs that is able to illuminate the here and now.

Kevan Collett, 'Carousel'

This dialectical carousel event is not progressive *per se*. There is no guarantee that the 'flash of knowledge' produced by the event enables a 'higher state of development'. Instead, it is an opportunity to see history differently and a response to the danger that the past becomes a part of "the homogeneous course of history" (1999a: 254). It is a relational event that establishes connections between different times and experiences. Benjamin thinks of these connections as being mimetic (see 1999c: 720ff), which brings us back to the image of the child on the carousel. In his view, it is children who often make the most spontaneous, ephemeral connections between times and experiences (see also Buck-Morss, 1989, and Cauchi, 2003). For Benjamin, children's ability to make the most creative connections, which he sees as a form of mimesis, points to precisely the type of revolutionary consciousness that is needed to imagine a time beyond the 'eternal return' of the capital carousel. Benjamin's child on the carousel, although part of the speed of the carousel, is thus an image of hope; a hope in a mimetic 'flash of knowledge' that would imagine a different speed of time.

* * * *

References

Adorno, Theodor W. and Max Horkheimer (1979) *Dialectic of Enlightenment*. London: Verso.

Augé, Marc (1995) *Non-Places: Introduction to an Anthropology of Supermodernity*, trans. John Howe. London: Verso.

Benjamin, Walter (1973) *Charles Baudelaire: A Lyric Poet in the Era of High Capitalism*, trans. Harry Zohn. London: Verso.

Benjamin, Walter (1974) *Gesammelte Schriften*, Vol. I.3, ed. Rolf Tiedemann and Hermann Schweppenhäuser (with Theodor W. Adorno and Gershom Scholem). Frankfurt/M: Suhrkamp.

Benjamin, Walter (1977) *The Origin of the German Tragic Drama*, trans. John Osborne. London: Verso.

Benjamin, Walter (1994) *The Correspondence of Walter Benjamin, 1910–1940*, ed. Gershom Scholem and Theodor W. Adorno, trans. Manfred R. Jacobson and Evelyn M. Jacobson. London: University of Chicago Press.

Benjamin, Walter (1996) *Selected Writings, Vol. 1*, ed. Marcus Bullock and W. Jennings, trans. Edmund Jephcott. Cambridge, MA: The Belknap Press of Harvard University Press.

Benjamin, Walter (1999a) *Illuminations*, ed. Hannah Arendt, trans. Harry Zohn. London: Pimlico.

Benjamin, Walter (1999b) *The Arcades Project*, trans. Howard Eiland and Kevin McLaughlin. Cambridge, MA: The Belknap Press of Harvard University Press.

Benjamin, Walter (1999c) *Selected Writings, Vol. 2*, ed. Michael W. Jennings, Howard Eiland and Gary Smith, trans. Rodney Livingston and others. Cambridge, MA: The Belknap Press of Harvard University Press.

Blumenfeld, Simon (1935) *Jew Boy*. London: Cape.

Böhm, Steffen (2006) *Repositioning Organization Theory: Impossibilities and Strategies*. Basingstoke: Palgrave Macmillan.

Braverman, Harry (1974) *Labor and Monopoly Capital: The Degradation of Work in the Twentieth Century*. London: Monthly Review Press.

Brodersen, Momme (1996) *Walter Benjamin: A Biography*. London: Verso.

Buck-Morss, Susan (1989) *The Dialectics of Seeing: Walter Benjamin and the Arcades Project*. Cambridge, MA: MIT Press.

Burawoy, Michael (1982) *Manufacturing Consent: Changes in the Labour Process Under Monopoly Capitalism*. Chicago: University of Chicago Press.

Cauchi, Mark (2003) 'Infinite Spaces: Walter Benjamin and the spurious creations of capitalism', Angelaki, 8(3): 23–39.

Caygill, Howard (1998) *Walter Benjamin: The Colour of Experience*. London: Routledge.

Deleuze, Gilles and Félix Guattari (1987) *A Thousand Plateaus: Capitalism and Schizophrenia II*, trans. Brian Massumi. Minneapolis: University of Minnesota Press.

Fukuyama, Francis (1992) *The End of History and the Last Man*. New York: The Free Press.

Godfrey, Richard, Gavin Jack and Campbell Jones (2004) 'Sucking, Bleeding, Breaking: On the Dialectics of Vampirism, Capital, and Time', *Culture and Organization*, 10(1): 25–36.

Hardt, Michael and Antonio Negri (2000) *Empire*. Cambridge, MA: Harvard University Press.

Harvey, David (1982) *The Limits of Capital*. Oxford: Basil Blackwell.

Lash, Scott (1999) *Another Modernity, A Different Rationality*. London: Blackwell.

Leslie, Esther (2000) *Walter Benjamin: Overpowering Conformism*. London: Pluto Press.

Lukács, Georg (1971) *History and Class Consciousness: Studies in Marxist Dialectics*. London: Merlin.

Marx, Karl (1973) *Grundrisse: Foundations of the Critique of Political* Economy, trans. Martin Nicolaus. Harmondsworth: Penguin.

Marx, Karl (1976) *Capital: A Critique of Political Economy*, Vol. 1, trans. Ben Fowkes. London: Penguin.

Marx, Karl (1992) *Capital: A Critique of Political Economy*, Vol. 2, trans. David Fernbach. London: Penguin.

Marx, Karl and Friedrich Engels (1948/1998) *The Communist Manifesto*. Woodbridge: Merlin.

Missac, Pierre (1995) *Walter Benjamin's Passage*, trans. Shierry Weber Nicholsen. Cambridge, MA: MIT Press.

Negri, Antonio (1991) *Marx beyond Marx: Lessons on the Grundrisse*. New York: Autonomedia.

Pietz, William (1993) 'Fetishism and Materialism: The Limits of Theory in Marx', in Emily Apter and William Pietz (eds.) *Fetishism as Cultural Discourse*. Ithaca: Cornell University Press.

Taylor, Frederick W. (1911/1972) *The Principles of Scientific Management*. New York: Harper & Brothers.

Toynbee, Polly (2003) *Hard Work: Life in Low-Pay Britain*. London: Bloomsbury.

Index